THIRTEEN

IS

MY

LUCKY NUMBER

BILL C. BIEGA

ISBN   1-57087-204-x

Library of Congress Catalog   95-71790

Published by
Syrena Press
P.O. Box 490
Plainsboro, NJ 08536-9998

Manufactured in the United States of America

99 98 97 96   10 9 8 7 6 5 4 3 2 1

To Lili

*who has always been at my side
through fortune and misfortune.*

*It is the mark of an inexperienced man not to
believe in luck.*

— Joseph Conrad

*Nature creates ability; Luck provides it with
opportunity.*

— François de la Rochefoucauld

FOREWORD

This is a story in which good fortune and optimism overcome dangers and adversities; a story in which moments of humor enliven times of hardship. It is not a history but a memoir of personal experiences for which historical events provide a dramatic backdrop.

I strongly believe that the course of our lives is subject to something out of our control. Call it Divine Guidance, protection of a Guardian Angel, fate, kismet, good luck or what you will. This story contains many moments which support that belief. Even the one chapter in which everything went wrong does not contradict this belief. I went into this undertaking with strong misgivings. However, I permitted myself to be persuaded to disregard the inner warnings. This shows that it is within our own power to disregard that guiding light or to take advantage of it. We are not alone; we share our life and space on earth with other human beings who can hurt us or help us, hate us or love us.

I thank all those good people who helped me, when in trouble, and gave me the opportunities for success, whether named in the text or not. Without them there would be no story.

Also, I thank my editors, Arlene Lewis and Vira Manchur Schwartz, for their assistance and valuable suggestions.

Bill Biega
August, 1995

CONTENTS

PART ONE
FIGHT FOR SURVIVAL

PART TWO
A NEW WORLD

◆ ◆ ◆

THIRTEEN IS MY LUCKY NUMBER

PART ONE

FIGHT FOR SURVIVAL

PROLOGUE

The pandemonium of warfare had died down. Only an occasional burst of machine-gun fire, the isolated crack of an isolated rifle shot, the *vro-oo-oo-m* of an exploding shell or grenade disturbed the dark night. The acrid smell of burning ruins had become so normal that it no longer registered in the brain as being anything unusual. I shivered in my tattered clothes. The nights were getting chilly as September drew to a close. The remnants of a wall sheltered me from the wind as I peered through the darkness over the field of rubble towards the broad avenue and the dark silhouette of the B.K.G., the National Economy Bank, the closest German stronghold. From there, I was sure, sentries were looking over towards the rubble on which I sat. I was the acting commander of a unit withdrawn to a secondary defense position. The battle had already lasted 56 days, which seemed an eternity. While I watched, the others rested in our quarters, the remains of the once famous sausage shop *Radzyminski.*

Only fourteen remained of the original 180 that had started out with such high hopes to take Warsaw back from the Nazis just eight weeks ago, on August 1, 1944. Two were girls, one of them my bride of six weeks, half were wounded as I was. This tiny squad was the last defense position between the front line, 200 yards to my left in the ruins of the once elegant Cafe Club and the cinema Coliseum, and the battalion reserve in a half-ruined house 100 yards behind me. If the enemy were to launch a strong attack now, we would probably not be able to hold out even till dawn. Our supplies of ammunition did not allow more than a handful of bullets for each gun. We were all hungry, reduced to a single daily meal of pancakes concocted from unhusked barley retrieved from the warehouse of a brewery. Meat had not been seen for weeks; all the dogs and cats and other animals had long since disappeared, even rats had deserted the hopeless wreck. Water was carried in buckets from the few wells that had been dug in the backyards of houses.

I shivered again and pondered my life that was surely to end any day now. It was indeed a miracle that I had survived this long. A life that had begun just 22 years ago less than a quarter of a mile away, in the flat of my Aunt Jadwiga, just beyond the bank looming dark against the late night sky.

My father had been a functionary in the Economic Section of the Ministry for Foreign Affairs. He had met my English mother while he was a student at the Ecole des Sciences Politiques at the University of Paris. She had stayed in the same pension while serving as secretary in the British delegation to the Versailles Peace Conference. They had married in London after his graduation with honors, and then came to Warsaw. When I was a year old my father was nominated to the position of Second Secretary in the embassy in London. My parents were a very happy couple and adored each other, but fate intervened. A year later, while on vacation in Caen, Normandy, my mother suffered a miscarriage while swimming and died from loss of blood. Father, anxious to provide me with good care, married another English woman, Baba Seely, a year later. They thought it would be better for me to live in the care of her parents in a small village, Sutton-on-Sea, on the east coast of England, rather than in a cramped flat in the big city.

I shifted positions on the hard rubble and remembered these carefree years. Summers in particular had been happy times. Then I had friends from among the families who rented summer homes. We dug sand castles, sailed model boats, and swam in the cold waters of the North Sea. The small local private school had given me a very good primary education. In the wintertime I read many books from my step-grandfather's library of classics. Then my father had returned to Poland. The party of Marshal Pilsudski, who had taken over Poland in a coup d'etat in May 1926, did not tolerate members of the opposition for long. His career in the Foreign Service came to an abrupt end in 1930. The marriage with Baba had also ended. As part of the international set Warsaw was enjoyable, but she was no longer happy to be just the wife of an impoverished early "retiree."

I shivered again, I wondered when my relief would come, it was getting colder.....No sign of life in the dark rubble in front of me.....I started thinking about those last enjoyable years before war destroyed our lifestyle.....Would I ever survive to see a normal life again?

1

INNOCENT YEARS

Yes, it would be wonderful to be care-free again. It was almost exactly nine years since I had returned to Poland from England, where I had lived almost all my life at a small resort village on the east coast. It was exciting for a 12 year old boy to travel all by himself on a ship. It was a small cargo vessel, *Lech*, that traveled regularly from Hay's Wharf, near Tower Bridge in London, to the Polish port of Gdynia. The voyage, across the North Sea, through the Kiel Canal to the Baltic, took three days. The ship carried only 12 passengers and the officers took good care of me and allowed me to spend many hours on the bridge. I stood there for hours, watching the helmsman who kept his eyes on the compass and turned the wheel, first one way, then the other, making corrections of course every few minutes. The watch officer scanned the horizon or paced back and forth on the bridge.

The captain showed me the charts and traced our course. At noon the sextant was brought out. They let me hold it and bring the sun down to the horizon by turning the knurled knob. Then the captain traced lines on the chart and pointed with his pencil at their intersection and said,

"This is where we are."

The idea of navigation by the sun and by the stars, voyaging over the seas to new and strange places fascinated me and I decided I wanted to be a sailor.

My father was waiting for me in Gdynia. He was a striking man, tall, broad-shouldered, with a very straight posture. His nose was prominent, his eyes blue, both Biega family traits. His hair was blonde with a light reddish tint to it, it had a tendency to wave but he always was careful to keep it smoothly brushed. He wore a moustache in which the reddish tinge was more noticeable, it was always neatly trimmed. He spoke excellent English with just a hint of an accent. He had an engaging smile, spoke softly, rarely raised his voice. He could be very firm in expressing his opinions, but was liked and respected by friends and adversaries alike, and particularly by women.

We took the train to Warsaw which was another exciting experience. The train was so different from those in England. Arriving in Warsaw in the early evening, we took a taxi to the comfortable five-room flat on the fifth floor of Gornoslaska 18 that my father had purchased when he was still in the Ministry of Foreign Affairs. From there, it was only a few minutes walk to the flat of Aunt Jadwiga who had a welcoming dinner ready for us. My cousins Janek and Marysia made me feel at home and during the next weeks helped me to learn Polish. Marysia, two years older than me, was learning French. I had also learned French at my school in England and this gave us a common bridge which made it easier for us to understand each other.

My father hired a pretty young lady, Miss Paczkowska, to give me daily lessons, not only in Polish, but also in those elements of schooling that I was missing and which I needed before I could enter high school — Polish history and geography. She spent four hours each day with me. She knew enough English to help me over some of the rough spots but insisted on speaking Polish most of the time so that I learned the language fast. All my studies and homework made time pass quickly.

In a few weeks the end of October arrived and the religious holiday of All Saints. On this day all businesses were closed to allow Polish families to remember dead friends and family. Special streetcars ran from every part of the city to the various cemeteries so that all families could make pilgrimages to the graves, place flowers and candles, and say a prayer. Our family visited the grave of my grandfather, whose distinguished career included a prominent role in the development of the Polish patriotic and sports organization *Sokol* (Falcon). His grave was marked by a beautiful memorial, presented by the organization, in red sandstone depicting a falcon standing on a pillar with its head bowed. This grave was located in the *Powazki* cemetery north of the city. This was also an occasion for me to meet my uncle Staszek and my other cousin Stasz Junior, three years younger. Uncle was a major in the Army engineers and lived with his family in officer's housing in the military camp just beyond the cemetery.

Christmas arrived a few weeks later. In Poland, Christmas Eve is the most important part of that holiday. My father and I always spent that festive event at Aunt Jadwiga's flat. When we arrived in the late afternoon a *choinka* (Christmas tree) had already been decorated. Aunt Jadwiga trimmed her tree with silver paper icicles and ornaments cut out of colored paper. A large silver star adorned the top. There were no electric tree lights, only a few candles in small metal dishes clamped to the branches. The candles were lit for only a brief period during the exchange of gifts. A manger, with animals looking at the cradle containing the baby Jesus, lay at the base of the tree.

Before sitting down at the table, the host and hostess shared a wafer, blessed earlier in the church, with each of those present; exchanging wishes and greetings of *Wesolych Swiat* (Happy Holidays). Then the first dishes were served; these included small pieces of herring arranged on squares of black bread, vegetable salad, and carp in a jelly with a mayonnaise or horseradish sauce. Numerous tiny glasses of ice-cold vodka were downed, particularly by the gentlemen, each glass being drunk to toast the hostess, next the host, then each of the guests in turn. In due course steaming cups of *barszcz* (clear beetroot soup) were served with *pierogi* (rolled crepes) or *uszka* (tiny dumplings) filled with cabbage and mushrooms. A hot fish dish, most likely *sandacz* (a fairly large fish caught in the Vistula River), followed after a brief pause. The dinner proceeded at a leisurely pace with much conversation. The sweet dishes did not arrive until at least eight or nine o'clock. These consisted of *kompot* (stewed prunes, apples, pears, and whatever other fruit might be available) and the cakes. A bottle of Hungarian Tokay wine would have been opened by now. The children, bored by the long proceedings, had already left the table to amuse themselves with the various toys, games and books that they had received.

The elders were now in very good spirits. Mr. Blaschke (who by profession was a cello player in one of the Warsaw orchestras) was coaxed into playing the piano, perhaps someone started singing carols. I remember that on one occasion Janek and I got hold of a bottle of Tokay and proceeded to drink most of it in one of the bedrooms. We were later discovered, both of us fast asleep. Shortly, Aunt Jadwiga and those guests still suitably sober left to attend Midnight Mass at St. Alexander's Church just across the square from the flat.

The other great family Holiday was Easter. Holy Week was a time for fasting and visiting the city churches to view the elaborate altars decorated with scenes depicting the Crucifixion and Resurrection. On Holy Saturday, the women took baskets of food to the churches to be blessed. A priest, who was a friend of the family, usually came to Aunt Jadwiga's flat and blessed the whole table which was already prepared for the Easter dinner. Late on Saturday evening the boom of the guns at the army barracks near the Lazienki Park and the ringing of the bells in all the churches commemorated the Resurrection of Christ. This also signified the end of the fast. The guests gathered at Aunt Jadwiga's flat shared a piece of hard-boiled egg that had been blessed and wished each other a Happy Easter. Then we sampled the collection of cold meats, hams, sausages, vegetable salads, gaily colored Easter eggs and cakes set out on the white tablecloth. Naturally this was also a proper occasion for numerous toasts, each accompanied by a swallow of cold vodka. All Easter Sunday and Monday it was traditional to go visiting friends and family, bringing good wishes and sampling the dishes every house had arranged on the table. Therefore the streets were full of people walking from house to house or riding in horse-drawn cabs *dorozki*.

By the end of spring I was sufficiently proficient in Polish to be able to go to high school, called *Gimnazium* in Poland. My father enrolled me in the prestigious *Sulkowski* boarding school located in the baroque palace of the Sulkowski family, which dominated the small town of Rydzyna. This town of perhaps 1,000 inhabitants was located a few miles from the German border, on the main railway line leading from Poznan through Leszno and Rawicz to the German city Breslau (called *Wroclaw* in Polish). This was only possible because my father was able to get a special reduced rate. At the time, he was struggling to build a new life out of the ruins of his diplomatic career. He could not afford the 2,500 zloty (about $500) tuition fee, to which must be added other expenses, clothing, travel, books. I started in the freshman class because of my problems with Polish. Fortunately, the basic schooling I had received in Sutton-on-Sea, together with the coaching of Miss Paczkowska, was so excellent, that after Christmas I was advanced to the next grade. My only real problems were with Polish as a subject. During my four years in Rydzyna I was always given double grading, one grade for content, another for grammar.

The director of this school was a man with a mission. A tall, imposing, rather heavily built man with a prominent nose, Tadeusz Lopuszanski wished to create a group of young men who would become leaders of the young Polish Republic. He believed that by immersing young boys in an isolated environment in which learning and team sports were almost the only available activities he could achieve this. Spartan conditions would eliminate laziness, selfishness and gluttony, which he considered the main sins of Poles. Therefore the food was nourishing but plain. We were not even allowed to receive any packages from home except on our birthdays. We were only allowed about 50 cents a month pocket money with which to buy cakes from the pastry shop!

As was customary in all schools in Europe, we wore uniforms. Our uniform, however, was designed not to "look" like a uniform. We wore "plus-fours", trousers buckled under the knee which were popular sporty dress in the '30s, and a single breasted jacket, both in a gray tweed-like cloth. Our shirts were white, normally without a tie. For special occasions we used a straight cut, orange-colored tie in a Polish ethnic pattern. We wore black shoes and gray wool knee-high socks. The summer uniform consisted of gray shorts with a light-gray shirt similar to those worn by Boy Scouts. Our gray-colored school cap, which we wore only when going to church or in inclement weather, was rather similar in shape to that worn by army officers, except the square cut cloth was soft, without the hard military insert. We would try to pull the loose cloth over one ear - this was the fashionable way.

For identification in the laundry, all our clothes were labeled with our personal number. My number was *thirteen*. This number 13 stayed with me all through my school years, marked on all my clothing and possessions. Friends joked, "Aren't you afraid? 13 is unlucky!"

"No, only stupid kids believe in this silly superstition. I'm different, for me it's a *lucky* number, you'll see," I always replied.

Many of the boys came from Warsaw or the eastern provinces of Poland. At the beginning and end of each term and at holiday breaks, a special coach was attached to a Warsaw - Berlin express, which was detached in Poznan and then coupled to the Poznan - Wroclaw express, which made a special stop at the tiny station about two miles from the small town Rydzyna. This third-class coach had wooden seats without any upholstery, common in pre-war Europe. Joseph Zwislocki, the grandson of President Moscicki, was accompanied by his mother, wife of the Minister of Transportation, on his first trip to Rydzyna. She of course came in a special private pullman car. His colleagues hassled him so much that, from then on he always traveled third-class with the rest of us.

Because of my foreign accent I was well known by all the school; I shared this distinction with Marc de Montfort who was French. Classes were small, there were less than 20 in mine. I developed friendships with Joseph Zwislocki, Alex Lempicki and Julek Geyer. Alex came from a family of landowners, now living in Warsaw. He was taller than me with a highly colored complexion and brown, tousled hair, a serious boy with many intellectual interests. Julek was blond and rather reserved, he was the son of a textile manufacturer. Our group traveled together in the same compartment going home for holidays, or we would like to be on the same team together, playing afternoon games. I also became very friendly with several older boys, a couple of classes higher. They were always willing to help me with some problem, or other in my school work. They also were interesting to talk to, and most important they were interested in talking to me, which is unusual in school; generally older boys are not interested in associating with younger ones.

There were certain teacher relationships that were closer than others. To begin with every teacher had a group of about nine boys for whom he was responsible; he was a counselor and guardian for that same group all through school. The same group also sat at one table for the three main meals.

My counselor was the teacher of mathematics, Romuald Wilkowski, a thin and rather short man, with a narrow face and dark eyes. He was a dour, humorless martinet, who did not encourage any familiarity from his charges. Meals at his table were always quiet with little of the joking and good spirits that were to be expected from a group of teen-aged boys. Initially, I had a good relationship with him, because mathematics was an easy subject for me and I was doing extracurricular work. Later I got discouraged at being pushed by him for more and more work, and I disliked his narrow mindedness, so I dropped extra mathematics work and spent all my free time working in the physics laboratory. Wilkowski was very disappointed and became very critical of me. A few years later I learned from another teacher, that Wilkowski had accused me before the Teacher's Council of all kinds of behavior that was not tolerated at Rydzyna, including smoking cigarettes. This accusation was completely false and I was never directly confronted with it. Nevertheless, he reduced my grade for mathematics from a Five[*] to a Four, and also reduced my grade for "Behavior & Attitude" to a barely passing Three.

Naturally, Arkadiusz Piekara, the Physics teacher, supported me before the Council, as did Marian Jasinski, the teacher of Polish. I had a very friendly relationship with both of them. I always had a Five in Physics, and as I said earlier I always received a dual grade in Polish.

I was especially interested in physics. In my second year I joined the Physics Club. Under the tutelage of Professor Piekara I started working on various projects. At the end of each project I had to prepare a paper and then make a presentation to a meeting of the club. These meetings were attended not only by club members, but also by other boys and some of the staff (after all there was no other entertainment in Rydzyna!). The most prominent member of the Physics Club was my friend Alex Lempicki who was doing some really interesting work. There was another advantage to working in the Physics Laboratory. When Professor Piekara was convinced that we were seriously interested, he gave each of us a small room to set up our experiments. Here we could hide away from others and enjoy privacy,

---

[*] The grading in central European schools ranged from 5 for "Excellent" to 2 for "Unsatisfactory".

which was difficult to come by in this school. Alex shared with me and Julek Geyer a dislike for team games, especially when the weather was cold and rainy. Julek had become seriously involved in chemistry with Professor Karczewski and also had his own little cubicle for his experimentation. So on cold rainy afternoons, while the rest of the boys were rushing around in the mud chasing balls, the three of us would secrete ourselves in our studios away from harassment by the other professors!

I had difficulty with sports which were heavily emphasized at Rydzyna. I had no training at all in gymnastics exercises and almost no experience in team sports, The only team game we had played at my school in England was cricket! Unfortunately the only sports I was really good at, and enjoyed — swimming and cycling, were not practiced in Rydzyna. I had brought my English touring bicycle to Rydzyna. On fine Sundays afternoons (the only day there were no team sports), I liked to go for long rides through the countryside exploring the woods and small villages. The country was flat and easy for bike riding. The German border was only about five miles away and one was supposed to stay away from it. Nevertheless, I made a couple of excursions along the deserted country roads in the vicinity of the border which was marked only by large stones, spaced about 200 yards apart. Where the roads crossed the frontier there were guard posts manned by German soldiers on one side, Polish frontier police on the other, a couple of hundred yards apart. Unfortunately, two days before the end of the first school year I collided with another boy on a bicycle and had to go to the hospital in Leszno with a broken collar bone. I spent about two weeks in the hospital, then Daddy came to take me home by train.

It was very hot in the plaster corset during July in the small rented flat on Sniegocka Street — Dad had been forced to sell his old flat. Of course I could not go swimming. During the week, while Daddy was at work, I sat at home reading books. I discovered Frank Harris's "*My Life and Loves*" on Daddy's bookshelf and read it with great interest, especially the explicit (for those days) descriptions of erotic adventures. It was certainly educational, but I doubt that Professor Jasinski would have approved of it! I remember a pianist exercising his scales, *do-re-me-fa-so-la-ti-do*, up and down, endlessly hour after hour, every morning. My cousins, Janek and Marysia visited me, or invited me to their flat to pass away the time, playing games and talking. In the evenings Daddy and friends took me to the movies and to operettas at the Summer Theater in the Saski Gardens.

It was a requirement for all new boys to attend the school's summer camp on Lake Serwy in northern Poland. The accident delayed my attendance until 1937. By this time I had completed the third year and most of the other boys were younger. It was a wooden house, with dormitories for 20 to 30 boys, and rooms for the teachers, some of whom brought their families. A fleet of rowboats and kayaks, all of which had been built by students in the school's woodworking shops, provided the main recreation. The rowboats were very classy ones, with real sliding seats like in racing sculls. Director Lopuszanski and his wife were also at the camp. Two of the rowboats were designed for twin sculls. Lopuszanski rode in one and his wife in the other, "volunteers" from among the students manning the oars. Swimming and rowing classes took up most of the first two weeks.

At school I was a duffer in sports, but in swimming and rowing I excelled. I easily won a swimming race across the lake and back, a distance of at least 1200 meters. The last 10 days of the camp were the most exciting. The boats were loaded on to horse-drawn wagons and taken to another much larger lake about 12 miles further north, Lake Wigry. From there we rowed across several lakes and then down the picturesque, wild Czarna Hancza River and finally back to the base camp along the Augustow Canal. Every evening we pitched camp, one or two larger tents for the teachers and several smaller ones, each for three boys. Our only problem — the mosquitoes which started attacking us as soon as the sun dropped toward the horizon. No one was spared the torment of continual bites. We spent the evenings sitting around blazing camp fires hoping the smoke would drive our attackers away, singing songs and telling stories.

A few weeks later, my father sent me with some friends of his to Worochta, a mountain resort particularly popular among people who lived in the south eastern provincial capital Lwow. It was a whole day's train journey from Warsaw. We stayed in an old wooden three story hotel *Skarbowka*, situated on a hill overlooking the village down in the valley of the river Prut. From the hotel we could see the

Czarnohora mountains a few miles away. A wide veranda completely surrounded the ground floor so that, on rainy days, one could still enjoy a walk without getting wet. Worochta was also the terminus of the railway line. Every evening everyone assembled at the station to see the new arrivals on the express from Lwow which arrived just after 9 o'clock. Several boxes of cakes and marzipan, from the famous confectioners *Zalewski* in Lwow also arrived on this train and immediately went on sale in the station buffet. Quickly, a line formed at the buffet to partake of these tasty delicacies. Afterwards the elders retired to the station restaurant to drink and dance to the music of a small band.

The day after my arrival I noticed a lovely girl, with short blonde hair and violet eyes. Wanda Vetulani was with her mother. Her father was a diplomat and she had acquired a sophisticated manner unlike most schoolgirls. Even though I was a year younger she was also attracted to me. Perhaps it was my English accent. We became inseparable. We spent every waking hour together, walking around the village, hiking up into the mountain meadows to lie in the sun, or splashing in the river. The water was cold, but we found pools of quiet water among the rocks which got heated by the sun warm enough for enjoyable bathing. Some of these pools were large enough to swim in, under a waterfall we found a place deep enough for diving. I was enraptured, I had never before met anyone like her. All too soon the holidays were over and our brief romance came to an end, we separated, she returned to school in Warsaw, I went back to Rydzyna.

School ended two weeks earlier in Rydzyna than in other schools. At the end of the first week of June all the students and accompanying teachers would spread out all over Poland on various camping, boating and hiking trips. A large map of Poland was painted on the wall of the indoor games hall. Every September the routes of each of this year's expeditions were added to the others painted in varied colors. In 1938, I and my friends Alex Lempicki and Julek Geyer, together with half a dozen others from our class, took part in a hiking expedition in the Eastern Carpathians. Our guide was professor Jasinski, whom we all liked because he was easy to talk with. He was interesting, liked to tell anecdotes and joke with us and we considered him to be a friend. We had a long train ride from Leszno to Lwow, which took a whole day, then a local took us into the foothills near Stryj. Next day we had another several hours on a narrow-gauge logging train up a valley to the base of the Gorgany mountains. This little train climbed the steep grades so slowly that we could jump out, gather flowers or fruit off the trees and then run and jump back on the train.

During the first week we traversed the Gorgany mountain range. The going was difficult, as the higher reaches of this range were composed of large rocks piled one on another. One afternoon we got caught by a thunderstorm while near the ridge line. We all crouched under boulders wincing as the thunderbolts kept crashing into the peak just above us. The nights were spent in hostels. When we finally came down into the valley of the Prut river at Jaremcze, we met another group from Rydzyna. Their leader had become ill. Jasinski felt that we were older and could take care of ourselves, and left us to look after the other group which was made up of younger boys.

We continued by ourselves, taking the train to Worochta, then a logging train to the slopes of the Czarnohora range. We traversed this range along the border to the point where the frontiers of Romania, Czechoslovakia and Poland came together. The second night we discovered that we had not husbanded our supplies well and we were already running short. Julek and I volunteered to go back to Worochta for replenishment and to meet the group at a hostel on a pass between two ranges. There was still hard spring snow on the northern slopes. Julek and I slid down the slopes at great speed but at the cost of wet pant seats. This was very exciting and saved us a couple of hours of walking. Then we double timed along the valley trail, several hundred feet below, to the logging railroad and just managed to catch the afternoon train back to the village. We spent the evening with some girls that we met in the village Youth Hostel, exchanging tall tales and flirting. With fresh bread and sausage in our knapsacks we embarked once more on the morning train. Just before dark we reached the rendez-vous, exhausted but pleased with our adventure. The next day we climbed the highest peak Pop Iwan, on the summit of which a new astronomical observatory had just been built. This was the only sign of civilization in this empty, wild country. The next day we met a lonely Hucul shepherd from whom we purchased some fresh sheep's milk cheese. Finally, we descended to the picturesque village of Zabie that runs for miles along a deep valley between the mountains. There we hired a horse-drawn cart to take us back to Worochta to catch the train back to Warsaw.

This area was still very wild and relatively uninhabited. The Carpathian Mountaineering Club had built hostels at various points, roughly one day's walk from one to the other. The main trails were well marked and there were good maps available. However no supplies were obtainable except in the villages in the valleys. The hostels were unattended and were equipped only with rough bunks, sometimes with straw filled mattresses, and stoves. A well or more often a mountain stream provided water. The only people we met were other hikers and occasionally a mountaineer shepherd tending the sheep and goats. These mountaineers, called *Hucul*, wore distinctive clothing, jackets made from sheepskins, broad rimmed black felt hats with colored embroidered bands. They spoke Ruthenian, a dialect more closely related to Ukrainian than Polish. The churches were Greek Orthodox, constructed entirely of hemlock wood with onion shaped domes on the church tower. All of this beautiful area was incorporated into Soviet Ukraine after the war and became very difficult for any foreigners to visit. Now the new Ukrainian government has relaxed these restrictions and is starting to encourage tourism once more.

During the previous year my father's financial circumstances had much improved. He was now managing director of one of the two evening newspapers in Warsaw, the one that was opposed to the government - *Wieczor Warszawski* (Warsaw Evening). The paper had a circulation of about 100,000, higher on Sunday. My father started a weekly magazine *Kronika Polski*, published in newspaper format, which quickly grew in size and was also sold in other large cities. He also introduced American comics to the daily paper. One of the strips was *Dagwood and Blondie* with dialogue translated into Polish. His long time friend Stanislaw Strzetelski had moved from the morning paper ABC to become chief editor of *Wieczor Warszawski*. The paper owned a modern printing plant at the west end of the main east-west thoroughfare Aleje Jerozolimskie (Jerusalem Avenue). The new high-speed rotary printing presses were fascinating to watch. The editorial and administrative offices were located in a separate wing overlooking the courtyard. One of the hazards of publishing an opposition newspaper was the censor who would blue-line parts of some news story which were deemed to be critical of the government. Inevitably, this would happen just as the press run had started. It was important not to delay delivery of the newspaper to the distribution points so the offending sentences were quickly ground off the printing plates and the paper would hit the streets with white spaces in the text. Naturally, the curiosity of the readers was aroused and gave rise to numerous rumors of greater harm to the government than the offending material would have been!

The success of the paper and of the magazine lead to Daddy being elected vice president of the Association of Publishers in the fall of 1938. With this base he also became a significant factor in opposition politics. He purchased a new car. It was a Chevrolet sedan, assembled in Poland in a factory owned by a joint venture of General Motors with a Polish manufacturer of locomotives and railway cars. As soon as I returned to Warsaw from the mountains, I started driving lessons. I enjoyed driving around Warsaw and to the suburbs with Daddy. He also had moved to a large spacious modern flat in a brand new building at 22 Narbutta Street. This building had garages for cars in a courtyard at the rear of the house, a novelty for Warsaw.

A few days after returning home from the hike in the mountains, I went again to England. Dad's second wife, Baba had a great affection for me. Many years later she confided in me that she fell in love with me when she first saw me, an orphaned baby, and then determined that she had to marry my father in order to have me. She had returned to England already before the divorce and had recently married Bill Murray-Lawes, a major in the Grenadier Guards and very well connected socially. His family still owned an estate close to Dover, high on the cliffs overlooking the straits. The day of my visit the weather was clear and we could see France from the house.

Bill, who was a member of the king's personal staff, took me to Buckingham Palace for a ceremony, the presentation of flags to a group of army veterans. It was a beautiful sunny day and the colorful ceremony made a vivid impression on me. I stood on the terrace of the palace with Bill, right next to the young Princesses Elizabeth and Margaret. I was not awed by them at all. The two girls didn't appear any different to me then any other girls of their age. They were dressed very formally with hats and gloves, but after all it was a formal occasion. They stood on the steps with all the invited guests watching their father and mother making the presentations and then reviewing the march past of the veterans. Bill also took me to his rowing club in Maidenhead on the Thames and to his old school, the famous Eton. I was impressed by this ancient school, all the buildings covered in ivy.

While I was in England, in July, my father married Hania Falecka, whom he had met while sojourning at a spa in southern Poland, called Truskawiec. They set off on a honeymoon trip across Europe in the new car. I met them in Paris. From there we continued across central France to Avignon and the Riviera. We stayed several days in a hotel in Cap d'Ail. I spent hours swimming in the deep blue sea and diving off rocks, until my eyes were completely red from the heavy salt concentration. Then we continued into Italy, stopping at many of the ancient cities until we reached Bellagio, on beautiful Lake Como, where again we stayed several days in the Grand Hotel.

From there we continued over the Gotthard Pass through Switzerland and on to Austria, which had been occupied by Hitler's armies earlier that spring. At the border between Switzerland and Austria I met Nazi officialdom for the first time. They confiscated some Swiss newspapers that we had in the car. In Innsbruck the city was a sea of red flags with swastikas. Some zealots had climbed the steep mountain face, that is visible as one goes down the main street, and had painted a gigantic swastika on the face of the cliff. This was very upsetting for the three of us, the atmosphere was so threatening that we left Austria as quickly as we could, even though Dad had planned to spend a couple of days in the beautiful mountains.

It was a relief to cross the border into Czechoslovakia and on to Prague, one the most charming of European capitals. We toured the most important sites but the tangle of tombstones, almost one on top of another, in the old Jewish cemetery is what I remember most vividly. From Prague to the Polish border is only a few hour drive. Here we were hassled by the Polish customs officials, who were not used to Polish tourists traveling in large cars. We had to unload all the baggage. They spent a long time going through the shirts, lingerie and dirty laundry. Finally they were satisfied that we were not smuggling anything and we went on to Cracow and back to Warsaw. It became clear to me during this trip that this was an unfortunate marriage, there were many quarrels already on this honeymoon which didn't augur well for the future. I believe the problem was very fundamental, Hania did not enjoy sex, she only wanted a husband who would be an attractive companion and provide her with a good lifestyle. She was also used to having her own way, but so was my Dad.

The summer of 1939 was spent under the threat of war. Several months earlier Hitler had occupied the Sudetenland, the border areas of Czechoslovakia. The British Prime Minister Chamberlain had journeyed back and forth to Germany and had acquiesced to the aggression to the shame of Britain and France. In return Hitler had promised that he had no more territorial claims! Only four months had passed before Hitler broke his promise under some flimsy pretext and had occupied the rest of Czechoslovakia. Shamefully, Poland had quickly grabbed a county adjacent to Cieszyn in Silesia, which had a large Polish population, and Hungary had annexed the eastern province Ruthenia, thus gaining a common border with Poland once again.

As was customary at the time, all senior high-school students received some elementary military training in what was called *Prysposobienie Wojskowe* (Preparation for the Army), commonly called PW. So that June, instead of wandering in the mountains, we spent four weeks in an army camp located on the Baltic coast. We drilled, marched back and forth on the parade ground, practiced target shooting, and engaged in long marches and war games.

After camp was over, I spent another three weeks on a farm near Wloclawek called Pieleszki. This estate, owned by family friends, was a summer home for a couple of dozen boys and girls, teen-agers mostly, all from Warsaw. The atmosphere was care-free and the food was plentiful. None of us gave any thought to politics and the rumblings of war. We spent the days riding horses, swimming in a lake, playing volleyball and eating fresh estate grown food. On at least one occasion we had a chance to sample the estate made fruit wines. They were stored in casks in a cellar under one of the farm buildings. One day the film got stuck in my camera and I needed a dark place to extract it. Someone suggested the cellar. Several of us went there and discovered the casks to each of which a rubber hose was attached. It seemed that we should sample the wines first. This we proceeded to do, going from one barrel to the next. They all tasted pretty good and soon we were all quite tipsy. After that my fingers seemed to get tangled up in the camera's mechanism, they were rather rubbery and it was too difficult to manipulate the film in the dark, and it got ruined. In the evenings we danced to music from a wind-up gramophone, played card games and flirted. Hania's nieces, the Treutler twins, were there, but at the time I was not interested in them, they seemed to be too young and unsophisticated. I spent my time with a girl who was a year older than me. She behaved in a rather superior way, but taught me how to dance.

From Pieleszki I went back to Warsaw and then by car with Dad and Hania to the Institute of Doctor Tarnawski in Kosow, almost on the Rumanian border. They were both going to take the cure, which consisted of a strict dietary regime, with morning gymnastics exercise sessions. This Institute had a long history. Dr. Tarnawski had founded it in the early 1900s. He believed that good health depended upon eating very light foods, dressing in loose, airy, clothes, doing vigorous gymnastics exercises and sleeping in rooms with wide open windows. This had been quite an innovation for those days before World War I when women wore corsets and voluminous clothes and men wore stiff high collars and vests under their jackets. The Institute was now under the direction of his son but the old doctor could still be seen walking around stark naked in the private garden of his home. Needless to say I was not on a diet and was one of the few to receive plates piled high with good food! As we had a car we also made a few excursions in the beautiful mountainous country and to Kuty, a picturesque town on the Czeromosz River, on the Romanian border. These excursions provided an opportunity to break the strict diet regime and indulge in a drink and some tasty tidbits.

We had planned to stay there till the end of August. Then I was to return to Rydzyna for my final year of high school. However all summer long the news became more and more threatening with every passing day. For weeks, Hitler had been increasingly belligerent in his rantings against Poland and in his demands. Then on August 21 the news hit us like a bomb. After secret negotiations, the German Foreign

Minister Ribbentrop had signed a treaty in Moscow with Molotow, the minister of Hitler's arch-enemy Stalin. It now became certain that an invasion of Poland was a matter of weeks or perhaps days.

Hastily, most of the men at the health spa (primarily business or government executives) packed and sought transportation back to Warsaw or some other city. We drove back to Warsaw almost without stopping, my father's hands gripping the steering wheel so hard that his knuckles were white against his tanned skin. His face was taut, all thoughts of laughter had vanished. Hania was frightened and smoked one cigarette after another. I sat in the back seat and wondered what was going to happen, I realized that my return to school, only a few miles from the German border, had suddenly become very unlikely. Pictures from war books that I had read flashed though my mind.

POLAND IS INVADED

When we arrived in Warsaw, the Polish army had already been mobilized and put on full alert. Everyone was hastily buying food supplies, putting up black-out curtains, pasting strips of paper over windows to prevent them from shattering. Teams of young men were digging trenches in the parks and in city squares to serve as bomb-shelters. Young men in uniform were crowding the stations to get to their units. My father, who was in the reserve, was called up and spent two days and nights together with thousands of other reservists at the central sports stadium. Because of his position as Director of one of Warsaw's principal newspapers, he was quickly released to take charge of this important means of communication.

Friday, 1 September 1939 - a date for future history students to memorize. Early in the morning, before 6 a.m., we awoke to the wail of sirens. In the distance we heard gunfire, anti-aircraft guns. We turned on the radio and learned that the war had started, that the Germans had crossed the frontiers in many places and that they had bombed Poznan, Gdynia and other cities. Hania became hysterical because we didn't have a gas-proof bomb-shelter, she raged that nobody had listened to her when she had begged that something be done in the cellars to prepare for war. Daddy dressed quickly and hastened to the office. About noon we saw planes high in the sky. We couldn't believe that they were German, but soon we learned that, unfortunately, they were. We heard the thud of exploding bombs.

Later we learned that the airfields close to Warsaw were bombed, but the radio announcers didn't admit the extent of the damage.

I went out and managed to buy some felt with which I struggled to seal the door of the bathroom (it didn't have a window), this was supposed to provide some protection in the event that the Germans dropped bombs with poison gas. All the while Hania kept complaining that this hadn't been done earlier. Then I went to see my friend Wanda Vetulani. She and her family were swiftly packing, her father was being sent abroad, to Turkey. The next day they were gone. I was never to see her again,

On Saturday the radio news was full of optimism and talk of victories and "turning the enemy back," but from other communiques it became evident that the Germans were advancing. The first fugitives from the western counties appeared on the streets. Without saying anything to anyone I put on my PW uniform, which I had last worn in the camp in June, and went to the local PW headquarters located in the army barracks, opposite the Legia football stadium. I was assigned to the group serving as messengers and telephone operators in the Mobilization Center under the stands of the stadium. My assignment - to be a messenger on the night shift. A group of Czechs, fugitives from their country overrun only a few months earlier, was being organized and outfitted.

Everyone was concerned about the lack of news regarding the intentions of our allies, France and England. Was there to be no action beyond delivering notes of protest? During the day some of the suburbs were bombed and, particularly, the Okiecie airfield. Black columns of smoke darkened the western sky. That evening I returned home, not having any duty that night. Father was not very pleased that I went off and joined up without talking to him first. He was very worried because from his newspaper sources he knew how bad the situation was, already on the second day of war.

Sunday, September 3rd. At noon the radio announced that England had declared war against Germany. Great joy everywhere, in spite of air-raid warnings, large crowds gathered in front of the British Embassy cheering and waving flags. That evening, when the news was broadcast that France, too, had joined the war, the crowds become even more enthusiastic. Crowds everywhere in the streets.

"Now the war will soon be over! We will show Hitler what war really means! We will be marching down *Siegesallee* and *Unter den Linden* before Christmas!" That's what people were saying, including some radio commentators. Nobody, not even the most gloomy pessimist, could imagine that the war would last six years.

It's amazing how many rumors spread around in times like these. For example, the next day rumors started spreading that the French had moved across the border into Germany, that they had advanced 50 kilometers and that Berlin had been bombed by the French and Polish air forces.

In the meantime it turned out that things were not going so well for us. Cracow and Poznan had already fallen. The Germans were advancing towards Lodz. In the north, Mlawy, only 100 kilometers from Warsaw, had also been taken. But people continued to be optimistic, " ... this is just the first impetus, we will soon show them! Our reserves are just entering the battle...."

In the meantime Warsaw itself was bombed for the first time. We could see the black clouds of smoke in several directions. Sad processions of refugees wended their way through the streets of the city, on foot with bundles on their backs or piled into hand-carts. The more fortunate were riding in horse-drawn farm carts, and rarely were refugees seen riding in motor vehicles. They all talked about being strafed by low-flying German planes. Rumors spread about poisoned sweets, exploding prayer-books dropped by planes[*].

Already, crowds of Varsovians were trying to leave the city. They were fighting to get on the few trains that were still running. The few that owned cars were loading them up to escape to the relative safety of the country. But nobody understood how bad the situation really was, they were unaware that the government itself was evacuating the city. On September 6th a great battle was developing near Kutno, only 100 kilometers west of Warsaw, where several divisions of Polish cavalry and infantry were trying to break through the surrounding pincers of Nazi armor. That same day, for the first time Stuka dive bombers screamed down over the center of the city dropping their

---

[*] These were all rumors, there was never any evidence that this had actually happened. They had no need for such childish tricks.

bombs on the approaches to the bridges over the river Vistula. Fortunately, they did not damage the bridges themselves.

During the night of September 7th to 8th I was on duty at the Stadium from midnight on. When I arrived at my post the building was already empty. Trucks were being hastily loaded and bonfires of papers were blazing. By dawn all was quiet. Nearly everyone had left. At the end of my watch nobody came to replace me. No orders were given to those of us still there. I waited at least an hour. At last we were able to reach someone on the telephone and were told to report to the PW Command Post because our units were leaving the city. Hastily, I returned home to pack my knapsack, to take a blanket, some clothes, some food.

Hania was hysterical. Dad came home, also under strain after spending most of the night at the newspaper. He was distressed that I was leaving. He didn't want me to go. He said it's foolish. But he didn't make any effort to stop me. I insisted that I had orders and must go with my unit. For him there was no question of leaving Warsaw. As long as possible the newspaper must be published. All through the 20 day siege the presses kept running, as paper supplies ran low the competing newspapers pooled their resources to put out joint editions, right up to the moment that the Germans came in and shut down the paper and padlocked the building.

I had to cross the entire city on foot because the trams had stopped running, or if there were any, they were overflowing with people hanging on all around them. The shops were all empty and shuttered. Small groups of people were moving in the direction of the bridges, on foot with push-carts, with knapsacks or suitcases. The luckier ones were on trucks, or in cars, or in horse-carts. All were streaming across the bridges over the River Vistula.

At the Command Post nobody was left except for a few lost souls like myself. Somebody said they had gone to Grochow - a suburb of Warsaw on the east side of the river.

"If you hurry you might catch them."

Somebody gave me a ride part of the way. In the early afternoon I reached Wawer, a partially wooded, residential suburb on the Minsk road. There I found a PW battalion, but from another command, many

boys from the Batory, Rey and Gorski high schools. From among them
- one arose from the ground and called out with joy:

"Bill!" It was my cousin Janek. From that moment till our sad
return to Warsaw six weeks later we stayed together.

During the next six days the PW battalion marched eastward
through Lukow, Miedzyrzec, towards Brzesc - the military garrison
and railway junction at an important crossing of the river Bug - a
distance of about 150 kilometers (95 miles). We marched at night,
spending the days in woods or villages. The days were hot, cloudless
skies providing perfect conditions for the Luftwaffe to bomb and
strafe the roads. We would see the results as we marched along,
starting as soon as the sun dropped lower towards the horizon. The
road was littered with broken wagons, burned out cars, broken
suitcases, corpses of horses, and a few human bodies not yet buried.
Our group consisted of several hundred boys, mostly 16 or 17 years
old. Dressed in the gray uniforms with dark blue collars of the PW, we
were not prepared for outdoor life. The uniforms, made of thin
material, were designed for summer camps and afternoon exercises in
the school playing fields. At night we were cold. We were lead by
school instructors and none of us were armed.

The first three days we were fed soup or gruel from army field
kitchens at our bivouacs. After that the field kitchens disappeared and
we fended for ourselves. In the villages, the women gave us whatever
food they could spare. In the day we dug up potatoes in the fields and
roasted them on fires. On the last day before reaching Brzesc we were
so hungry that we dug up some sugar beets from a field, cutting them
up and eating them raw. Twice we were bombed by planes, but
luckily lost no one. We were hidden among the trees or in barns in a
village. We were not the object of the attack, the planes were just
strafing the roads and the villages at random. They were flying so low
that there could be no doubt that the pilots could see that they were
strafing civilian refugees. There were no troops to be seen on the road
or anywhere close to it.

The last three nights we could see the glare of burning towns and
villages to the north of us. We could hear gunfire and see the flashes
of bursting shells on the horizon. We passed through the little town
of Lukow in which all the houses had been burnt to the ground, just

the chimneys stood out as black, ghostly shapes against the starlit sky. We had no real news, no idea what was happening. We were told that we were being evacuated to eastern Poland and that the army was retreating and would make its stand along the river Bug. There were of course the usual rumors, the French were sending help through Romania, and so on.

Most of the time we were cold, tired and hungry. The first couple of days we had marched along sandy country tracks. Later we marched along a gravel road, which was easier and we made faster progress. I soon had holes in my socks. Somewhere I got some cloth and wrapped my feet with long strips to prevent blisters. Finally, in the late evening of the 14th, we reached the outskirts of Brzesc and sat by the roadside for a long time in a freezing, cold wind. In the middle of the night we crossed the bridge over the river and reached the railway station. A field kitchen gave us our first warm food in three days. Then we were loaded on a train of box cars, which traveled the rest of the night and all the next day to Kowel, a railway junction on the line going south toward Lwow. The train made frequent long stops during which we anxiously watched the skies. Fortunately for us the Luftwaffe was busy elsewhere.

In the late afternoon we reached Kowel and unloaded, then marched another 7 kilometers south of the city to a school summer camp. There were many refugees from Lwow from whom we learned that the Germans were coming from the south (across the mountain passes from Slovakia) and were already approaching that city. The following morning we were marched back to the Kowel station and loaded on to another train, this time made up in part of passenger cars. The Luftwaffe bombed the town but did not hit the station. Shortly after the air-raid the train left eastward. The train moved slowly through the swampy birch forests of Polesie all night long.

Midday of the 17th the train reached Sarny, a small town and a railway junction, only a dozen miles from the border with the Soviet Union. We were able to buy some food, each for himself. After a stop of a couple of hours the train started moving again slowly, this time in a southerly direction. In front of us and behind us were other trains full of troops. In the late afternoon planes flew over dropping leaflets. At first we thought that they were Polish, then we saw the red five-

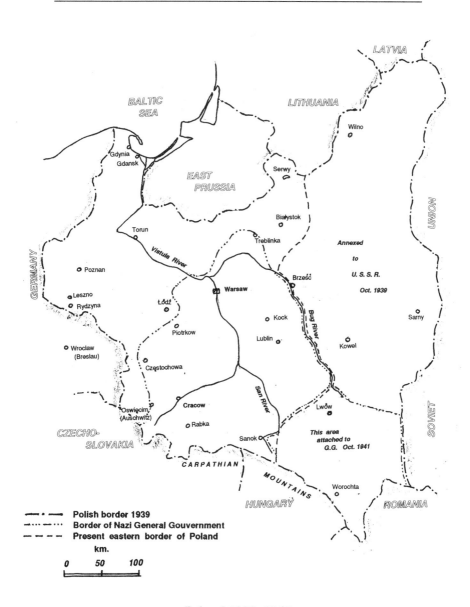

Polish border 1939
Border of Nazi General Gouvernment
Present eastern border of Poland
km.

0   50   100

Poland 1939-1945

pointed stars on their sides. None of us saw any of the leaflets, they fell far away from our car, so I have no idea what was in them. After moving forward for a mile or so the train came to a halt, stood for a while, then jerkily moved forward some more. Finally, it stopped again and stood still the rest of the night. When the sky lightened at dawn, we could see other trains in front of us and behind. Soldiers were already unloading their gear.

Then we were told that the Soviets, or Bolsheviks as we called them, had crossed the frontier. We were in despair. It was now clear that the situation of Poland was hopeless. We did not know what the intentions of the Bolsheviks were, but we were sure that they were not friendly, even though we were unaware that the German-Russian treaty, signed in August by Ribbentrop and Molotow, contained a secret addendum agreeing to divide up Poland along the line of the river Bug. We all sat dejected, our eyes downcast, hardly a word was said, what could anyone say. One of the younger boys started sobbing. Then our group leader gave us a pep talk.

" Don't despair. We aren't giving up yet. Remember that whatever happens our Allies will defeat Germany, I'm sure of it. Poland has survived greater calamities in the past. What we must do now is to survive so that we can fight back when the proper time comes. The Bolsheviks have announced that they are going to occupy all territories east of the Bug. That means we have to get out of here and get back beyond the Bug. Now, all of you, get up, get your stuff together, let's go. Now!"

We and all the troops unloaded from the trains and started marching cross country back towards the west. Janek and I discussed the situation and agreed that come what might, we must stick together and make our way back to Warsaw to find our families. That night our PW group stayed in a village in which the people were friendly and shared what little food they had with us.

During the next few days, on passed through several villages inhabited by Ukrainians who were very unfriendly. They were reluctant to part with any food and watched silently as we passed. On the 20th there was an exchange of fire with some group in the village of Troscianiec. At the entrance to the village a wooden arch had been erected with signs welcoming the Soviet Army. Our PW group had no weapons, but the accompanying military unit, which was part of the special frontier defense force, engaged the attackers. After subduing them, our troops took supplies of food from the houses and then set them on fire.

The following morning, September 21, we were attacked by Soviet planes while we were crossing an embankment over a marsh, near the village of Maniewicze. Several of the soldiers were wounded and some horses were killed and supply-wagons were destroyed. Now the intentions of the Soviets were quite clear. From now on our leadership concentrated on avoiding any Soviet troops. Once more we started the routine of marching at night and lying low in the woods during the day. Our officers must have had good information about the movements of the Russians. We kept changing direction, once going westward, then north and again doubling back toward the south. We were in an area of Poland which was totally devoid of modern paved roads. Even so we kept to field tracks and woodland trails, away from the main routes. Twice during our daytime bivouacs we saw Soviet tanks passing along a road. However the troops accompanying us withheld their fire and kept under cover. We no longer needed to worry too much about aerial observation. The good weather had deserted us. It became cold and a steady drizzle added to our misery. On the 24th we crossed the Kowel-Brzesc railway line, along which we had traveled just nine days earlier.

Just after dawn on the 26th of September we recrossed the river Bug in the vicinity of Wlodawa. At this point the river was only about a hundred meters wide and quite shallow. The horses and wagons and the artillery forded the river. We were ferried across on small boats. The peasant on our boat told us that the previous day German troops had crossed the river at the same place, also going westward, obviously withdrawing from the territory assigned to Russia by the treaty. We were on very short rations and hungry most of the time. Janek and I talked all the time about the wonderful meals his mother cooked. But now again the villagers were friendly and shared with us what little food they had. In one village we found a Polish plane hidden under a covering of hay. After consultation with our officers, the plane was dragged out and the pilot took off flying close to the ground and heading south. No doubt he was hoping to reach neutral Hungary. I doubt that he made it.

The night of the 28th we continued our march through the small town of Parczew which was still burning after being bombed, we didn't know by whom, Germans or Soviets? We also learned that Warsaw had surrendered after a three-week siege. We realized that this was probably true, but still, we did not want to admit to ourselves that this could be true. If we did, what was the point of continuing on? We had reached the vicinity of the small town called Kock, about 100 kilometers south-east of Warsaw. After three weeks of marching and traveling on trains we had almost returned to our starting point! This was also the last pocket of resistance in Poland. Spread over a wooded area some 15 kilometers (10 miles) in diameter a collection of cavalry, infantry, artillery, frontier police, under the overall command of General Kleeberg, was surrounded by the Germans. The date was October 1. The war was only 30 days old. It seemed like an eternity.

That night 13 of us, including Janek and me, were bivouacked in a small village in the woods. In the morning when we awoke the rest of our group had moved and left us behind. We got together and were marching along this country path through the woods when we smelled food cooking. We came into a clearing to find a Polish army field kitchen. We were very hungry and glad to get some hot soup. An officer organized us into a group and gave us some rifles and a few rounds of ammunition. For four more days a desultory kind of activity continued. For an hour or two our artillery fired shells at some unseen target. After a while the enemy artillery started firing back. Hastily, the horses were harnessed to the guns and they were pulled away to another position. We lay in the foxholes that we had dug and watched the salvos advancing across the meadow towards us. Each line of explosions came closer and closer to us. To our relief the next salvo passed over our heads and crashed into the trees behind us. The falling shrapnel sounded like hail. Then again there was silence. Apparently, the Germans were in no hurry to attack. We have nowhere to go anyway. Nobody has anything to say. What is there to talk about?

On the evening of October 4, close to the village of Krzywda, we were told that General Kleeberg had capitulated. The cease-fire was to take effect at dawn. We were each given rations and pay. Suddenly, the distant guns opened up and shells started falling into the clearing in the woods where we had been assembled. Several were wounded, including Janek. A piece of shrapnel hit the top of his head (we had no helmets). He was conscious but bleeding. I helped him and another wounded boy to the first-aid station in the village, where someone bandaged his head. In the morning German ambulances arrived to take the wounded to a field hospital. The Germans were the victors. They were well-fed, clean-shaven. Their uniforms were clean and fresh. They were happy that the fighting was over. One of the medical orderlies, with a big smile of anticipation on his face, told me:

"England is not going to fight, I will be home at Christmas. This the Fuhrer has promised!"

The field hospital that Janek was taken to (and I persuaded the German ambulance orderlies to take me along as well) was in a small town, Garwolin, in a school building. There was a shortage of beds and many of the wounded were lying on straw mattresses on the floor. It was a Polish army field hospital with Polish army doctors and medics. Some German soldiers watched over things. However at this point it could not be said they were guarding us. I was allowed to come and go as I pleased. It was obvious that this situation would not last very long. With the money we had been paid on the last night of freedom, I managed to procure some civilian clothing for Janek and myself, from a butcher in the town. They were filthy and ragged, but wearable. I also made an arrangement with a farmer to take us to Warsaw. In a couple of days Janek was strong enough to travel and the farmer had found some more passengers. Knowing that there would be a shortage of food in Warsaw which had undergone a three-week long siege, I also procured some *slonina* (pork fat), some bread and a container of milk.

Early in the morning, just as it started to get light, I helped Janek out of the field-hospital to the waiting cart. The German sentries paid no attention to a couple of young boys in filthy clothes. The journey to Warsaw took about seven hours. Although there were military patrols on the road, none of them bothered us. There were hundreds of displaced people wandering around at the time and the Wehrmacht at the moment seemed relaxed and pleased with the rapid defeat of the Polish army and not yet prepared for occupation and police duties.

As we approached Warsaw our anxiety increased. What would we find when we got home? What had happened to our homes and families? The increasing signs of mass destruction, as we rolled into the outer suburbs, were not reassuring. Our driver let us off in the suburb of Praga on the east bank of the river. I do not remember at all how we got across the river and how we reached our homes. I suppose we were in a state of shock at the sights that we saw. The streets were full of rubble. The overhead wires of the trams were lying all over the place. Not a single building was unscathed. At the very least the windows were broken and the facades were pockmarked from shrapnel. Many houses were empty shells with blackened holes where the windows had been. Others were partially collapsed as a result of a direct hit by bombs or shells. Most had at least one hole in the roof or walls from shell impact.

We finally reached Narbutta Street. Janek's mother was then living in a flat in Aleje Niepodleglosci which was a little further down Narbutta Street. As we learned later, Aunt Jadwiga and Marysia had spent the last two weeks of the siege with my father and Hania, because their flat had been damaged by a shell. We were overjoyed to reach number 22 and find it relatively unscathed. We went up the stairs and I had a joyous reunion with Daddy. We hugged and kissed each other, then looked at each other and hugged again. Janek learned that his mother and sister Marysia were also all right and had just returned to their own flat, so he quickly left for a reunion with them. Our flat was unscathed except, of course, all the windows were broken. The building had received two direct hits, but one was in the rear wing and the other in the roof. Both Janek's family and mine had survived the first stage of the war and the siege with minimal losses. We were very fortunate.

My father had maintained the publication of the newspaper throughout the siege. Of course as paper supplies dwindled, it was reduced eventually to a single page. In the very last days he joined forces with his competitor, Antoni Lewandowski, the managing director of *Dobry Wieczor* (Good Evening), to keep the news flowing. He also was a member of a Citizen's Committee that was trying to maintain essential services for the besieged city under the leadership of Mayor Starzynski. For his role in maintaining the morale of the fighting city my father was awarded the *Krzyz Walecznych* (Valiant Cross). As soon as the Germans entered the city after the capitulation they took over all printing presses and closed them. A few weeks later they removed from the buildings of Wieczor Warszawski all the equipment, printing presses, linotypes, and any other equipment that could possibly be used for publishing. Then, they allowed my Father to return to the empty buildings and the offices. In the case of the large modern building and presses at Marszalkowska 3, which were the headquarters of the pro-government Dobry Wieczor and several other periodicals, they took over the entire premises for the publication of German newspapers and magazines in the Polish language. Most of the editorial staff of Wieczor Warszawski had left Warsaw at the end of the first week of the war. It had been intended that they set up publishing of the newspaper in south-east Poland in the event that Warsaw would be captured.

This became impossible with the Soviet invasion. They and many members of the government and leaders of the political parties, who had been in the same position, managed to cross the border to neutral, but friendly, Romania. From there they made their way to France. A Polish government-in-exile was established in the town of Angers on the river Loire. Many army units also managed to reach Romania and became the nucleus of the new Polish Army in France. Other units reached Hungary where they were interned. The Hungarian government, fearful of the Germans, officially refused to let them proceed further. Nevertheless, many Hungarian officials were not too zealous in guarding the internees, and large numbers made their way through Yugoslavia to France. By the spring of 1940 close to 100,000 Poles had reached France from Romania and Hungary and formed the new Polish Army to continue the struggle against Nazi Germany.

Before my return to Warsaw, Hitler had reviewed a victory parade of the German troops along the tree lined avenue *Aleje Ujazdowskie*. Naturally the streets had been cleared of all Poles, so we could not witness this final humiliation.

3

UNDER NAZI OCCUPATION

The reality of life in Warsaw after the siege, the first weeks under German occupation, was grim. In the middle of October, winter was coming and most homes were left with paneless windows. There was little fuel, even less food after the long siege. People were in a state of shock and still did not realize the full extent of the situation. They could not face up to the fact that the new reality might last many years. On the contrary, everyone fooled themselves into believing this to be only a temporary state of affairs. Nobody believed that the Allies were in reality so weak and had no great desire to fight. In the meantime everyone was so busy trying to gather new food supplies, searching for window glass and coal, and, for those whose flats were badly damaged, working to close up the gaping holes in the walls and the roofs before winter closed in. Therefore they had little time to really think about the more distant future. The present urgent needs were too great.

Those who had no home at all, those whose houses had been totally destroyed by fire or bombs, or the refugees from the western provinces who were not permitted by the Germans to return home, had the added necessity of finding clothes, a temporary home, a bed to sleep in and blankets to cover themselves at night. The Treutler family belonged to this category. Hania's twin sister, Wanda had left Warsaw on September 6th with her mother and her twin daughters,

Lili and Hala. They had gone south and spent the time of siege in a village about 100 miles from Warsaw, near Garwolin. When they returned in mid October they found that their house had been completely destroyed by fire, and with it, of course, had gone all their possessions. They were only able to recover some silver and jewelry that had been locked in a wall safe. Blackened by the heat, they could be restored.

They had spent a few days in our flat on Narbutta Street before my return. Then they had found refuge in the flat of some friends who had fled to Romania in the first week of the war. They also inherited the friends' maid, Puncia and their dog, a boxer called Rygo. Unfortunately, this flat was located in the elegant Avenue Szucha, opposite the modern building of the Ministry of Finance. This area of Warsaw had suffered very little damage and was a district of large mansions, elegant apartment buildings, parks and embassies. The Gestapo decided to establish their headquarters in the Ministry and to take over all the houses in the avenue and the neighboring streets as residences for the Gestapo officers and personnel. After only a few days in this flat, Aunt Wanda, her husband and the twin girls Hala and Lili (plus the maid and the dog) were given one hour to leave the flat and allowed only to take one suitcase each.

For the time being they moved back in with us. The flat at 22 Narbutta was a large one, in a modern building, had only two bedrooms, a fairly large living room and dining room and a servants room by the kitchen. Somehow we all fitted in as best we could. Quickly a close relationship developed. The girls and their mother were sleeping in what was normally my father's room, which he shared with me. During this period I slept on a couch in the living-room, my father shared Hania's bed. During the day we all had work, but in the evenings there was nothing to do except sit and talk. We sat together in their room, on the large couch, that made up into a double bed. We played games, talked and flirted. At this time I divided my attention equally between Hala and Lili. I had difficulty telling them apart, they were so alike. They were attractive tall girls with blond shoulder length hair, cut in the popular page-boy style. They had good figures and beautiful, long legs. Their blue eyes were slightly elongated, almost almond shaped, arched eyebrows which seemed to be always asking a question. To add to the difficulty, they always dressed identically. Soon I discovered that Hala had a tiny pock mark on the side of her nose and started recognizing slight nuances in the way they talked and reacted. They only stayed about three weeks. A friend of Wanda's, Mr. Grabowski, lived in a very new large block of flats at the edge of the hill looking over the valley of the Vistula. The street was aptly named *Na Szkarpie* (On the Cliff). A neighboring flat was vacant, the owners having fled the country and arrangements were made for the Treutler family to take it over for the duration.

In the meantime, I had been in touch with some of my friends from Rydzyna, particularly Alex Lempicki. Early in November the schools reopened. We both enrolled in a well-reputed private Lyceum called *Mazowiecki* which was located near Plac Unii Lubelskiej, not far from Narbutta Street. Conditions in the school were very crowded, because many other refugees from other schools outside Warsaw also enrolled in this school. The crowding didn't matter because we only managed to go to school for about three weeks. One afternoon the teacher announced that the German authorities had issued a decree closing all schools above the 6th grade.

This was one of the first decrees of the newly formed "General Gouvernement" of Poland to introduce the "New Order" ordained by Hitler. Poland was to be systematically destroyed. Poles were declared to be a *Sklavenvolk*, a nation of slaves. Therefore any schooling other than the very basic was unnecessary. At the same time the news started spreading of the mass arrests of the intelligentsia. Virtually all the professors at the venerable University of Cracow were arrested during one weekend at the end of November. Many of them subsequently died in concentration camps, particularly *Oswiecim* (which later became called *Auschwitz*). An order was issued forbidding the possession of radio receivers. They all had to be handed in. The next order forbade Poles to own automobiles, they too were confiscated. All printing presses were placed under police control. The printing presses of all newspapers were physically removed and taken away to Germany. Only one newspaper in the Polish language was allowed in Warsaw and it was operated by the Nazi occupation government. Poles in general boycotted this propaganda newspaper. Throughout the war, nobody in our family ever bought or read a newspaper or magazine (except of course for the underground press which started developing later in 1940).

The first Christmas of the war was a very miserable one for most people. It became bitterly cold. Fuel was scarce and to add to the discomfort many windows were still without glass, boarded up with plywood, perhaps a small hole with a piece of glass gave some light. Double glazing existed only in the few lucky houses which had avoided damage. Therefore, the cold was felt even more acutely. Fortunately, at this time food was still in good supply, although the prices continued to rise.

Just after Christmas the first incident occurred in Wawer, an eastern suburb, that later was to become all too familiar. At night the SS troops surrounded a group of houses, arrested all the men, and then executed several of them. The pretext was that a German soldier had been attacked. My father decided that I should go for the rest of the winter into the forest. This had been arranged by Antoni Lewandowski, the publisher of *Dobry Wieczor*, the rival newspaper to my father's *Wieczor Warszawski*. It was his modern plant at Marszalkowska 3 which had been taken over by the authorities to publish the new German operated newspaper and magazine publishing company. Although rivals, he and my father were good friends. So early in January I and Staszek Brzosko, Mr. Lewandowski's nephew, went by train to Ceglow, about 50 miles east of Warsaw. We lived the next two months in the house of a forester, Czeslaw Darkowski.

Staszek and I slept in the attic under bearskins. In the attic the temperature was always below freezing. In the morning it took a few moments to gather the courage to slip out from the warmth of the skins, then we dashed down the stairs to the kitchen in which the stove was always lit. In the forest there was no shortage of fuel! We shared the chore of drawing pails of water from the well, bringing them into the kitchen where we carried out our morning ablutions. After breakfast we went to the forestry office, just across the road, where we received our work assignment for the day.

Our job was marking trees to be cut and making an estimate of the cubic content of the logs. We worked in a team of five. One carried a hatchet and marked the selected tree. The second then stamped serial numbers using a tool with a wheel on it which contained all ten digits from 0 to 9. The numbers were rotated, smeared with black paint and using the tool as it were a hammer he would hit the tree as many times as there were digits in the serial number. The third measured the diameter of the tree. The fourth would write the data down in a note book, in the bitter cold this perhaps was the hardest job, his fingers were freezing and it was hard to hold the pencil and write legibly.

The team leader was an experienced woodsman. His job was to select the trees to be cut and estimate their height. Clear cutting of forests in Europe was limited to small sectors of mature growth. To promote growth the forests were selectively thinned out by selecting a percentage of trees to be cut in each year. The snow in the woods was deep, in places almost up to our waists. Frequently, we had to walk an hour or more along a forest trail to reach the area to be marked. The days were short so we would be out no more than five hours. In spite of the cold we enjoyed the work. It was cold but dry, in the forest we were sheltered from wind. When we returned we were very tired and had a tremendous appetite. There was not yet any shortage of food in the country, so we ate very well.

Towards the end of February my father wrote that I should return to Warsaw. The teachers in the various schools, working with the parents, had organized clandestine school groups to continue our studies. We met in groups of five or six in each others' flats. I was in a group together with my friend from Rydzyna, Alex Lempicki. The teachers came to these groups and lectured us, handed out study assignments and checked our homework. With this arrangement we made very fast progress in our work. Nobody goofed off. We were all anxious to learn fast while we had the opportunity, everything was so temporary, who knew what tomorrow might bring? The element of secrecy and danger added a spice to the learning. We had our own codes for warning, if for some reason it was not felt that it was safe to meet in the previously arranged place at the set time. Each student would arrive at the meeting place five minutes apart, and after class would leave the same way. One of us sat at the window watching the street to warn of any unusual activity outside. At the same time through-out Warsaw (and of course elsewhere in Poland) probably hundreds of such school classes were taking place. Our group was the senior year, we were preparing for the final examinations called *Matura* in Polish, the equivalent of the *Bac* in France or Matriculation in England.

By the end of May we were ready for the tests. One morning our group teacher came, set us down apart from each other and then handed out the questions which covered the whole gamut of required study in high school, Polish literature, history, geography, mathematics, physics, chemistry, biology. Three to four hours of complete silence followed. Each of us writing our answers to the questions, or essays as the case might be. At the end of the allotted time the teacher collected our work and took the papers away for checking. A few days later the group assembled again, as I remember, in our flat in Narbutta Street. Our teacher read out the results. We had all passed! We had a couple of drinks, toasted each other and thanked the teacher. One required subject for matriculation was missing, a foreign language. Each of us promised to make up in the chosen language by self study and to report to the teacher when we felt we were ready for the final test to be given by a language teacher, whose name would be announced at that time.

While we were studying feverishly, the war had taken a very serious turn. The "phony" war had suddenly ended in April with the Nazi attack on Denmark and Norway. The first reaction in Warsaw to this news was a sigh of relief. Now, we thought, the Allies will have to react and Hitler will soon find that he has bitten off more than he can chew. Instead, the minuscule force sent by Britain and France to assist the Norwegians was itself quickly chewed up by the Germans. Our dismay turned to gloom after the lightning attack into Holland and Belgium, the surrounding of the British at Dunkirk and the rapid advance of the German panzers around the Maginot Line into France itself.

In Poland the situation was deteriorating rapidly. The Germans had established the "General Government" of Poland under Hans Frank with headquarters in the ancient city of Cracow, which had been untouched by the September war. All of western Poland had been incorporated into the German Reich. This included all of Silesia, the Poznan area and Pomorze, which once before had been incorporated into Germany[*], as well as a large slice of central Poland including Lodz, the center of the textile industry and the second largest city of Poland. In Western Poland all semblance of Polishness were being eradicated. In the GG, as the "General Government" was usually called, ration cards had been introduced and the police grip on every day life had tightened. Daily arrests were taking place, people would leave their flat in the morning to go to work or look for food in the country and disappear without a trace. To cut down on the smuggling of food into the city, groups of people, particularly in the vicinity of the railway stations or the open air market places, would be surrounded by police, loaded into lorries and carted off to temporary camps on the outskirts of the city. Many would then be loaded on to trains and taken to Germany as slave laborers. Only those who were too old or who had good valid work-cards certifying that they were working for the various administrations or industries would be spared and return home after several days of worry.

A new privileged group of people had suddenly been established, the *Volksdeutsch*, Polish citizens of German descent. There were a few who were opportunists and saw a chance to get jobs, better rations, and avoid persecution by signing up as *Volksdeutsch*. However there were very few who did so. Of course there were German families who had never been assimilated into Polish life, who legitimately were German people (many of these had been spies for the Germans - the so called "second column" - prior to and during the September campaign). However the majority of Poles of German origin with German names resisted pressure from the Nazis and refused to accept *Volksdeutsch* identity cards. Lili's father, Stefan Treutler, whose mother spoke German better than Polish, was called into the German police several times and induced to accept the "V" card, but he refused. In the areas that had been incorporated into the Reich, those with German names who refused were frequently arrested and were lucky if only their property was taken away from them and then they were expelled to the G.G. (as the General

---

[*] In 1793 Prussia, Russia and Austria had occupied Poland dividing its territory among them. Poland regained its freedom in 1918 after World War I.

Government area was called). The father and uncle of my school friend Julek Geyer, a prominent industrial family in Lodz, were shot when they refused to sign the pledge of German citizenship.

In the spring of 1940 Jews were required to wear yellow Stars of David on their clothing. And little by little they were moved out of their own flats and moved into crowded houses in the predominantly Jewish district of Warsaw, the so-called Nalewki district. The building of the "ghetto" wall did not start until the following year.

The situation in Russian occupied Poland was even worse. The news from Wilno and Lwow and other towns of eastern Poland was horrifying. Whole families were being taken out of their homes in the middle of the night and carted off to Siberia. Living conditions were much harsher than in the General Gouvernment. A steady stream of refugees was crossing the border to the G.G. where they were relieved to reach this haven of relative "safety."

In this atmosphere of despair I returned to the forestry at Ceglow. The administration of the forest was now in charge of a young *Volksdeutsch*, Marcinkowski, who did not outwardly appear to be pro-German. Presumably, he was one of those opportunists. In any case he behaved quite decently towards me and the others in the forestry. Shortly after my arrival, the news of the fall of Paris came and finally on June 23 Petain surrendered. We were stunned. I was in a state of shock. This was one of the few occasions in my life that I actually cried in public. The Volksdeutsch showed me the newspaper. I just stood there with tears running down my face, then turned round, left the office and went back to my living quarters. This time I was not living at the forester's house but had a room in the home of one of the forest workers in the village, Mienia. There I stayed the rest of the day.

I had placed so much hope in the belief that France and England would defeat Germany that this cruel disappointment was almost more than I could bear. I tossed and turned on my narrow bed in despair. Were the Nazis really invincible? Were all our hopes in vain? Finally I fell into an exhausted sleep with many bad dreams. In the morning I gritted my teeth and decided that there was no alternative, I had to keep on hoping, in the meantime it was necessary to keep on with daily life.

Work in the forest was quite different in the summer. The weather was beautiful and hot. Again we worked in a team of five. Now most of our work was marking and measuring the logs. The trees that we had marked in the winter had been felled, all the branches and the bark removed. We climbed over the piles of timber and measured the diameter of the each log, its length taken with a tape measure. Frequently, particularly on rainy days, I was given the job in the office of calculating the volume of the lumber and recording it in reports. I became quite proficient with an abacus which was the calculator used throughout eastern Europe and Asia until quite recently. The typical abacus had ten wires in a wooden frame, on each wire ten beads were strung. Each row represented a group of numbers, one row digits, the next tens, then hundreds, and so on. Addition and subtraction were quite easy to master. In the office the only sound was the clicking of the beads as they were flicked from left to right and back again. Multiplication and division were more difficult.

I also did some work redrawing maps of the forest. My great-grandfather, who had been a surveyor in Sanok, would have been proud of me! In Poland, as in other European countries, the forests were operated much like farms. The average time it took a tree to grow to maturity was between 100 and 150 years, depending upon type. Therefore the forests were divided into strips and about one hundredth was cut each year. Additional young timber for firewood, mine props, paper mills, was culled by selective individual cutting. This thinning out of the forest strengthened the remaining trees and reduced the dangers of disease and forest fires. The Germans needed timber for the war effort and decreed that the cutting of the Polish forests was to be tripled. The foresters sabotaged these efforts by, deliberately, marking diseased and crooked trees for felling. I am sure that Marcinkowski was aware what was going on but, at least while I was there, he paid no attention.

During the winter, a cavalry officer, who had evaded being taken away as prisoner of war, came to the forest and was also working with us. His name was Makalinski. The origin of his name was MacCallum. His ancestor, an artisan, had been brought from Scotland to Russia by Peter the Great. His grandfather had settled in Poland and changed his name. We became good friends. He had become heavily involved in the new underground movement that had been developing during 1940. Frequent visitors, mostly girls, kept appearing with dispatches for him. Unfortunately, he was too much of a cavalry officer and was not very discreet. Shortly after I left Ceglow in September, he was arrested, and as I learned later from his sister, he was taken to *Oswiecim* (Auschwitz) where he died in late 1941. I suspected that our Volksdeutsch administrator had observed the activities of Makalinski and reported him to the Gestapo.

During this summer, twice a week, I walked to the bakery in another village 3 kilometers distant, to collect my ration of bread. The warm, black rye bread tasted so good that I would consume a good portion of my ration during my walk back home! The forester's niece who was my age came from Warsaw for the summer. Although we flirted she had her eyes on the dashing cavalry officer and was not interested in me. This same summer Lili and Hala had also gone to the country, where it was easier to get good food and safer than in the city. They were staying at a farm near Celestynow. One weekend I borrowed a bicycle and pedaled the 30 kilometers or so to visit them. They were indeed eating well on the farm and to my surprise were both quite pudgy! Needless to say, as soon as they went back to the restricted diet of Warsaw they quickly lost the extra kilograms.

Early in September, I was called back to Warsaw by my father. The Nazi occupiers had suddenly decided that the war was going to last longer than they had planned. England, contrary to the Fuehrer's expectations, was putting up a stiff resistance. The Battle of Britain was not going as easily as Goehring had promised. Therefore they were going to need a cadre of technicians, not only plain slave laborers. Abruptly, they agreed to permit certain vocational high schools and technical academies to reopen.

One of the schools that was re-opened was the technical college named Wawelberg. Before the war this school was a three-year school for technicians, with two departments, mechanical engineering and electrical engineering. Although not at the university level it had a very solid reputation. I enrolled in this school together with several hundred other young lyceum graduates. I think that the enrollment in Wawelberg school was at twice its prewar level. Many professors of the Warsaw Politechnika (the technical university) were engaged as "instructors." The result was that the curriculum of studies was not that of Wawelberg, but that of the Politechnika. For some strange reason the German authorities never caught up with this subterfuge. A couple of times during the next three years the Germans made frequent sudden inspections of the classes. We were prepared. For example, during a mathematics lecture, the professor would suddenly switch from a discussion of, say the theory of arrays, to a very mundane discussion of calculating the bending moment of a steel rod, which a student technician should be learning.

After the war I was told that the German administrator of the Wawelberg school, who had been sent from some university in Germany, was not a true Nazi. Apparently, he realized what was happening, but was sympathetic and kept his knowledge to himself, and in fact assisted in the cover up by warning the teachers when the Gestapo was coming for another inspection. I believe this explanation to be plausible. Otherwise it is difficult to understand how this deception on such a large scale could have succeeded. The following year (1942) the enrollment in the school increased so dramatically that the Wawelberg school was moved from its cramped premises into the buildings of the Politechnika itself. We were thus able to utilize the spacious lecture halls and all the laboratories of this institution, most of which were still equipped with all the original instrumentation.

Enrollment in this school officially sanctioned by the Nazi administration had one other personal benefit. Each student received an identity card specifically stating that he was exempt from compulsory labor. This was good protection against the sporadic roundups by the German police to feed the ever growing demand for slave labor on the German farms and in the factories. On at least two occasions I had the personal opportunity to verify the value of this card.

Lili and Hala still had one more year of secondary school. They participated in *komplety*, the clandestine study groups organized by their own school teachers. The following year they both enrolled in a "nursing school" organized by professor Zaorski. In reality it was a medical school which actually operated in the buildings of the medical college of the university, with university professors teaching the fledgling "nursing students". Close to the end of the war the authorities realized that somehow the "nurses" were never completing their "two year school," and the school was closed. But its purpose had been fulfilled. Many students had completed one or more years of medical school. After the war, whether in Poland or abroad, the students of this school as well as those of the Wawelberg Technical School were able to continue their studies virtually from whatever level they had achieved. In my own case, since I had graduated from the Wawelberg School, when I finally arrived in London, I was able to pass the examinations of the Institution of Electrical Engineers and thus legitimize my status as a graduate electrical engineer.

In the meantime the Polish Underground movement was becoming better organized. Initially soldiers and officers of the army who had avoided being sent to prisoner-of-war camps had formed the nucleus of an underground military organization to continue the fight against the enemy. At the same time civilian leaders, business men, such as my father had also been organizing a civilian resistance organization. My first attempt to get into contact with the underground was just before leaving Ceglow. I had talked to Makalinski and he had told me whom to contact in Warsaw. I made the contact in an office and was told to return on a certain date. When I returned to this office and asked for the same person I was told she had gone away. I came back once more and was given the same answer. Later I learned that Makalinski had been arrested, possibly the young woman I had contacted had disappeared to avoid arrest, or had also been arrested herself. I never found out.

Several months went by. Finally, almost a year later, in the late summer of 1941 Stasz Brzosko, my colleague from the forest approached me. Very shortly afterwards, I was enrolled in an officer-cadet's training course. In our group of five with me were Stas Brzosko, pseudonym "*Socha*", Julek Herman (pseudonym "*Czarny*" which means Black) and two others whose names I have forgotten. When I was sworn in I assumed the pseudonym "*Palak*". This name had no significance; when I asked to choose a name I looked out of the window and saw a tram passing by. In Polish the pantograph, the device that picks up the electric current from the overhead wire, is called *palak*. On the spur of the moment I chose this as the name by which I would be known in the organization for the next three years. This training course was part of a group called *Szare Szeregi* (literally the Gray Ranks).

Our group of five met two or three times a week in different flats for three hours or so at a time. Our instructor was a young Polish officer. We went through the basic instruction that was given in the prewar officer-cadet schools. Of course we were spared the field exercises and sadistic treatment normally given young officer aspirants by the professionals. So we learned about basic army organization, map reading, principles of field movements, weapons etc. All this was theoretical, except handling of weapons. We learned how to handle pistols, grenades and sub-machine guns working with the real thing. We also learned about German army organization. We had two excursions into the country to the forests which lay not too far from Warsaw and were reachable by suburban narrow-gauge trains. There in the forest we were able to carry out some rudimentary exercises in movement in terrain. However we never actually fired any weapon. All of us had basic training in the P.W. at our respective high schools before the war, which had included target practice with small caliber rifles.

Our training also included material that had never been taught in prewar officers' schools, guerrilla warfare tactics, how to make and use *molotoff cocktails* (fill a bottle with gasoline, stuff a rag into the neck, light the rag with a lighter, then throw under the treads of a tank, or even better lob it into the open hatch). We found out later during the Uprising how effective these simple weapons could be if aimed carefully. We also studied specific buildings or enemy targets. One of those that we studied was the Central Post Office, which later on turned out to be our actual target. In December 1942 a senior officer visited our class and gave us an examination. Shortly afterwards, all five of us graduated and were given the rank of corporal-cadet. Each of us was assigned a group of five or six volunteers for further training and preparation for the eventual uprising against the German occupiers.

The meetings were all organized with careful precautions, similar to those that we had used for the high school study groups. The telephones still worked in Warsaw and were commonly used for communications. Of course you had to consider that potentially every conversation was being monitored. We used carefully prepared codes so that every communication would sound like a normal harmless conversation. We had several warnings, meetings were canceled at the last moment, but we were lucky, we never had even what might be called a "close call". We all were equipped with good papers, a German *Ausweis* (identity card) certifying that we were students in German-recognized schools, or working for essential services, so we could move about relatively safely. Nevertheless a number of friends or acquaintances were caught, sometimes quite innocently. They just happened to be in a building or in a street-car that was surrounded by the Gestapo and SS and all young people arrested for no particular reason. In many of these cases the best documents could not save them. Good documents however were essential for safety, because you could be stopped at any time by a German or Polish police patrol for checking of papers, and a frisking for weapons or contraband.

In the spring of 1941 a Polish policeman left an official letter requesting that I report to Police headquarters. At first there was some consternation at home. But after some thought my father and I decided that no danger was involved. Obviously, if they wanted to arrest me or deport me to Germany they would not have left a letter. It was better to go and find what it was all about. One morning I went to Police headquarters, after showing the letter I was escorted in to the office of a German police officer. He told me that a request had been received from some official in Italy, that I should be allowed to go there. If I wished to go I would receive a pass. I was completely surprised and didn't know what to say. I was told to go home, think about it and return within two weeks to give my decision, yes or no. That evening, at home we discussed the matter. The name of the Italian official was unknown, but my father supposed that he might have some connection with American friends who were trying to get me out of enemy territory (America was still neutral at the time, as was Italy).

My father made no effort to influence my decision in the matter. For several days and nights I thought about it and finally decided not to avail myself of this opportunity to get out of Poland. Accordingly I returned to the police headquarters where I was asked to sign a paper acknowledging, that I had received the offer and declined to avail myself of it. I think that the reason for my decision was rather romantic. I felt that if I left I would be like a rat deserting the sinking ship, I felt an obligation to stay with my father and my friends. My father was very proud of me that I had decided to stay with him. After the war I found that it was Bill Murray-Lawes who had asked some American friends of his to arrange this chance for me to get away. The Church teaches us that we all have a free will to make the choices which determine our lives. Personally, I always felt that chance or luck, *kismet,* generally decided what happened to you. However this time I did have a free choice to decide my future destiny. Sometimes at night, particularly later in prison camp, I would dream what would I be doing at that moment if I had accepted the offer?

My father had found a way to earn a living. With some of his acquaintances he had set up a factory of condiments in the empty building of the *Wieczor Warszawski.* The main product was a soya based sauce like the famous "Maggi". The bottles were even similar. This gave him and several other people a source of income. Even more important it enabled him to get the necessary papers with the essential German police stamps certifying him as an important producer of foodstuffs. His secretary, Janka Mazurkiewicz, was his right hand in this operation. She lived with her husband close by on Narbutta Street, and they walked together the mile and a half to the office, across the open space of the Mokotowskie Fields, every day in every kind of weather.

This business only kept him partly occupied. As a person with a long background in the political life of Poland, very soon after the collapse he was deeply involved in the civilian side of the resistance movement. I knew very little of what he was doing. In the resistance movement the less you knew about somebody else's activities the safer they were in the event of your being arrested. Similarly, he knew little about my activities, other than knowing that I was involved in some way. It was inevitable that these activities could not be kept completely secret from one another, as we were living in the same flat. In this flat I held meetings of my group. From time to time he also held meetings with some of his people. Before agreeing to have any meeting we would consult with each other to find out if the way was clear. Implicitly, it also meant that the other should stay away from home during this meeting, to avoid knowing or recognizing any of the participants. We had to keep Hania, my step-mother, ignorant of all our activities. She maintained the household, purchased and prepared the food, and read hundreds of books that she borrowed from a lending library. She knew that something dangerous was happening, she was aware of the strange people appearing at all hours of the day and whenever one of us had a meeting she went to visit friends or stayed in her bedroom. She lived in a perpetual state of terror.

After the war I learned a little more of the details of my father's activities. He was active in continuing his work in the *Stronnictwo Pracy* (Labor Party). This party, in spite of its name was not Socialist, but similar to the Christian Democratic Party in post-war German and Italy. This political party participated in the Polish Government in Exile in London. In the Underground a corresponding organization was working under the name of *Delegatura Krajowa* (Delegated Home Government). Its activities were limited, of course. However they worked on consolidating the several military resistance groups, that had sprung up spontaneously, into a cohesive *Armia Krajowa* (Home Army). They worked on coordinating the numerous school activities. There was also a Judiciary which passed judgment on various war criminals, both Germans and Polish traitors. In particular with regards to the latter, judgments were passed and punishments, including death sentences for particularly heinous crimes, were decreed and swiftly carried out.

My father was Assistant-Director of the Department of Documentation under minister Olszewski until the summer of 1942. During the next two years up to the Uprising (and afterwards until arrested by the "liberating" Russians) he was Secretary of the *Rada Jednosci Narodowej* (Council of National Unity) and was the recording secretary of its Main Committee. In this capacity he participated in all the key meetings of those responsible for leading national affairs in Poland.

An important function of the underground government was to keep the government-in-exile in London informed of all important details of life under the occupation. This included collecting information relative to all war crimes perpetuated against the population and documenting evidence to be used against the Nazi war criminals, preparing position papers on various aspects of life and government in the future liberated country. I played a small role in this effort. I did some research for my father and helped in making translations and typing some of the documents which were later transferred to microfilm. Communications with London were maintained by radio and also considerable documentation was sent to London by couriers. Among the better known couriers were Jan Karski and Jan Novak, both of whom have written books about their experiences.

To inform the population news sheets were published and distributed. At the beginning, these news sheets were simply typed and crudely copied. As time went on the organization was perfected and well printed eight page newspapers were distributed in thousands of copies, particularly in Warsaw, but also in all smaller towns. The largest of these was the *Biuletyn Informacyjny* (Information Bulletin) which reached a circulation in the tens of thousands by 1944.

In the meantime every day life also went on. I attended school and studied. I had capitalized upon my knowledge of English and was earning a little by giving lessons to people who could afford to pay. During the winter of 1940-41 I had started to give lessons at first to only about three different pupils, twice a week. As I developed a routine and gained more proficiency I was able to command higher fees and increased the number of my pupils. The largest number I had at any one time was six. There was a lack of good textbooks, most of those that were in existence were extremely boring. So, with time I developed my own course materials, trying to make the work as conversational, and related to every day life, as possible. This way, by the summer of 1942, I was able to cover all my own expenses and, eventually, contribute towards the support of the household.

My days were now very fully occupied, studies at the Technical Institute took up the mornings six days a week and a couple of afternoon hours working on laboratory projects. I gave English lessons in the afternoons twice a week and on Saturday mornings. Two evenings a week and several hours each weekend were occupied by officer's school. Of course I also had homework to do and getting from one place to another took a lot of time. The trams were erratic and generally over-crowded, walking was a good way of getting most places. Fortunately, Warsaw is not a very large city and most of my activities at this time were concentrated within a two mile square area between the Mokotow district, were we lived, and the center of the city.

Not much free time was left, most of it was spent with Lili. After she and her mother and sister had moved from our flat on Narbutta Street to the flat on Na Szkarpie, we saw each other quite frequently. When I returned to Warsaw from the forest in Ceglow and started attending the Wawelberg Technical School we started seeing each other several times a week and telephoning daily. In the spring of 1942 they were evicted again by the Germans. They moved from that flat (this time they were allowed to take all their belongings) and found a temporary home in a small villa on Filtrowa Street, which was just a few blocks from the Politechnika. It was also just 10 minutes walk across the Mokotow Fields from our flat. Now we were spending some time together almost daily.

During 1940 and 1941 the grip of the Germans had increased on life in Poland and Warsaw in particular. The number of Germans. civilian, military and SS living in Warsaw had steadily increased. They selected the most modern residential blocks for themselves and evicted the Polish tenants or owners at will. Thus in the summer of 1940 we had been evicted from our lovely flat on Narbutta Street. We were fortunate to find another smaller flat in a fairly modern smaller building at Lowicka 60, just a few blocks further from the center, close to the last stop of the tram line No. 3. This flat consisted of a living room and two bedrooms plus a kitchen and a servant's room. My father occupied one room, Hania the other, I used the servant's room. During the winter the only source of heat was a kind of Franklin stove in the center of the living room. From it a long black sheet-metal pipe lead to a hole in the window that overlooked the rear yard. This pipe helped to contribute a fair amount of heat to the flat. From 1942 on, electricity was very limited. Usage was rationed. I found a way to by-pass the electric meter so that we did not exceed our ration. This method resulted in a very low voltage so the lights were dim, and the electric radiant heater in my room and Hania's bedroom barely glowed, but did take some of the chill out of the air. In 1943 the Germans started disconnecting the electricity altogether, except in the central part of the city where many Germans were living (*Deutsche Wohnunggebiet*). In our area we were provided with electricity for only two hours a day. For illumination we used carbide lamps, which were very smelly but produced a fairly bright light. During the last two winters I did all my homework by this light.

During this same time the pressure on the Jews had been increasing. First they were obliged to wear yellow Stars of David on their clothes or on an arm-band. Then they were evicted from their homes and flats and forced to move into the already crowded Nalewki district, which for the last 100 years had been populated almost exclusively by poorer Jews, workers, shopkeepers, artisans. This overcrowding was increased by the transportation of Jews from other Polish towns, especially those in Western Poland which had now been incorporated into the Reich itself, to Warsaw. The next step was the building of a wall around this district which occurred towards the end of 1941. The Jews were no longer permitted legally to live outside the "Ghetto," as it was called. They only left through the few gates in work parties under guard. Early in 1942, large groups started to be removed to camps in Eastern Poland, in particular to the infamous Treblinka. It was not until later in 1942 that rumors started to spread about the mass murdering of the Jews in the gas chambers of these camps. In prewar Poland there were about 3,000,000 Jews (about 10% of the total population). At least 300,000 lived in Warsaw, a city of about 1,200,000. It is reported that before the mass deportations to the death camps started, almost 500,000 had been crowded into the cramped quarters behind the walls of the "Ghetto."

Thousands died from malnutrition and sickness. The rations assigned to the Jewish population were even more meager than those of the remainder of the Polish population. Most of us however were able to supplement our rations with food bought in the black market, mostly smuggled in from the surrounding countryside. In the "ghetto" supplementary food sources were non existent. The German guards at the gates prevented any contraband from entering. Although the daily work parties had some possibility to acquire extra food, the gate sentries would search them when they were returning. A very small number of Jews managed to lose themselves with the help of Polish friends in the general Polish population already early in 1940. This involved considerable risk for those who hid them and assisted them in any way. However in the city with large numbers of refugees, both from eastern and western Poland crowded into the four and five story apartment buildings, it was easier for this subterfuge to be successful than in smaller towns and villages.

As mentioned above, the Jews from Warsaw and other towns in Poland were being transported to Treblinka, about which, initially, we knew nothing. The camp to which Poles were sent, who had been arrested, many times for no reason at all, was Oswiecim (Auschwitz) which figures prominently in the post war stories of the holocaust. In actual fact, during the first three years of the war, most of the inmates of Oswiecim were not Jews. It was not until 1943 that the gas chambers and crematorium were built in a new camp at Birkenau close to Auschwitz. Up to that time thousands of Poles had died there from malnutrition, sickness or had been hanged or shot. In 1943 the transports started arriving with Jews from other camps in Germany, such as Dachau, Belsen, Theresienstadt, Ravensbruck. German technicians had now developed a gas as an efficient way for disposing of all those camp inmates who were no longer useful for work, the old, the young children, the sick and weak.

The relative ease of hiding groups of strangers in the apartment blocks of the large city became utilized by the underground organization to provide half-way houses for Allied prisoners who had escaped from prisoner-of-war camps in the eastern part of Germany. I was involved with one such group in early 1941. An elderly, aristocratic lady who lived in a large flat on the third floor of a large building in central Warsaw was hiding three English airmen who had escaped from a camp in Pomorze not far from the Baltic Sea. They were waiting for arrangements to be made to conduct them further on their way home. It became a major problem arranging exercise to keep them in reasonably good physical condition for their long journey. Several times I took them for walks, one at a time. Understandably they were much more nervous about walking along the crowded streets than I was.

A key player in all these clandestine activities was the *dozorca*, the equivalent of the French *concierge*, the person who resided in a small apartment at the entrance door to every apartment complex. Every person entering the apartment building had to pass the small window through which he, or she, could be observed, and if necessary questioned. This was where you asked for information if you didn't know where the person you wanted to visit, lived. The *dozorca* was also supposed to check that every person residing in the building had registered with the police. Fortunately, most of them were Polish patriots and asked no questions of anyone. Also they were paid only very small cash salaries and in these hard times were too busy trying to augment their incomes to pay much attention to their official job. Nevertheless this was an additional danger one had to be aware of.

In June 1941 the Germans started their offensive against Russia. This was not entirely unexpected. For several weeks there had been an extraordinary movement of military convoys eastward through Warsaw, both by truck and by rail. During the spring the Germans had over-run first Yugoslavia, then Greece. At the end of April the British paratroopers evacuated Crete. With the Balkans now under Nazi control, they were free to go after Russia. Stalin apparently had not expected Hitler to attack Russia, at least not so soon. The Soviets were living up to their agreement with Hitler. Every hour at least two long freight trains carrying grain or oil to Germany passed along the main railroad through Warsaw. Russian grain and oil had been shipped to Germany all through the winter. In the spring of 1941 wheat was sprouting and growing between the rails!

Certainly, the Russian army was no match for the onslaught of German tank divisions completely experienced in the technique of blitzkrieg. Within weeks the German armies had taken Kiev in Ukraine, swept through the Baltic states to the outskirts of Leningrad, and by early October were within artillery range of the capital, Moscow. This rapid advance was remarkable considering the distances and the lack of good roads for bringing up supplies. Nevertheless at this crucial moment, the forward movement had to stop for lack of supplies. Before the armies had regrouped and brought up ammunition, food and fuel to the front lines, the Russian winter set in. First the rains of November reduced the terrain to a sea of mud, then the bitter cold and the snow stopped any further forward movement. Hitler, like Napoleon 129 years before, was defeated by the sheer vastness of the Russian land and the bitterness of the winter, for which the German soldiers were no better prepared than Napoleon's legions had been.

For Poles the Russian campaign had a profound influence. All of Poland was now occupied by one enemy. Those in eastern Poland who had survived the savage deportations to Siberia were able to communicate with their families in the General Government. Food supplies in Warsaw became easier, even the official rations were increased. For a while the pressure of the Gestapo and SS was reduced. They were too busy pacifying the newly occupied territories. For those who had been deported to Siberia or were suffering in Gulags or Soviet prisons, the hope of freedom softened their suffering. Thousands had already died from sickness, frost, malnutrition or had been brutally murdered.

But now, the Soviets desperately needed help from the "capitalists" in the west. They agreed to release all the Poles held in camps throughout Siberia and allow them to leave Russia. A Polish mission arrived from London and established headquarters in Kubyszev on the Volga river. During the winter and all through 1942, a steady stream of Polish men, women, and children made their way across Siberia to Iran where Polish refugee camps had been set up. From there they were moved to Lebanon, Egypt, Palestine, and Kenya. A new Polish Army, the Second Corps, was established. The men and the younger women were enrolled in it and trained. This army unit took part in the battles in North Africa and the campaign through Italy, including the battle for the monastery of Monte Cassino.

Close to 12,000 Polish officers and NCOs from the regiments and divisions caught in Eastern Poland by the Russian advance in September 1939 had been interned in camps. Then they had disappeared. All inquiries by the Polish mission directed towards the Russian government were met with a stony silence. In the spring of 1942 German soldiers discovered mass graves in the forest of Katyn, not far from Smolensk. Delegates of the Swiss Red Cross and also representatives of the Polish Red Cross were brought to the site to witness the exhumation of the bodies of the missing officers. Soviet propaganda immediately sprang into action to accuse the Germans of this war crime. British and American communists and socialists, of course, followed this lead. However the evidence was overwhelming. Diaries found on the bodies, the state of decomposition, the Russian bullets that had been used to shoot each of the officers in the back of the head, and finally testimony of the local population, who had seen the transports being lead into the forest and had heard the shots, all established without any doubt who was responsible for this crime, and the exact dates when it had occurred. The publication of this evidence (which had been obtained from the Swiss Red Cross) by the Polish Government in London resulted in the Soviets breaking all diplomatic relations with the Poles late in 1942. This halted all further evacuation of Polish refugees from Russian territory and the Polish Mission in Kubiszew was closed.

On the war fronts, 1942 started as a very depressing year, in spite of the momentary pause in the early winter the Nazi juggernaut continued its advance through Russia; in North Africa Rommel was threatening the Suez Canal. The entry of America into the war at the end of 1941 encouraged us, we knew that beleagured England would now receive increased supplies. But the long series of Japanese victories in Asia and on the Pacific dashed our hopes again. Not till autumn did we receive any encouraging news to lift up our spirits.

In spite of all the problems of everyday life in Warsaw, the shortages of all commodities, food, coal, clothes; in spite of the constant danger of arrest, or being seized for no reason at all and taken to a camp for subsequent deportation to forced labor in Germany, or even worse, to a concentration camp such as Oswiecim (Auschwitz); we still tried to enjoy life as much as possible. Relaxation was limited. There was no radio (the possession of a radio receiver was a crime). We boycotted all publications coming from the printing presses operated by the Germans. Therefore we did not read newspapers or magazines. Some cinemas were open but showed only German films, therefore we boycotted them also. The Germans tried to open a theater to show selected Polish plays, but we boycotted that also, and the few actors that participated in this endeavor were ostracized.

Most of the prewar cafes and restaurants were open and some new ones were established. Those that were not patronized by Germans were all full. In many of them actors, actresses, musicians provided entertainment. For example in the large Cafe Lardelli at the corner of Polna and Koszykowa Streets, the musicians of the Warsaw Philharmonic played every afternoon. Their repertoire was limited by the authorities to works by German composers, but that was acceptable to us. We didn't consider Beethoven or Strauss to be Nazis! The coffee was made from a mixture of grain and acorns, but the cakes were acceptable and tasted sweet. Sitting in a cafe had an element of danger in it. We risked that the cafe might be surrounded by the police and any one arousing their suspicion, whether possessing good documents or not, could be dragged into the waiting trucks and taken to a camp or to the Pawiak prison. But we took the risk to meet other people, listen to music, and in winter time it was warmer than at home.

Most socializing however was done at home. Anyone's namesday was an opportunity for a party. Nobody had any food to spare, so it was an accepted practice, when invited, to bring some food or a bottle. Anyone who had a flat larger enough to accommodate several couples with space left over for dancing was assured of having frequent company. Among the students of the Zaorski medical school any occasion was a good one for a party. Because of the curfew, which in winter months was from eight o'clock until six in the morning, these parties often became all night affairs. At such occasions it was normal for the boys to bring a liter of vodka and each girl brought a dish of food.

During the summer months those that could would try to go into the country for a few weeks or even weekends, even though travel was both difficult because of the limited and overcrowded trains, and dangerous because of frequent raids by the Gestapo and SS, who stopped trains to check all documents. In the summer of 1941 I was able to go to a village near Grojec, about 50 miles south of Warsaw, for about three weeks. An older colleague from Rydzyna was convalescing there from a severe stomach ulcer and invited me to keep him company. I enjoyed the peace and quiet and reminiscing with him about old times at school. I also took advantage of this time to complete a crash course in German literature to fulfill my final requirement for obtaining my certificate of Matriculation.

In 1942 Lili and I, Hala with her boy-friend Sten and two other couples went to a village not far from Rabka, in the foothills of the Carpathian mountains, for a two-week holiday. Needless to say, all our parents were horrified but were unable to dissuade us. The journey was a difficult one. This was an overnight journey standing packed like sardines in the corridor of the Warsaw - Cracow train, then change to a local for another three hours. We did not go all together but split up and went on different days and trains. We occupied an empty summer home and took care of our own provisions, collecting berries and mushrooms in the forest. Here in the country, far from any large city we were also able to get quantities of eggs, fresh vegetables and milk, even a chicken or two and a couple of times a piece of meat. The relaxation in peace and quiet in fresh air and the fresh food fully justified the hassle of getting there.

Where was the money coming from to support daily life and these relaxations? Food was rationed and the rations got progressively smaller as the war dragged on. All other necessities such as soap, textiles, clothing, shoes were also rationed and in increasingly short supply. Rationed goods were at controlled prices. Salaries in all official jobs were also frozen. Widows and old people were getting their pensions which allowed them to buy rations and pay their rent (also frozen). But all this was woefully inadequate. An underground economy sprang up as it always does under such circumstances. The farmers smuggled food into the cities in spite of the efforts of the police. Of course, as the shortages and the difficulty of smuggling increased, so did the prices. Textiles, leather and other articles somehow found their way into the black market, many German bureaucrats and police becoming quite wealthy in the process. These goods found their way to the ultimate consumer through several hands, each making some profit. Others established small enterprises to produce the goods that were needed, or provided services at a commensurate fee. For example many women, widowed or whose husbands were in camps or prisons, maintained their families by baking cakes, sewing clothes, smuggling food from the country, or serving as a link in the chain providing some type of goods to the underground economy.

Transportation had become a major problem in Warsaw. There were of course no private cars (except for Germans), no buses, no taxis. Streetcars (trams) provided the only public transportation. Even their number was reduced by mechanical breakdowns and lack of spare parts. Therefore the trams were terribly overcrowded. The front of the trams was reserved for Germans, the remaining passengers fought to get in. As they trundled along, passengers hung on from the windows, on the bumpers and braced on the couplings in between the cars. Needless to say, there were many accidents. For those who could afford it there were a few horse drawn cabs, which had survived from prewar days, but as the supply of fodder diminished and the poor horses got thinner and thinner the number of *dorozka* also dwindled. Enterprising people will always find a solution for any problem. Soon rickshaws appeared in the streets. In fact these were three-wheeled bicycles with a seat that could accommodate two passengers. As time went on someone came up with the idea of providing an electric motor to propel the rickshaws. The motor was driven by current from a battery that was charged at night. The speed and range of these pedicabs was very limited but it provided transportation for the affluent and a source of income for the entrepreneurs who built the vehicles and for the young people that pedaled them or drove the electric versions.

What of our families? Lili's mother and father both had jobs as accountants, under the pressures of war-time life they had become estranged and finally separated. Aunt Jadwiga lived in her flat with Janek and Marysia not far from us. She continued to work at the Institute for the Blind. The pay was, of course small, I don't know what she did to make ends meet. Janek and Marysia both completed their schooling by participating in clandestine classes, just as I had done. Both I and my father would drop in to see them from time to time, but not nearly as often as we should. Uncle Staszek's wife, Genia, together with young Staszek, then 15 years old and baby Maciek, had left Pulawy and gone east as the German army approached. They, like thousands of other refugees, were then caught by the Soviet invasion of Poland and suffered through the bitter winter of 1939. In the late spring of 1940 they found their way across the border back to Warsaw. Genia was a dentist by profession and was able to make a living. Staszek was not much of a student and I don't believe he was able to complete his secondary schooling in the difficult conditions that were existing at the time. I saw very little of him during these years. However in 1943 he left Warsaw and joined the partisans in the Holy Cross mountains in the center of Poland. In this heavily forested area quite large armed groups of different political persuasions were successfully operating during 1943 and 1944. In 1943 Genia was arrested under circumstances the details of which I never learned. As a matter of fact we didn't learn of her arrest until several weeks later. She was taken to the infamous concentration camp at Ravensbruck in northern Germany and was subjected to barbarous treatment and medical experiments. She survived but was a broken and sick woman as a result.

PREPARATION
FOR BATTLE

With the New Year of 1943, hope stirred anew in the suffering peoples of occupied Europe, particularly in Poland. The tide of war seemed to have finally turned. The Americans had crossed the Atlantic and were pushing the Germans back to Tunis in North Africa. The British had broken out at El Alamein and were advancing across Libya. The German army was surrounded at Stalingrad. Allied air raids were increasing against German cities. Although we knew little about the war in the Pacific, we did know that the Japanese at last suffered defeats at Guadacanal and the Battle of Midway.

A dozen couples gathered in a house in an isolated residential area surrounding the old Mokotow Fort to greet this hopeful New Year. In small groups we reached the end of the No.3 tram line and then walked the mile across the fields, our boots squeaking in the frozen snow. The girls laden with food; the boys with vodka and beer. An almost full moon in a clear, cloudless sky shone down on the road. We all gathered before the curfew hour of 8 p.m. Most were students from the Zaorski Medical School, a few from other schools. In spite of the scarcity of food, there was enough for the whole night of reveling: *Bigos* and *barszcz, kielbasa*, vegetable salads, black bread; some of the girls had baked cakes. Music was provided by an electrically driven gramophone. The records were an assortment of various personal favorites brought for the occasion. The house had electricity because of its proximity to the radio transmitter *Warszawa II*, so we had light all night. Its isolation allowed us to make as much noise as we wanted. Vodka flowed freely, and we danced all night long — we could not leave until 6 a.m. even if we wanted to. It was a weary group that, a few at a time, trudged back through the snow to the end of the tram line, in the gray light of dawn.

As it became clear that the turning point of the war had passed, that now slowly but surely the Germans and their Axis allies, Italy and Japan, were being beaten back, activities in the Polish Underground increased. The number of people, young and old, who were actively engaged in some facet of it, steadily increased. Even as some got caught, imprisoned or executed, many more took their place. The organization grew not only in numbers, but also in its effectiveness. The numerous independent military groups had been knit into a single organization, *Armia Krajowa*, universally called AK. Only two organizations refused to join. One was a group organized by politicians of the extreme political right, the other comprised of radical socialists. The latter was infiltrated by communist agents. The former, even if it was later accused of being "fascist," was just as violently anti-Nazi as the others.

Personally, I also became more active. Previously I had been a student. Now graduated from Cadet school with the rank of corporal-cadet, I was assigned my own group of six, a section. It was my turn to be an instructor, to pass on my acquired knowledge. I was responsible for the preparation of this group for the final attack on the Germans. I met with this group once a week for training, passing on instructions from above, and transmitting gathered intelligence up the command chain. The section leaders would meet about once a month with the platoon leader to work on plans for action, review new instructions passed down from the leadership, and study new weapons.

It was inevitable that in turn I would recruit Lili. Girls and women had been active in the Underground from its beginning, mainly as couriers and distributors of the underground press. With the approach of the final battle, there was an urgent need for a medical corps to take care of the inevitable casualties. Lili, being a medical student, could play an important role here. So, after a period of initial training in the fundamentals of army discipline and the specific requirements of military first-aid, she was assigned her own section of girls whom she taught medical basics. The girls also received some rudimentary training in handling weapons, military procedures, and methods of communication.

In the spring of 1943, at Passover, a week before Easter, the Jews in the Ghetto rebelled against the Germans. They had finally realized what was happening to them. As I have said earlier the Nazis were systematically removing Jews by the train load to camps in Eastern Poland, principally Treblinka and Sobibor. It had now become proven that as the trains arrived, the majority were taken to a "bath-house" in which the shower-heads sprayed, not water, but cyanide gas. The bodies were then removed and burned in large furnaces. Evidence of this had been obtained by the Underground and passed to London. It was later learned that this intelligence was deemed to be so preposterous that it could not be true[*]. It seems that the Elders in the Ghetto did not believe it either, they thought that these trains were taking them to camps but did not believe they were being systematically murdered. Therefore they cooperated with the Germans in selecting the daily quotas for loading into the trains. Finally, it was realized that the unbelievable was true. The decision was reached that although a fight was doomed to failure, it was better to die fighting the enemy than be passively lead to the slaughterhouse.

The fight lasted nearly three weeks. The Jewish fighters were able to inflict substantial losses on the Nazi forces who had to fight them house by house. Unfortunately, many of these troops were not actually Germans, but units made up largely of Ukrainian and Latvian SS troops that had been created after the Germans had taken these countries from the Russians in 1941. Soon the area fell quiet, the blazing houses burned out and the huge cloud of black smoke finally died down. All that was left of a couple of hundred city blocks, inhabited towards the end by half a million people, were heaps of blackened rubble.

---

[*] Jan Novak went to London carrying this information. Churchill sent him to Washington to brief President Roosevelt. His information was ignored.

Poles have been criticized loudly by Jewish writers and publicists, particularly in the United States, for not providing assistance. This is not true, the small quantities of arms and ammunition that the Jewish fighters had, were provided by the Polish Home Army. The only way of communicating with the Ghetto was through the sewers, and that was not easy. Many of them had been blocked or booby-trapped. Some Jews managed to escape from the Ghetto by this route and were assisted to safety by the Polish Underground. We agonized over our impotence, a gloom fell over all our meetings and social gatherings. The cloud of black smoke hung over the city, at night the sky was red from the flames. Several diversionary attacks were carried out by the AK, the largest on April 23rd, but they had no overall effect. We were certainly in no position at this time to mount a major military effort. And it would have been doomed to fail, as it eventually did even under much more favorable conditions, a year and half later. The Allies had not yet set foot on the European continent. In the east, the Russians had just started an offensive on the river Don, 1,000 miles away.

In the spring of 1943, Lili's mother Wanda, through her connections, was able to find a flat at Wilcza 58. The flat was new, built just before the war, with two spacious, light, airy rooms. Several flats in the building were occupied by Volksdeutsch, so the building received a decent allotment of coal and the central heating worked sufficiently well to keep the flat tolerably warm even during the coldest days. They had one other advantage. The location was right on the border of the "German residential district" and they enjoyed the luxury of electricity at all hours of the day and night. This flat was only a few blocks from the Politechnika, and also close to many of my other activities, so I became almost a daily visitor. As was common in Warsaw, there was a tiny alcove in the kitchen with a narrow bed intended for a maid. As my home was much further away in the south of the city, my heavy schedules made it difficult to reach home before curfew. I became a frequent occupant of the maid's bed.

In the kitchen, in the ceiling above the sink, there was a small trap door giving access to the plumbing in the flat above. There was just enough room in this space to hide an automatic pistol and some grenades that had been assigned to me for training purposes. Of course, neither Hala nor Wanda had any knowledge of this. That this was a secure hideaway, although clearly visible, was proved much later. The flat was miraculously spared destruction during and after the Uprising. When Wanda was forced to leave the city, she hid her silverware in this same place, only the big soup-ladle would not fit. The flat was occupied afterwards by German soldiers, and later by Russians. When Wanda returned several months later she recovered her silver unscathed.

Towards the end of 1943 our company, which was now known as the 2nd Company of the Kilinski Battalion, was approaching full strength. The company consisted of three platoons, each with three sections, plus a medical section and courier section. I received a promotion to platoon leader and was now responsible for three sections. About this time we were assigned the area that we were to capture during the planned uprising against the Germans. Our primary target was to be the Central Post Office. We studied the target and prepared plans how we should take it. The Central Post Office occupied almost a whole city block, with the front facing Napoleon Square. Just as we were preparing for the final show-down, so were the Germans. Towards the end of the end of 1943, the paramilitary defense Force in the Post Office was reinforced by regular army soldiers and machine gun emplacements were built commanding the square and the side streets. What had earlier seemed an easy target, now became much more difficult. While we might be equivalent to a regular army company in number of bodies, we lacked the rudimentary fire power necessary to deal with a regular army unit in what was now becoming a fortress.

As 1943 continued on into 1944, the frequency of indiscriminate street roundups also increased. The lucky ones, possessing good papers issued by the authorities to those employed by enterprises producing essential goods and services and to the students in the technical schools authorized by the General Government, were generally released after a few hours. The rest were loaded onto transports to the Reich to work in German factories or on the farms. The most unlucky ones were those who got sent to concentration camps or to the Pawiak prison of the Gestapo.

In retaliation, attacks on Germans and various acts of sabotage increased. In some cases these brought instant reaction in the form of surrounding the area where the attack had occurred and arresting anyone without the proper papers, particularly young men. In a few cases there were immediate executions, but more typically those arrested were taken to the Pawiak Prison for interrogation by the Gestapo. Once arrested it was very rare for someone to be released, although some German officials were able, for suitable ransom payments, to obtain the release of someone for whom the Gestapo had no further use. Those whom the Gestapo could not break down and could find no substantial evidence against them, would be shipped off to a concentration camp, generally Oswiecim (Auschwitz), Majdanek or Ravensbruck. Only those that were initially strong and healthy survived these camps for any length of time. In any case they disappeared and it was difficult to find out what had happened to them. Periodically, large posters were put up on the advertising kiosks with lists of names of "hostages" who had been executed as punishment for "attacks by criminal elements against the Reich." The appearance of a loved one's name on one of these posters was generally the only news the family had of their fate.

The Feast of All Saints, November 1, is a day in which all Poles honor the dead by visiting the cemeteries to place flowers and burning candles on the graves. Our family always congregated at the tomb of my grandfather in the Powazki cemetery. A handsome tombstone, a rose colored granite column upon which a falcon stood with its head lowered, had been presented by the international *Sokól* (Falcon) organization of which he had been a co-founder and long-time vice-president. On this day in 1943 not only the graves in all the cemeteries were decorated with flowers and candles, but also flowers and candles appeared in the streets at places where, during the last four years, executions had been carried out by the Gestapo. All day long the candles flickered and the flowers lay there, for some reason the police did not react.

Nevertheless the mood of Varsovians became more buoyant as the underground newspaper *Biuletyn Informacyjny* brought news of the German retreats on various fronts. In July 1943 Sicily was invaded by the American 6th Army and secured a month later. A month after that the Italian army surrendered. Now the Allies were established in Southern Italy. One immediate advantage of this was that the flights of British and Polish planes with supplies or couriers to Poland became more frequent. Our frustration grew again as the advance through Italy bogged down south of Rome at Monte Cassino. It was not until six months later in May 1944 that a breakthrough was made with the participation of the Polish II Corps under General Anders.

In the meantime I continued my studies at the Wawelberg Technical School. Lili and Hala studied in the Zaorski Medical School. My role as professor of English also continued. I had now five classes held in other peoples' homes twice a week. Two or three times a week I met with my three sections carrying out training. The soldiers of each section were responsible for providing a secure location for these meetings. Most of them were in the area just west of the city center. One location was in the building of the prewar Ministry of Trade on Elektoralna Street. This building was now used by the Office of Weights and Measures of the General Government. Mechanical workshops were located in the basement of this building. Many of the mechanics were members of different underground groups and some used the equipment for making parts for guns. I think that they were being paid to work overtime by the unsuspecting Germans!

Other groups within the AK organization were assigned the active diversionary activities against the Nazis. They carried out attacks against Germany army supply depots to capture weapons and ammunition, they carried out attacks against German police units, and successfully rescued several groups of prisoners that were being transported from prisons to concentration camps, they carried out death sentences issued by the underground courts against traitors and Germans responsible for heinous crimes. These activities received a lot of notice, that is they were reported in the underground press. Many of us who were engaged in the more mundane activities, training and preparing plans for future action, became restless. We also wanted to participate in some kind of immediate action. I mentioned this to the officer who had been our instructor in Cadet School, when I met him by chance. My friend, Julek Herman was also impatient. A couple of times we were called upon to provide back-up for other groups engaged in some action.

Finally we were given an assignment. The Judiciary had passed out sentences of death against some traitors. One of these was a Polish police officer, Skomorowski. We were given a copy of the sentence, and a description and photograph of the man. Julek and I recruited three other fellows from our sections who had also been grumbling. We discussed a plan of action. One at a time, relieving each other on a regular basis, we staked out the Polish police station opposite the Central Railway Station for several days, mainly late afternoons, up to the curfew time. This was late November and it was cold and rainy and very miserable standing around in doorways for hours on end. Because my shoes had become very worn and leaked, my feet were continually wet and cold. I was also nervous because the area was heavily patrolled by police, both Polish and German. We were unable to make positive identification. The one time we thought we had him, he jumped in a car and sped away. We were determined to get the job done, but without taking any unnecessary risks. After three weeks without any result the assignment was taken away from us. The next team to whom the job was given was successful, but also unlucky as one of the team members was killed in the action on January 12.

In March we were given a new assignment. This one was a Volksdeutsch living in Zurawia Street, only two blocks away from Lili's flat. He had been responsible for the arrest and later execution of several members of the resistance and their families. The Underground Court had passed sentence of death. As before we were given a photograph. For several days we watched his apartment from an adjacent stairwell and we were able to make a positive identification. Each of us in turn followed him from his flat to his office in one of the government buildings in Czacki Street. Every day he followed exactly the same routine, so we were able to prepare a simple plan of action. To minimize the danger to local people, we decided to carry out the execution close to his office. For the escape route we found a building in Czacki Street which had three different exits to other streets. We carefully walked through an exercise, making sure that all the exits were open in the morning and, apparently, unwatched by police.

On the chosen day everything went like clockwork, exactly as planned. Julek and I followed the target down the street from his home, each on opposite sidewalks. At the tram stop we waited anxiously, noting numerous uniformed Germans waiting on the same corner. We got on the same tram that he did (although in the rear section assigned to Poles). As expected he got off at his usual stop, crossed the main street and proceeded up the side street towards Czacki Street. We now followed him, one behind the other. As we approached his office we nervously looked in every direction. My heart was beating furiously as the moment of action approached. Miraculously, there were no uniformed police or German soldiers close by.

Just as we passed the gateway of our selected escape route, I stepped forward, Julek next to me. We each got off two shots at close range. The target jumped in the air and fell face down on the pavement, blood spurting from his back. We turned around, walked back quickly to the gateway and entered it, trying to look as unconcerned as possible. Then we paused and turned around to see if anyone was following us. The people in the street were quickly dispersing to get out of the way before police surrounded the area, no one was paying any attention to us.

Germans dashed out of the office building and surrounded the site of the execution, but, fortunately, we had been successful and avoided detection. Quickly we passed through the courtyard to one of the other exits. There a third team member was waiting with a bag of plumbing tools, took our guns. Then we separated. The whole operation took less than a minute. Following different circuitous routes we all arrived back at our home base. We slumped down exhausted from the tension. Slowly my pulse rate returned to normal. Julek and I debated whether we had killed the enemy for sure and decided that the wounds were most likely mortal. This was the first time that I had killed anyone. Did I have any feeling about it? No, I had been given an assignment to punish an enemy who had been responsible for the death of innocent people; I felt elated that I had carried out this assignment and relieved that we had not suffered any losses ourselves. We drank a glass of vodka to celebrate the successful conclusion of our assignment and then dispersed.

Through all this there was still time for fun. In the summer of 1943 one of our friends rented a cottage near the village of Swider. This was only about an hour by train from Warsaw and many of us would spend a few days there, or even go for brief weekend. The cottage was twenty minutes walk from the station, in a pine forest, close to a small river which even had a sandy beach. For the overflow crowd there was a stable with hay which made quite comfortable sleeping. Lili and I spent several days in this idyllic place. For a brief time we banished all unpleasant thoughts about the realities of life from our minds. We spent the days lying on the sand in a forest clearing getting a warm tan, or splashing in the river with our friends. At night we enjoyed each other and forgot everything else. Unfortunately, the idyll came to an end too quickly and we returned to ugly realities.

On the Eastern Front the Russians had pushed forward to the river Dnieper and Kiev, the Ukrainian capital, was liberated in November 1943. In January 1944 the Russians crossed the prewar borders of Poland. As the Soviet Armies pushed forward into Poland, the Polish Underground units in eastern Poland had been assisting the Russians by sabotaging supply lines behind the German front line. However when the Soviet Army overran the area of the underground units, the Underground Army commanders revealed themselves and were promptly arrested and the soldiers were disarmed and shipped off to the interior of Russia. The disclosure of this treachery hit us in Warsaw like a torrent of ice water. What shall we do now? There was much discussion of the situation in every cafe, at every meeting. The general consensus was:

"This cannot happen in Warsaw. Our Allies will support us, they will force Stalin to respect us."

As the events revealed, this was naive thinking. Stalin would not even allow Allied supply planes to land at Russian airfields for refueling. But this we did not yet know. We continued in our self-delusion.

In April 1944, Hala and her boy-friend Sten were married. Wanda was very pleased. She respected Sten, and at least once told Lili that she should find someone like Sten who was a medical student and sure to be successful. Wanda was suspicious of me (not without some reason). Now that Hala had moved in with Sten, and Wanda was also away quite often with friends of her own, Lili and I frequently had the flat to ourselves and much more freedom of action. On several occasions, my father took advantage of this to use the flat for meetings of the Council of National Unity and for a mail-drop. As soon as my father arrived, Lili had to leave not to see any of the participants in these high level gatherings. After the specified time period she returned and carefully removed any traces of the meeting, crumpled pillows or any strange matches or cigarettes.

About this time I received a British light machine gun which had just been delivered by aerial drop. It was still encased in its protective wrapping. Lili and I spent a whole Sunday removing the protective grease from the gun and preparing it for action. It was almost as difficult to remove the grease later from our hands as it had been from the gun. Fortunately, the flat had plenty of hot water and we could take our time cleaning each other in the shower. Now we were faced with the problem of where to store the weapon. I carefully wrapped it in brown paper, then put it into a potato sack and hid it in the corner of the cellar under a pile of potatoes. Later I carried it to training classes a couple of times, then returned it to the Company Commander.

On June 6, 1944, the Allies landed in Normandy. Rome had been liberated the previous day. In Warsaw we waited nervously, until it was clear that the bridgehead had been firmly established. Then we all broke out a treasured bottle of vodka and celebrated, we were now confident that the long war was finally approaching its end. A few days later I took the final examinations at Wawelberg and turned in my Diploma work. Just in time as events were moving rapidly towards the climax. During July the Soviet Army had been pushing the front back towards Warsaw and the Germans in Warsaw were in a panic. Civilians and families were packing up and leaving. Convoys of retreating troops, particularly, ambulances, passed over the bridges and along the main east-west thoroughfare, Aleje Jerozolimskie. The tension increased with every day, we knew that the moment of destiny was close at hand.

UPRISING

With every passing day the front lines moved back toward us. The signs of the German retreat became more obvious. The day of reckoning was fast approaching. Our euphoria and excitement increased with every new issue of the underground press; on every front our Allies were victorious. In Normandy the bridgehead broadened. In Italy the advance continued north of Rome. In Warsaw the preparations for the final battle continued; although the shortage of weapons and ammunition remained a major concern. The clandestine factories redoubled their efforts producing grenades and the crude, but effective, sub-machine guns, called *Blyskawica* (Lightning). Every favorable night, sorties from Allied airfields in Italy dropped more supplies at various drop zones in the forests, particularly in the Kampinos Forest north of the city. Individual units worked on their own to improve their armaments, carrying out attacks on soldiers at night to steal their side arms or breaking into isolated warehouses, railroad cars or trucks.

In the middle of July, Lili told me that one of her girls, Danuta, who worked as a maid in the Hotel Polonia (reserved for German officers), had reported that an officer wanted to sell some weapons. Danuta set up a meeting with him in one of the rooms of the hotel. I undertook this mission with considerable trepidation. Even though I entered the hotel through a side-door, I still had to pass a hall full of gray-green uniforms. I felt that I was walking into a trap. I climbed the stairs and entered the designated room. The officer was standing there. Suddenly, I realized that he was just as nervous as I was and my confidence returned.

"I am an Austrian," he said. *"Alles ist kaputt. I will nur nach Hause,* (Everything is over. I only want to return home)."

He gave me a list of rifles and ammunition that he could supply, twelve rifles complete with several thousand rounds of ammunition. The rifles were Belgian and used different ammunition than the standard German type used also in Polish pre-war rifles. I wasn't sure that this was a useful purchase and started bargaining. Finally, we agreed on a very much lower price. Then, I agreed to meet again the following day. Meanwhile, I contacted our Company Commander *Frasza* (Franciszek Szafranek). He agreed to the purchase and supplied me with the required cash in German marks. The following day, I returned to the same room in the Hotel Polonia. The rifles were stacked in the clothes closet and the ammunition was packed in parcels, each the size of a loaf of bread. I examined the supplies carefully and made sure the ammunition really fitted the guns. When the Austrian came into the room I gave him the brown paper bag containing the money. Quickly, he looked inside the bag but didn't count the money, then said, *"Danke* (Thank you)," and left the room. I waited about ten minutes and Danuta came in; I recognized her because I had trained Lili's section in military routines and handling of weapons. We discussed how to get the stuff out of the hotel and agreed upon a plan.

The next day a team was organized to transport the weapons to a safe house. Danuta, and another girl from the same section, brought them down to the rear of the hotel in bags of dirty linen. Boncza and Zak* brought a handcart to the exit door. Two other boys and I were the guards watching the approaches from either side of the hotel exit. Once the "linen" was loaded we went ahead, the two girls leading the procession. If either saw danger, for example a police patrol, she was

---

* These were their pseudonyms. Boncza was Staszek Nestrypke, the younger brother of a friend from the school in Rydzyna. Zak was a high school student. He had been the plumber who took our guns after the execution, described in the previous chapter.

to drop her handkerchief. The biggest difficulty was crossing the main street, Aleje Jerozolimskie, because an army convoy was passing on its way to the front. We had to wait nervously about 15 minutes for a break in the traffic, looking around in every direction. Then we quickly crossed to the other side. The handcart was pushed along the street, the guards walked along the sidewalks on either side. It took us about 45 minutes to reach the storage place and everything went off without a hitch. At the end we quickly dispersed; each going his or her own way. All three days I had been at a high pitch of anxiety. When it was all over, completed successfully with no problems at all, I was elated. I was also amazed how calmly Danuta had handled her part in this episode.

By the July 26th, the German retreat was in full swing. At German offices some files were being feverishly packed and loaded into trucks; others were being burned. In the German *Wohnunggebiet*, families were standing in the street with suitcases waiting for transportation westward away from the approaching Soviet armies. We could hear Russian artillery in the distance. Apparently, the Russian radio was inciting the Poles in Warsaw to rise up immediately against the Germans. This did little good because Poles had no radios; they had been confiscated in the fall of 1939. The fliers of the minuscule communist underground organization P.A.L. (Polish People's Army) repeated these announcements for the few that bothered to read them.

On July 27th, the German authorities demanded that 100,000 people report the following day to dig defensive works along the river. This message was repeated every few minutes over loud-speakers that had been installed on the streets many months before. Immediately, the headquarters of the Home Army issued orders for all units to assemble in their previously assigned action stations by the night of July 28. My unit's action station was at Marszalkowska 130 in a bank office on the 2nd floor. By about 7 p.m. we were all assembled, about 40 of us, with our weapons, awaiting further orders. Frasza, our company commander, reviewed the details of our planned attack with all the platoon and section leaders . We, in turn, relayed the pertinent parts to our own troops. Guns were cleaned and readied for action, but not yet distributed. Then we settled down for a nervous night of waiting, talking in groups, speculating what would happen. We all dozed in fits and starts, lying on the floor wherever we could find space. We munched on sandwiches; there were insufficient facilities to prepare any warm food.

Early in the morning, we were told to return to our homes, but to remain in a state of alert. It is amazing that, in the conditions existing in occupied Warsaw, it was possible to assemble over 30,000 young people and their supplies into quarters with only several hours notice and without arousing the suspicion of the enemy. We all dispersed; leaving the premises one by one. Those who lived close by carried weapons and supplies with them, to have them quickly available. Most returned to their normal activities, but we were all very anxious knowing that we could be called back at any moment.

I kept in close personal contact with my section leaders to make sure that they and their people remained on the alert. As I moved around the center of the city, I was alarmed by the evidence of increased German patrols in the streets, it seemed that they were aware of the impending insurrection. The movement of retreating army units had ceased, on the contrary large convoys and armored units were moving eastward over the bridges. These were unfavorable signs but at the same time the activity of the Soviet air force increased. Every night bombs were falling on railroad installations and military installations in the suburbs. Even during the day, Soviet planes were flying over the city and some dog-fights with German fighters occurred. The underground press reported that a tank battle was blazing only 12 miles from the city center, so close that we could hear the rapid gun fire. The tension rose from hour to hour.

The new alarm was early in the morning of August 1, ordering all units to be back in their action stations by 3 p.m. that same day and setting the hour of attack, "W" hour, at 5 p.m. Because of difficulties in getting the orders to all people in such a short time, and because of the disruption in public transportation due to German troop movements, some of us couldn't arrive at our designated places before the action started. I, myself, did not receive the orders until after 9 a.m. and was unable to contact several of those on my personal alert list. At about 2 p.m. Lili and I reached our command post.

Frasza was already there, very agitated because of the slow arrival of his troops and the difficulty of carrying out our designated plan with so many missing. We were all very tense, nobody smiled, faces were grim. I counted my troops over and over again, greeting each new arrival with relief. This time there was no pulling back, the moment of truth had arrived. Weapons were distributed to the troops and hastily checked once more. Lili and some of the boys and girls, together with volunteers from the upstairs apartments, started breaking holes through the walls in the cellars to create connecting tunnels from building to building. Imagine her surprise when, through one of the holes, our good friend Mirek Ferster emerged! He was stationed with a unit in the adjacent building.

"W" hour, the moment we had been preparing for during the last two years, had finally arrived. We had hoped that a fast surprise attack would help us overcome superior forces in spite of the lack of sufficient weapons. Unfortunately, the large numbers of young people hurrying through the streets aroused the suspicions of the Germans; who were already very nervous. Already at 4 p.m., sporadic shots were exchanged between German patrols and various groups. Therefore at 4:35 we received the order to move to attack. We adjusted our red and white arm-bands, the only article of military uniform that was common to all of us. We were all in civilian clothing, dressed in whatever each of us had available when the call for assembly had reached us. Lili was attired in gray trousers and a brown sports jacket, I wore gray flannel trousers and a light-gray windbreaker. We picked up our meager supply of arms and ammunition. I carried an automatic pistol and two grenades, several of our sections had rifles and two had machine pistols, either British Sten guns or Polish fabricated "Lightnings."

I lead my platoon down the stairs and out into the street. We dashed along the street, about 50 yards to the corner. On the opposite side of the street stood my unit's first objective — the building of the P.K.O. (Postal Savings Bank). Another of our units had proceeded us and was already entering the bank, which was only lightly guarded by some German army auxiliary personnel. They were taken by surprise and in a few minutes the entire bank was under our control; only half a dozen shots were fired.

Simultaneously, the remaining units of the 2nd Company of the Kilinski Battalion were to secure other prominent buildings in the immediate neighborhood, particularly the 16-story Prudential Building on Napoleon Square, and some Polish police stations* on adjacent streets. All of these were lightly defended and within a couple of hours all had been taken. At the same time the 3rd Company was to capture the Gorski School, which was the barracks for an Auxiliary Army Unit made up of Ukrainians. This they also accomplished.

The next step in the plan was for both companies to attack the Main Post Office, which was a tougher nut to crack. In recent weeks the fortifications had been strengthened and additional armed units had been added to defend it. Seeing that the situation at the P.K.O. was under control, I moved on with my sections to our next objective, to secure the buildings facing Napoleon Square which is three blocks long and 100 yards wide with a grass lawn in the middle. I took my platoon down Jasna Street, where we exchanged shots with two Germans, hitting both of them, to Sienkiewicz Street and then to the corner of Napoleon Square. The corner building was occupied by a German para-military unit. After a brief skirmish, they managed to escape from us across the square to the Post Office. Now we were pinned down by machine gun fire from the bunkers across the square.

One of the fleeing Germans dropped a box with ammunition in the street close to the curb. I decided to try to retrieve it. I crawled out of the doorway and edged along the sidewalk to the shelter of a large concrete container, which had once held flowers. Lying prone on the sidewalk, I reached out with a broom to try to snag the box. Suddenly, the machine gun in the bunker opened fire. One of the bullets hit my left hand. It was a little after 6 o'clock and I had been in action less than two hours. I felt a tremendous searing pain and then nothing. Blood was spurting from the area of my wrist, someone pulled me back towards the building, then I lost consciousness. From that moment, I remember very little until several hours later.

When I recovered from the shock and loss of blood, I was lying in a bed in one of the apartments on the second floor of the same

---

* Most of the Polish policemen joined us, only those who had blatantly cooperated with the Germans, put up any resistance.

building. My left arm was bandaged, also I had some bandages on my left leg where I had been hit by shrapnel. My arm was in pain but I was relieved to see that most of it was still there. I was told by the woman, who was looking after me and another wounded man, that the fighting outside was heavy, that the attack on the Post Office was still in progress. She sounded worried. Finally, as evening approached, cheering and rejoicing voices sounded throughout the building.

The woman was jubilant as she ran into the room crying, "The Post Office had been captured! We have won! We are free!"

For the first time since my injury I was able to smile. I joined in the jubilation, wincing every time I moved my left arm.

Many prisoners had been taken together with large stocks of supplies and weapons. The entire square and several blocks around it were now firmly in our hands. Polish red and white flags were flying, over the post office, on top of the Prudential high-rise and on balconies of surrounding buildings, for the first time in five years!. In spite of sporadic sniper fire, people flooded out into the streets to rejoice. For the next few days people in the midtown area believed that the battle had been won.

Everyone, men, women and children pitched in to build barricades across the streets to provide protection from the snipers and to provide a barrier against any German counter-attack. Posters appeared with instructions from the Polish civil authorities and freshly printed newspapers were passed from hand to hand. The supply of electricity had not been cut off, the power station was firmly in our hands. Water was also available and, for the moment, there was no shortage of food.

My unit, the 2nd Company of the Kilinski Battalion, was now garrisoned in the Post Office and was attacking the Germans still holding the Holy Cross Church and the University. Lili and her platoon of girls, nurses and messengers, were also quartered there.

Later that evening I was moved to the field hospital that had been established in the basement of the P.K.O. It was filled with more than a hundred wounded fighters and civilians, most of them from the "Kilinski" Battalion. There were not enough beds; I and many others were lying on blankets and mattresses on the floor. The doctors and nurses had their hands full. Lili was busy at work here and we had a joyous reunion. However, the state of my wounded hand was a cause of concern. This hospital was under the command of Doctor Zaorski, who had established the clandestine medical school in Warsaw University. Zaorski took one look at my hand and announced, "Hopeless, it will have to be amputated."

The operating room was filled by more urgent cases so I received a momentary reprieve. I was shocked, in spite of the pain I didn't want to lose my hand permanently. I begged one of the professor's assistants, a young surgeon Mirek Vitali, to take a look. He carefully probed the wound and saw that, although all the wrist bones had been completely fragmented, and particles of my wrist watch were imbedded in the wound, the tendons and nerves seemed to be, miraculously, in one piece.

He said, "It doesn't look good, but there is a slight chance we can save it. I'll try to do what I can."

He had just been put in charge of a new, smaller field hospital that had been set up in the basement of a stationery store at Moniuszki Street 11, opposite the Adria Night Club. The next morning I and several other wounded were moved from the P.K.O. to the new location. Here we even had beds to lie on. Dr. Vitali* put my hand together as best he could without the benefit of X-ray and with only primitive equipment. My arm was encased in plaster of Paris with a small window over the wrist for changing dressings. Whenever Lili had a free moment she came to visit me, at least once a day.

Frasza, the Company Commander, had also been wounded during the fighting for the Post Office, on the afternoon of the second day. My friend Staszek Brzosko was now the acting Company Commander. Frasza lay in the next bed and we wiled away the time discussing all the events of the previous days. We, and all the other wounded, were apprehensive about the future.

The failure of the Soviets to maintain their offensive and come to our assistance was ominous. Even Soviet planes had vanished from the air space over the city. True, none of us considered the Bolsheviks (as we continued to call them) to be our friends. But they were allies of

---

* Mirek Vitali later became a famous orthopedic surgeon in England and received many awards for his work for the rehabilitation of crippled soldiers.

our Allies, and common sense seemed to indicate that political differences should not prevent them from taking advantage of the bridgehead we had created on the west bank of the Vistula. We still felt sure that any day their offensive would resume, but nagging doubts disturbed us.

Several days later we were both making good progress. I had even been able to walk with Lili's assistance to the P.K.O. for my arm to be X-rayed. When I returned, and Lili had gone back to the Post Office, Frasza asked me, "I've watched you two for some time. You're both obviously very much in love, why don't you get married?"

"Yes, I love Lili and she loves me," I answered. "We talked about getting married many times during the last weeks, but it just wasn't a very practical thing to do in these difficult times. We plan to as soon as this is all over - if we both survive."

He asked, "Why don't you do it now?"

"How could it be done?" I responded.

"I will ask the Battalion Adjutant."

He proceeded to write a note which he sent with one of the couriers. Early the following afternoon a messenger brought him a note. He read it, smiled and said, "The arrangements have been made, your wedding will be tomorrow morning in the paper shop upstairs. I have sent a messenger to Lili to tell her!"

Rysia Vitali, the doctor's wife and constant assistant, made arrangements to get me a suitable uniform for the ceremony. Lili was in a stage of shock when she received the totally unexpected message, but her friends rallied to help her, gave her a clean blouse and skirt. My father came by visit me (his office in the Government Secretariat was only a few blocks away on Mazowiecka Street). When I told him the news he was vehemently opposed.

He said, "This a ridiculous thing to do, you have no home, no job, no way of supporting a family..." and more in the same vein. All the usual parental objections.

Patiently, I explained, "Dad, you know that we've been in love for years. Tomorrow we might all be dead, so all the old rules don't mean anything. At least we'll be together as long as we can. Perhaps we'll survive somehow, let's hope and pray we do. Then we'll figure things out together."

He went away quite angry, but after reflection he realized that I was right. In the morning, he came to the ceremony and gave us his blessing.

Thirteen was still lucky for me. That was the date of our wedding day — August 13. A field altar was set up on bales of paper in the store upstairs. The borrowed uniform was pushed and pulled onto me over the plaster dressing of my left arm. Finally, I was ready just as Lili arrived with an honor guard composed of six of her girls, holding a bouquet of rather wilted gladiolus in her hand. An attack on our positions had occurred that morning so none of my colleagues, not even the best man, Stas Nestrypke, could come to the ceremony. However, the Propaganda Section, which was quartered in the night club Adria, just across the street, sent over a film unit. The entire ceremony was filmed, to the annoyance of the Battalion Chaplain, who disliked the bright lights and noise. Lili saw the whole film, two days after the ceremony, in the Cinema Palladium, which at that time was still operating*. This was the first wedding during the Uprising and we became celebrities, our photographs have appeared in many magazines and books about the Uprising.

We exchanged wedding rings, not gold but brass curtain rings. After the brief ceremony the Chaplain wrote up the marriage certificate using our assumed names of *Palak* and *Jarmuz*. My father had the presence of mind to say that the time of secrecy had passed, the document must be in our real names, otherwise later on we would have serious problems proving we were legally married. A new document was typed up and signed by Chaplain Corda. Then, all the participants and the other patients enjoyed a wedding breakfast composed of French sardines and paté on biscuits captured from the stores of the German garrison in the Post Office. The obligatory toasts were made in vodka.

The attack had been beaten back. Lili and I ducked behind the barricades, which were under constant sniper fire, to the Company command post, where another party had been prepared in the luxurious suite of the chief postmaster. More toasts were drunk, then

---

* Miraculously this film survived the war and a clip was inserted into a film about the Warsaw Uprising which was shown on American television in 1976.

we ducked back past the barricades to the hospital. My bed was already in use. "Biega, if you are well enough to get married, we don't have room for you! We need your bed for the more seriously wounded."

Once more we returned past the barricades, with our heads low to avoid sniper fire, to the Post Office. We spent our wedding night on the floor of the ante-chamber to the office of the chief postmaster. Our nuptial bed was a mattress on the floor. We did not have much privacy; all night long, messengers tiptoed past our bed into the suite which was the company command post, but this did not bother us. I was in pain so I did not feel very amorous and we contented ourselves by cuddling together, shortly we fell into an exhausted sleep.

The next few days, although resident at company headquarters, I was still on the detached list as a wounded person. A tiny room on the fourth floor of the post office was given to us. Every day I returned to the hospital for a change of dressings. But after all the exertion of the wedding and moving around, I was very weak and spent most of the next few days in bed in this small room, with Lili looking in on me when she had a moment free from her duties. In the meantime the casualties were mounting. My good friend and best man, Stas Nestrypke, was killed in the final successful attack to capture the area around Holy Cross Church.

August 15 has always been a holiday in Poland, it is the day in which the Virgin Mary is honored and it is the feast day of the Polish army. A High Mass was celebrated in the courtyard of the post office by Bishop Adamski. It was attended by a number of officers from the staff of General Bor-Komorowski and Colonel Chrusciel and all the soldiers not on the front lines, as well as by many civilians from the surrounding area. It was an occasion for Thanksgiving that we had been successful in capturing a major part of the city. It was also an occasion to pray for Divine help in gaining victory. At the end of the Mass the voices of the congregation singing the patriotic hymn *Boze cos Polske...*, and then the national anthem, echoed from the walls surrounding the courtyard. It was an emotional moment. Tears appeared on the faces of boys, girls and elders alike. Lili and I held hands and were too moved to even sing.

On the 20th I returned to active duty, but still with a headquarters function, relieving Brzosko to take care of fighting matters. In the meantime the aerial attacks were becoming more vicious. The German *Stuka* dive-bombers had concentrated their efforts, until now, on the Old City and other areas outside the city center. Now the Stuka started dive-bombing targets closer to the center, systematically attacking specific city blocks each day. We evacuated all personnel from the upper floors of the post office to the ground floor, which felt safer than it really was.

By this time we had consolidated our positions in the city center. The 12 story PASTA Tower housing the central telephone exchange had been captured after a 10 day long siege. Several other German strongholds had also been captured; many prisoners taken as well as substantial quantities of heavy weapons and ammunition were obtained. Even two armored cars had been captured and for a brief time were placed in service with Polish flags painted on the sides. The Germans had been beaten back from the area near the Central Station and also from Aleje Jerozolimskie between Nowy Swiat and the station. The two halves of central Warsaw were now effectively reunited.

One evening, Lili and I went to visit her mother, Wanda. Streets in her neighborhood had been little damaged so far, in spite of the heavy fighting around the Politechnika only two blocks away. She had learned about our wedding from a postcard which we had sent by the mail service operated by the Boy Scout organization. She congratulated us and was very happy to see one of her daughters. I don't know whether my role in restoring Lili to her had any influence on her feelings towards me. She certainly did not evidence any great warmth in her greeting. We had no idea about Hala's plans or movements.

All of us celebrated the liberation of Paris on August 25th. But that was a bitter sweet celebration. We all knew that we too could have been celebrating if the Soviets were not such enemies. Stalin's desire to destroy any resistance to the spread of the Soviet Empire throughout Europe overcame any tactical considerations. To further his political ambitions, the Soviets gave up the tactical advantage of the bridgehead we had established, which had cut all direct communications between the German forces to the west of Warsaw with those on the east bank of the river Vistula.

I met my father who had become very pessimistic. Being privy to the deliberations of our leadership and the exchanges of communications with London, he knew that we could not expect any real outside assistance. The Polish Prime Minister, Stanislaw Mikolajczyk, flew to Moscow and met with Stalin on August 3 and 9. His pleas for help fell on deaf ears. Churchill and Roosevelt both appealed to Stalin, they were ignored. The Home Government and the Commander of the Home Army agreed on September 9 that negotiations with the German Army for a surrender were essential and that, in the meantime, periods of cease fire should be negotiated to allow the civilian population to leave the doomed city. However none of us troops knew this, nevertheless it became obvious to anyone that we had little hope.

The Germans were closing in. The fate of the Old Town had been effectively sealed with the loss of the western part of the city under the heavy attack of two SS armored divisions. By August 7 these troops had reached the Saski Gardens cutting off the Old Town from the center. Several Polish counterattacks were all unsuccessful. The offensive continued against the Old Town from all directions. The narrow streets and the density of the old buildings reduced the advantage of the enemy's superior forces. But the ancient buildings collapsed one by one from the onslaught of bombs dropped from above and the explosions of heavy mortar shells. Incendiary bombs ignited the old timbers, lacking water it was impossible to extinguish the flames. Hundreds of fighters and civilians died each day under the rubble. Inexorably, the defenders were pushed back.

Finally, the ruins of the Old City were totally overrun on September 2 and about 4,500 survivors evacuated through the sewers to the center, most still carrying their weapons. Another 800 managed to reach the northern district Zoliborz. The German troops systematically killed the wounded that they found in the cellars of the ruined buildings, often burning them to death with flame-throwers. The survivors among the civilian population were transported to concentration camps.

The fall of the Old Town opened up the northern railroad line and the road crossing the Vistula and allowed the Germans to re-establish direct communications with their troops on the east side of the

Vistula. Worse, it allowed them to bring into position the enormous 18-inch howitzer mounted on railroad cars, which had been used previously for bombarding heavily armored positions on the Russian front. These one ton shells started falling on the houses in the center. The shell traveled slowly and made a loud noise, a high pitched rumble like heavy furniture being pushed across a rough wooden floor, hence the nickname — *szafa* (cupboard). Fortunately, there was only one and the shells were fired once every five to ten minutes. When the *szafa* was heard coming in close by, everyone froze awaiting the impact. A four story brick building hit by this shell would collapse in a great cloud of dust and smoke, burying everyone that survived the explosion itself.

The uprising had now lasted five weeks. Our supply situation was becoming desperate. The Germans had blown up the pumping stations so that now we were short of water as well as food and ammunition. Old wells in the courtyards were put back into service for the first time in half a century. Other new wells were hastily dug. British planes tried to get through to us with supplies. Drop zones were marked every night by burning barrels of rubbish set up in distinctive X patterns. The planes flew from southern Italy carrying a heavy load of fuel for the 1,600 mile round trip, consequently, they could carry very little weight in supplies. The losses were heavy. Many of them were shot down by German artillery fire as they came in at low altitude to drop the parachutes as accurately as possible into the drop zones. The Soviets continued to refuse permission for Allied planes to land on their airfields for refueling.

The insurgents were now separated into four groups cut off from each other — the northern district of Zoliborz — the center of town which included the low lying Powisle district along the western bank of the Vistula and the power station, which was still operating and provided electricity to the center — the southern district of Moko-tow — and a small enclave along the river south of the bridges (Czerniakow). Zoliborz was completely cut off, the remaining three still maintained contact with the center through the sewers. Radio communications were maintained in part by relay via London! The signals of our small transmitters were too weak to be heard only a few miles away, but could be picked up by the powerful amplifiers in

England, which then retransmitted a strong signal back to Warsaw. Small insurgent groups in the surrounding country had tried to break through the surrounding cordon of German troops without success. The dead were buried wherever it was possible to dig a grave. Every grass courtyard or plot of grass in the centers of the squares, became a cemetery. Wooden crosses on each grave were marked only with a name, if known, or pseudonym, or just a date and the name of the army unit if the identity was unknown.

Communal soup kitchens fed soldiers and civilians alike. As long as the supplies of flour lasted, bread was being baked and distributed: first, to the fighting units, then to the hospitals, finally, to the civilians. Anyone who was not in a fighting unit and was physically fit, was engaged in some activity for the common effort. Long lines snaked along the streets, ducking under barricades, or clambering through ruins, carrying sacks with provisions from warehouses under attack or in danger of capture, to safer storage in the center. Others were carrying containers with water from the wells to the hospitals and kitchens. Much of this activity took place at night when there was less danger from snipers and the Stuka dive bombers. Many were working in the printing and distribution of newspapers, which continued to be published daily. We were short of food and ammunition, but not of paper and ink, even postage stamps were being printed. Young boys and girls carried messages and letters, Boy Scouts operated the postal service. Other work teams, which included German prisoners, dug through the rubble of buildings that collapsed after being hit by the 18 inch shells or the aerial bombs, searching for survivors and any articles that needed to be salvaged.

On the 5th of September, the Stuka dive bombers started a systematic attack on the area around the post office. Most of the soldiers of our company, who were in reserve or off duty, went into the air raid shelter built by the Germans. Some kind of premonition made me admonish Lili and several others close to us, including Staszek Brzosko, "Don't go to the shelter! Please, listen to me, stay here!"

One of the bombs fell through one of the large windows of the central hall and exploded in a stair-well just a few feet from our headquarters room. BOOM — a deafening explosion. Numerous noises of falling objects. Rubble fell on us. It became completely dark, smoke and dust swirled around us. Someone cried out. Then silence.

When I picked myself off the floor my ears were ringing from the concussion. The air was so full of dust and smoke that I could not see more than a couple of feet. Except for some scratches that were bleeding, I seemed to be OK. I groped around and found Lili, I could barely recognize her. A layer of gray dust covered her completely, even her face and hair, her jacket and shirt were torn. The rest of the group were in the same shape. Only one had been hurt by the typewriter which had been hurled off the table by the force of the explosion, but, fortunately he was only cut and bleeding and had suffered no serious injury.

After the dust had settled a little, we crawled over the rubble to determine the extent of the damage. When we emerged from the wreckage of the walls surrounding our room, we were stunned to see that, although the main structure of the Post Office was standing, a portion of the south wall had collapsed. A crater in the floor under the rubble revealed that the concrete roof of the bomb shelter had collapsed from the direct hit. Not a single sign of life came from the couple of dozen of our comrades who had sought security there. Quickly, rescuers came with crow-bars and picks, but there was not enough manpower to deal with the heavy blocks of concrete. There was little hope of finding anyone alive. The only survivors were those that were with me and some others who had been in a different part of the building, farther away from the explosion. We were told to move in with the Third Company which was quartered around the corner in the Gorski High School.

Lili and I picked our way past the barricades to my father's office which was only a block away. He couldn't recognize us at first. Then he managed to find a bucket of water and a towel and some soap and helped us clean ourselves off and obtained a couple of clean shirts for us to wear. After some rest and some food we returned to our group at the Gorski school.

I obtained a group of German prisoners to dig into the rubble in the vain hope that some survivor might be found. This operation went on all night long. Truly a scene from Dante's Inferno — bearded prisoners, most stripped to the waist, the sweat on their bodies

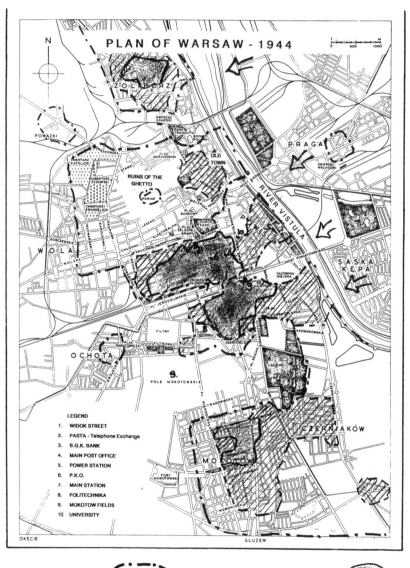

Aug. 3   Under Polish control

Aug. 26   Polish area

Sep. 26   Final Polish area

Sep. 12   Soviet Forces advance

Warsaw 1944

gleaming in the light of the flaming, smoky torches that provided the only illumination, worked with iron bars and pickaxes to clear away the enormous blocks of concrete, grunting and groaning from their exertion. One by one we extracted the bodies and laid them out, covering them with whatever scraps of material we could find, bits of curtains and blankets. The force of the explosion had torn their clothes off. As dawn approached, Lili found a volunteer to continue supervising the work and dragged me away to get some sleep.

This rest did not last long. Lili woke me up to convince me that the Gorski School and its large concentration of AK combatants would undoubtedly be the next target. This made sense considering the pattern of the bombing during the last few days. Staszek Brzosko had returned to the front line; therefore, I was the senior officer on the spot. I communicated our fears to the officers of the Third Company and told them that I was moving the resting remnants of our company, to a partly demolished building on the corner of Widok Street, closer to the front line. I reasoned that there we would be safer from the bombing, most of the area between that street and the main east-west axis of Jerozolimskie Avenue was already a pile of rubble from earlier bombing. This turned out to be a good decision. That same morning, about 11 a.m., the school was hit by several bombs and many more were killed.

During the next several days the Nazi armored units advanced steadily from the Old Town area. After very heavy fighting they pushed the AK out of the Powisle district cutting us off from the river. Heavy fighting developed along Nowy Swiat Street and the Second Company suffered heavy losses. Brzosko was wounded and I became the acting commanding officer of what was left of the unit. On September 8 or 9, we were withdrawn from the battle and placed in reserve. My command was now down to 14, including Lili and another young woman from her section, most of whom had previously been wounded, as I had been. We were the only ones of the 160, that had started fighting six weeks earlier, who could at least hold a gun. The victorious battles for the Post Office, Holy Cross Church, PASTA, the aborted attempt to capture the University and during the last few days the fight to capture the Cafe Club, commanding the crucial corner of Bracka and Jerozolimskie, not mentioning a number of smaller engagements, had all taken their toll. During the final three weeks of the Uprising we stayed in reserve, quartered in the ruins of the two story house on the corner of Widok and Bracka streets.

Technically, we were in reserve, separated from the front line by the width of Bracka Street and the even-numbered houses opposite us. On the 10th of September fierce fighting broke out in the back of these houses but the German attack was repulsed. That evening a woman across the street cried out that Germans had entered the cellars of the house. I grabbed a pistol, a couple of my men grabbed grenades and we dashed across the street, followed by Lili with a Walter 9mm automatic pistol in her hand. We searched the cellars and the ground floor and found no one except some of our comrades from the Third Company resting, exhausted after a another long day of fighting.

The next day, at noon, two German tanks penetrated Bracka Street right up to the barricade in front of our position. Hastily, I sent a messenger to battalion Hq. to request a PIAT*. Our position was a second floor balcony, protected with mattresses, overlooking the narrow street. The tanks could not elevate their guns sufficiently to hit us, they fired off a couple of shells into the buildings further down the street. We hurled grenades down on them, unfortunately, not causing much damage, but the tank-crews hastily backed out of the dangerous position in the narrow street, just as the PIAT crew arrived. They only had two projectiles, and decided they couldn't get a good enough shot and were loathe to waste their last two rockets. This was the last active action that our tiny group saw until the end.

On September 12 the Soviet army resumed the offensive that had been broken off the same day the Uprising had started six weeks before. Soviet planes reappeared over the city and dropped some bombs on German positions. At night small single engine planes flying at low altitude dropped small quantities of food, weapons, and ammunition without parachutes. Most of these supplies were damaged by the drop and were unusable. On September 13 the Germans pulled their troops back from the suburb of Praga on the east side of the river Vistula and blew up the bridges. Soviet troops now faced

---

* These very effective British anti-tank weapons had been dropped to us by air.

the city from across the river, too late because we had been pushed away from it except in one small area south of the bridges. Some elements of the Polish troops in the Soviet Army made two attempts to cross the river, but received inadequate artillery support and lacked sufficient boats to put enough men across. They suffered huge losses from the heavy fire of German artillery and the attempts were driven back.

Convinced that the Polish forces were doomed and, consequently, no longer a danger to Moscow's plans for communist domination of Central Europe, the Soviets finally acceded to pressure from Washington and agreed to permit a single flight of American planes to land on Russian airfields. On a bright sunny day, on September 18, the contrails of a large group of planes appeared over the beleaguered city and the white parachutes started dropping like petals from trees. It was too late, the area in our possession had been so reduced in size, and the drop was made from such a high altitude, that most of the supplies fell into German hands. This was the only attempt to provide large scale air-drops—too little—too late.

In the meantime the Germans were relentlessly pushing all around the perimeter of the city center, and every few minutes another one ton shell from the heavy gun would drop on a building, or increasingly frequently on ruins. However air attacks were reduced by the presence of Soviet fighters. One by one the Germans finished off isolated pockets of resistance in the outlying areas. However in the center activity died down. We had run out of men and ammunition; the Germans sensed that they had only to wait for us to give up and were reluctant to go in for any more hand-to-hand fighting to retake another mound of ruins. Several cease-fires had been declared and planes dropped leaflets urging the civilians to leave the city and promising safe conduct. The Polish authorities also pasted posters on the walls, indicating that the civilians could leave. A few thousand took advantage of this offer, but after all the atrocities that had happened during the previous weeks, most were unwilling to believe the promises made in the leaflets.

The remnants of the "Kilinski" Battalion were being reorganized into a last ditch offensive company made up of those who could walk and had at least one good arm. We maintained watch on our balcony and in an outpost in the rubble overlooking the broad avenue and the

B.G.K. bank from which an attack could be expected. We were constantly hungry. All the food that was left was unhusked barley and some white fat in cans that had been captured from a German army warehouse. It had an unappetizing smell and flavor, and we called it "monkey grease." But it did serve to make pancakes from the barley, which were more appetizing than gruel. Lili had brought some sugar from her flat, which we sprinkled on the pancakes. We also used the "monkey grease" to make lamps to give us some illumination at night. Our small group had more time to talk; we wondered what was going to happen to us. We realized that only a miracle could save us and were resigned to our fate, but were determined to keep on going as long as possible. To keep the gloomy thoughts away we cheered each other with stories of happier times. The ruins in which we dwelt had housed the well known sausage shop Radzyminski. As we ate our dwindling rations we talked longingly about *kielbasa*!

However the situation was hopeless, and on October 2, after several days of negotiations, the Polish commander General Bor-Komorowski surrendered to the German commander SS General von dem Bach. Under the terms of the surrender the German army recognized the Polish insurgents as combatants in accordance with the Geneva Convention, which provided that the survivors would be taken to prisoner-of-war camps, under the care of the German Wehrmacht. The Allies had already pushed the German armies in the west back into Belgium toward the boundaries of the German heartland, just as the Russians were approaching East Prussia. The German Army commanders recognized that they had lost the war even if Hitler didn't. Finally, they had decided to treat the defeated with respect, because they remembered Stalingrad in which the German army had also held out for many weeks against overwhelming odds. Some of them undoubtedly began to face the possibility that they, too, might soon find themselves in a similar situation.

Until quite recently the German troops, which were mainly SS units mixed with detachments of auxiliary military units composed of Ukrainians and Latvians and serving under SS command, as well as some units made up of Soviet nationals taken prisoner in 1941 and 1942, had been less magnanimous. Most of the Underground fighters who had the misfortune to be taken prisoner during the early days of the Uprising had been executed on the spot, either shot or hanged, frequently after being savagely beaten. When the Nazis retook the western suburb of Wola in the first week, they killed all the wounded and most of the staff of two large hospitals. As late as the third week of September, a number of prisoners taken in the Powisle district along the river Vistula were executed.

My father and most of the *Delegatura Krajowa* were now on the south side of Jerozolimskie Avenue. Lili and I took advantage of the cease fire to cross over and visit him and also Lili's mother. We were in a much happier mood. The fighting was over and we all thanked God that we had been spared. The future was uncertain but we could hope and pray that it would be a better one. Lili and my father convinced me that now was the time to return to a field hospital to ensure that I would go to that type of prisoner-of-war camp where I might get reasonable care for my wounds. Therefore on October 3, Lili and I both reported to a hospital to which most of the Second and Third Company wounded had already been transferred.

From here we watched as our comrades assembled in the streets the following day and marched off in long columns to the western district of Wola where they surrendered their weapons. Then they marched on to the cable factory in Ozarow, 15 miles west of Warsaw, from where they were transported to various POW camps in Germany. According to German sources the total number of prisoners that surrendered was 15,300. Another 5,000 wounded were later transported from the field hospitals starting on October 8. Our Uprising, started with such great hopes 64 days before, was over. We had not achieved the freedom for which we had been fighting but we had fought valiantly against overpowering odds and had inflicted significant losses on the enemy. According to official German records they had suffered 26,000 casualties. The Polish losses were much higher. Including the civilian population, it is believed that the total casualties were probably around 300,000 dead and wounded, however the actual number will never be known.

As we waited for transportation, the civilian population was lead out of the ruined city to Pruszkow, where tens of thousands of men, women and children were held for days with very little food. From there some, mainly older women, including Lili's mother and aunt Jadwiga, were allowed to leave. Some managed to take advantage of the overall confusion to escape into the fields and, eventually, to find their way to villages and small towns. The majority of the younger men and women were loaded into trains and taken to Germany to work as slave labor on farms and in factories.

My Father, together with the civilian leadership of the Home Government, *Delegatura Krajowa*, managed to reach the country outside Warsaw and then make their way to the provincial town of Piotrków, where the survivors of this group went back into action, under the leadership of the Government Delegate Jan Jankowski. There they continued to run underground Poland until the Soviets came and liberated them and then promptly arrested them. But that is another story.

Hania had been taken with other civilians from the Mokotów district to Germany. Lili's sister Hala had been working in one of the hospitals in western Warsaw and managed to hide away when it was occupied by the advancing SS troops who proceeded to massacre all the wounded and most of the staff. Her husband, Sten had been severely wounded in the fighting in the north part of Warsaw, Zoliborz. They managed to find one another several weeks later in a hospital near Lowicz. My cousin Janek had been fighting in southern Warsaw in Mokotow, had been evacuated to the center through the sewer, then after the capitulation went into the prisoner of war camp Stalag IVA at Muhlberg. My close family had miraculously survived a major catastrophe.

PRISONER OF WAR

arsaw was empty and deserted. Only the wounded in hospitals and the medical staffs remained. Germans troops were systematically searching the ruins and the remaining buildings for any people that might be hiding in them. At the same time any property worth taking was loaded into trucks. All remaining buildings, except those in sufficiently good condition that they could be used by the troops defending the Vistula crossing against the Red Army, were being blown up. Hitler decreed that not a stone should be left standing in Warsaw.

The house, in which Lili lived, at Wilcza 58 was almost untouched. It would be used by the Germans and spared from destruction. As it was not far from our hospital on Lwowska Street, Lili went there and extracted some clothes, towels, blankets and photographs. On October 10 a convoy of army trucks and ambulances took us down Raclawicka Street, past the ruins of the Politechnika, to a railway siding west of the city. The long train consisted of the typical European, dark red, short four-wheeled freight cars. Red Cross emblems, painted on the sides and roofs, marked it as a hospital train used by the German army for transporting its wounded from field hospitals on the eastern front. There were several rows of wooden bunks with straw filled mattresses in each wagon; a small cast iron stove stood in the center. Lili and I climbed into one wagon together with Mirek and Rysia Vitali and several other doctors and walking wounded. We were greeted by a German soldier, an elderly gray-haired medical orderly, who throughout the journey was pleasant and helpful. Loading took a long time, many of the wounded being in critical condition. Among the "passengers" there were several children, and I saw two cats and a bird in a bird cage! Under the terms of the surrender, the doctors were allowed to take their families with them to the prison camp. Late that night the train pulled slowly out of the siding, our journey had started into the unknown.

The following morning the train pulled into another siding parallel to a street with street car tracks. It turned out that we were in the outskirts of Lodz, Poland's second largest city, only 100 miles from Warsaw. Armed SS troopers in their ominous black uniforms surrounded the train. We were loaded into waiting street cars, which took us through city streets, then out along a cobble stone road in the outskirts. We were forced to alight and enter a field surrounded by a tall barbed wire fence. Inside the compound stood rows of long wooden huts which were filthy inside; there were no beds, only dirty straw on the floor. This was obviously a concentration camp, not one suitable for wounded soldiers. I was stunned, as were my comrades. So much for honorable surrender and treatment in accordance with the Geneva Convention. We had been naive to believe the Nazis. We sat outside in despair. Luckily, the weather was sunny and warm, otherwise the situation would have seemed even more tragic.

After several hours we were told to get back into the street cars which took us along the same city streets, back to the train. I learned later that there had been a major altercation between some Army officers and the SS. We never learned what exactly happened, but, fortunately for us the Army won. Among the conditions for the surrender of Warsaw was the stipulation that:

"... control, transportation, housing and guarding of the prisoners of war shall be solely under the jurisdiction of the *Deutsche Wehrmacht* (German Armed Forces)." (Paragraph II.(9) of the agreement)."

The news of our presence had spread quickly through the city. Lodz had been incorporated into the Third Reich shortly after the occupation of Poland and many Poles had been banished to the General Government. However a large part of the Polish population had been allowed to stay to work in the textile mills, so vital to the German war effort. During the return trip from the camp, people ran along the streets throwing packages containing bread, fruit and vegetables through the open windows of the street cars with little interference by the police. At the train the SS guards had been replaced with Army soldiers in their familiar gray-green uniforms. Beyond the cordon of sentries small groups of local people were standing, who had also brought food packages. Some of the more severely wounded had never been unloaded from the train as no suitable transportation had been made available. The train stood at the siding all night; finally, early in the morning it moved off westward. We traveled slowly through the provinces of Silesia and Saxony, standing often for hours in sidings while other trains carrying troops and freight passed us. On the train we were well fed, that is we received the same rations that German soldiers would have received. Our orderly heated the food for us and dished it out on enameled metal plates. Presumably, the same was happening in the other cars of the train. Several of the critically wounded died during this journey which lasted three days.

Finally, we pulled into a siding next to a pine forest. We had arrived at Stalag IVB, located near the small German village of Zeithain, a few miles east of the river Elbe, about half way between Dresden and Leipzig. Our welcoming party included the camp commander Stachel in the rank of *Oberst Arzt*, which translates as Colonel Doctor. He was a typical Prussian army officer, slim, erect, dressed in an impeccable uniform, shining riding boots and carrying what looked like a riding crop. When he saw the doctors' families alighting from the train complete with children, cats and pet birds, he turned around and left in disgust. This was too much for a proper, German professional army officer.

Those of us who were walking had to pass through the showers where we were liberally doused with some kind of chemical which was supposed to get rid of any lice we might be carrying. I don't know how the severely wounded were handled. Then we marched to the compound which was to be our home for next several months, a distance of about a mile.

The camp was built in the form of a right-angled triangle. A mile long compound containing Soviet prisoners formed one arm of this triangle. The second arm included the compound set aside for us at the apex, a compound for Italians who had been imprisoned since Italy withdrew from the war a few months earlier, then a small section containing about 30 Russian women officers and, finally, close to the showers and supply depot, a small section housing about 40 Polish soldiers captured in the 1939 campaign and suffering from TB. The railroad line formed the base of the triangle. Ammunition dumps were placed in the forest between the rail line and the rest of the camp. Obviously, the Nazis hoped that the presence of allied prisoners would deter any attempts to bomb these military supplies.

The camp itself was similar to all those that have been seen in such films as the "Great Escape." A double barbed wire fence, with watch towers every 100 yards or so, formed the outside perimeter. A 20 yard wide area criss-crossed with barbed wire made any approach to the fence very difficult. Any attempt to approach this area resulted in shouted warnings "Halt!" from the guard towers. The latrines were located close to the outside fence. They were open to the elements and cold. A concession was made for the women, a series of closed latrines were built for their use. Inside the camp there were about 40 identical wooden huts, each housing about 120 inmates in long rows of two-tier wooden bunks. A cast iron stove, in the center, provided the only source of heat and the means for cooking or heating water.

One hut near the center of the camp was used for assemblies, another served as the cook-house. A third hut was turned into an operating room, dispensary, and store room for medical supplies. There was also a laundry. Two huts in the center of the camp were occupied by the doctor's families, another two by the nurses and other medical personnel. The seriously wounded were housed in the huts closest to the doctors' quarters. The less seriously wounded occupied the remaining huts, with the women at one end of the compound, the men at the other. Virtually all the equipment for the operating room, a portable X-Ray machine, and some basic dental equipment, had been brought on the train from Warsaw. To a large extent the medical supplies, bandages etc. had also been salvaged from Warsaw. The Germans supplied very little.

The camp guards were all convalescent German soldiers, limping or with eye patches or suffering from asthma or some other disease. The senior in charge of the guards was a limping, grim faced noncommissioned officer, sergeant Stolz. He was a typical master sergeant of the old school who was very unhappy at being stuck in this camp and was determined to take it out on all of us. All work inside the camp was performed by the inmates. A senior person was assigned responsibility for discipline in each hut. The Polish compound had its internal commandant, Colonel Strehl, who was a Polish army colonel and a doctor. He was responsible to the Germans for the camp's discipline. There was also a liaison officer (Major Nizankowski) selected by the camp inmates, who served as the person who took any grievances to the German commander and also passed on information from him to the prisoners.

The weekly routine soon settled down. Once a week all the walking inmates were marched to the showers, the men one day, the women another. Before leaving the gate we had to count off, but we always managed to get the guards befuddled and ending up with the wrong count. When we came back the count was repeated and never agreed! Once a day we lined up by the kitchen hut and collected our ration — two pieces of black bread, a small cube of beet jelly, a tiny cube of margarine, a canteen can of some watery soup with maybe a couple of pieces of turnip, or spinach floating in it, and a couple of small potatoes. In the morning we could also get some weak coffee made from grain. We were always hungry with this kind of diet and reluctant to do more physical exercise than absolutely necessary. As winter approached it became more and more difficult to keep warm. Each hut received a weekly ration of soft coal, enough to have a fire burning for three or four hours a day.

Shortly before Christmas, we received a shipment of Red Cross packages. The quantity received was only sufficient to provide one package for four prisoners. These were typical 10 pound American Red Cross parcels which contained a can of powdered milk, a can of meat, coffee powder, sugar, canned fruit, vegetables, cookies, chocolate bars, and of course cigarettes. This small quantity of luxury items raised our spirits and made it possible to celebrate Christmas. During the next three months we received three more Red Cross shipments. In one of them were British packages which naturally contained tea and cocoa, but the vegetables in most of these were turnips, to the disgust of the recipients. Another shipment came from the Swedish

Red Cross which contained butter and cheese in addition to other articles. Just after Christmas a shipment of warm underwear, long-johns, long-sleeved tee-shirts and socks arrived. The nursing staff distributed to those in greatest need as the quantity was not large enough to go around. We also received a shipment of books. I still possess a leather-bound volume of Byron's poetical works from this consignment, which I was reading at the time that we left the camp.

Soon after we arrived at the camp we were given postcards that we could use to communicate with families. These were two part cards, half of it served for the reply. Lili and I had agreed with our parents on an address of friends in Poland that we would use to establish contact. We both received replies and learned that they both had succeeded in getting out of Warsaw safely, and were in Lowicz, where Lili's mother had a cousin. My father even managed to send us a small parcel with some food, which we received just before Christmas. Lili received a card from her sister telling us that she and her husband, Sten, were safe and had found sanctuary in a small town at the house of Sten's sister-in-law. It was a relief to get news and re-establish contact, which was broken again almost immediately.

The Soviets resumed their offensive early in January 1945. They crossed the Vistula quickly, both north and south of Warsaw and occupied the ruins of the city, which the Germans abandoned without firing a shot; to avoid being surrounded. Within a few days the rest of Poland was taken over making any further communication impossible. The last card received came from my father in Piotrkow and was dated January 10, 1945.

We also learned that my step-mother Hania had been deported to Halle in central Germany and received her address so that we were able to exchange several cards with her. Ironically, the only one of our family to be killed was my uncle Staszek who had been a prisoner of war since October 1939 and who, theoretically, was isolated from the hazards of the violent times. By mistake, an Allied bomb was dropped on his camp in Dessel on September 27, while we were still fighting in Warsaw. This sad news was given in my father's first post-card.

A few weeks after arrival in the camp the cast was removed from my arm, and although I used a sling for my hand for several more weeks, with regular therapy I was gradually regaining the use of my fingers. Most of the other wounded were gradually recovering. I think that there were no more deaths. Those that had survived the ordeal of transportation eventually recovered. In the spring the Germans started examining the wounded and sending those that had recovered to Stalag IVA in Muhlberg, just a few miles away. This was a large POW Camp containing many Americans and British. About a thousand Poles from the southern part of Warsaw were also in this camp including my cousin Jan Brodzki, with whom I was able to exchange postcards.

Life continued with no great problems other than the general discomfort and lack of food and a plague of bed bugs. Finally, after many weeks of complaints, the camp authorities set up a program of fumigation. One by one each of the huts was evacuated for 24 hours, and some kind of gas was used to rid them of the pests. This improved the problem, although it did not entirely solve it. The smell of the chemical had also pervaded our clothing and mattresses, even though it was cold we kept all the windows open for several days to try to get rid of the stink.

To occupy the time various kinds of activities were organized. Early in 1945, a show was put on by an enthusiastic group of amateur entertainers. Small groups were meeting regularly for various kinds of studies and discussions. I was asked by some of the doctors to give them English lessons, which I did three times a week. The camp regulations, enforced by *Feldfebel* Stolz, forbade any intermingling of the sexes. The doctors' families were exempted from this rule, and were living together in cramped quarters in the huts reserved for them, stretching blankets and other materials around bunks to give them some semblance of privacy.

A curfew was enforced between the hours of nine at night and six in the morning. No lights were permitted in the huts during these hours and, of course, nobody was permitted outside. The searchlights on the watchtowers played back and forth cross the camp to enforce these rules. However there were constant air-raid warnings during which the searchlights had to be switched off. Needless to say, couples were always finding some way to get together, and occasionally they were caught and, at least the men were banished to solitary confinement for several days. Zeithain was probably the only POW Camp in Germany which recorded at least two marriages, and in which one baby was born.

Lili worked as a ward nurse for the first few weeks. Then a dental clinic was set up and Lili transferred to it as an assistant. I allowed Lili to use me as a guinea pig. She replaced a couple of fillings, and did such a good job that they lasted for several years. This dental clinic also provided us with the opportunity to meet in private for an hour or so at least once a week. Lili also visited me in my hut, which, technically, she was able to do as a member of the medical staff. One of Stolz's guards caught us sitting on my bunk. I was reported to the Camp Commandant. The Duty Officer, a young Captain in the Medical Corps accepted my explanation that we were married. He decided that the rule against women visiting male huts must be enforced, but that husbands could visit their wives during specified hours in the afternoon. From that moment there was a regular parade of husbands to the women's huts. With the sympathetic cooperation of Lili's immediate neighbors, I even managed to spend a couple of nights with her. It was tight quarters in the narrow bunk, fortunately, it was the lower one. Our lovemaking had to be very restrained considering the close quarters, other women above and on both sides, but we still enjoyed being close to each other for the night.

There was little incentive for any one to escape from the camp, although it was not difficult because of the poor training and physical condition of the guards. It was a much greater problem to get anywhere once outside without any identity papers. Just after Christmas, two men took advantage of the weekly visit to the showers to escape. Because of the general confusion in the counting of heads, I don't think the Germans knew that any one had gone. However, before they were able to get to Polish territory, the Russian offensive had reached the eastern borders of Germany. Three weeks after their escape, hungry, cold and tired, the two turned up at the camp gates and asked to be let back in. They spent several weeks in solitary confinement and then were sent to another camp. Several weeks later another escaped, but got picked up by the police and taken to jail in Dresden. One night there was a massive bombing of Dresden and the jail was destroyed. In the confusion he escaped. Not knowing where to go, he returned to the camp. He had no identification of any kind, and for a long time the guards would not let him in! It took a long time to convince them that he was an escaped POW.

As spring approached our spirits were boosted by the signs that the end of the war and our release from confinement was rapidly approaching. We had very limited access to the news. Of course, the guards passed on to us any news favorable to them, specifically, about the first successes of the December offensive in the Ardennes, later named the Battle of the Bulge. Nevertheless, some information did get to us, in part from the Italians who either had a radio receiver or managed to get news when they were working on the farms. The frequency and intensity of Allied air raids also increased. At night we could see the glare of blazing cities and hear the rumble of falling bombs. During the day the contrails of high flying bombers arched across the sky.

By now the German guards had become very lax in their discipline, they also knew that the end was near. Even the dour Stolz lost his desire to harass us. It is a Polish custom on Easter Monday morning to sprinkle water on every one. The German guards all got their share of *Smigus*, Stolz was not spared and reacted only with a growl, "*Verruckte Polnische schweine* (Damned Polish swine)." A few months earlier, such an incident would have resulted in arrest and detention in solitary confinement for several weeks.

Towards the end of March, a group of French officers, evacuated from a camp in western Germany, arrived in Zeithain and were put into some huts in a compound between us and the Russians. Three Polish officers, Lichomski, Duchateau and Krystek, who had been captured in 1940, were among them. They had a hidden radio receiver and, although physically separated by a double row of barbed wire fences, they were able to supply us with daily news bulletins. We learned about the Yalta meeting of Roosevelt, Churchill and Stalin that occurred in February. Although at that time we did not know any of the details, the fact that Europe had been divided up into "spheres of influence" made us very unsure of our future. In any case we started discussing what to do should the Russians reach us before the Allies. Many of us agreed that we should try to break through to the Americans or at the least reach the camp at Muhlberg to enlist the support of the British and American prisoners there. A group lead by Lieutenant Deren, made up mostly of men from my hut, started putting together a detailed plan for a break out from the camp at the appropriate moment.

The Russian offensive of late January had stalled again roughly along the prewar frontier of Poland and Germany, then down through central Czechoslovakia to a point east of Vienna. In the meantime by March 20 the Allies had crossed the Rhine along a broad front. In early April the Allies were driving across Germany towards us and on April 12 patrols had actually crossed the Elbe River near Magdeburg. At the beginning of April the Russians resumed their drive westward. The following is quoted directly from my diary:

"April 13, Friday - My lucky day! The American offensive is advancing at lightning speed, reaching Erfurt - Weimar - Brunswick - Coburg - Wittenberg. The 1st Army near Leipzig and Halle. Besides real news the camp is full of rumors. A joyful atmosphere in the camp. Everyone is sure, contrary to earlier fears, that Zeithain will fall into the hands of the Allies rather than the Russians. The chances seem about equal. But we're on the wrong side of the Elbe.

"April 14. - Clear signs of the approach of the war. At 14.00, out of a clear blue sky, American two-engine fighters with strange double fuselages dove down and bombed a train standing at the camp station. They raked the supply depot in the woods with gunfire. Great advances all along the line. Bridgehead across the Elbe at Magdeburg (60 km from Berlin). I predict that by Wednesday the Americans will reach the Elbe close to us. Last night the petrol factory at Riesa was set on fire by bombers.

"Sunday the 15th. - Dr. Longin, who a few days ago had been sent to another POW camp Altenburg, returned. He told us that he arrived in Leipzig on Friday evening and stayed in the home of his escort. But Altenburg already occupied by the Americans, so they could'nt go further. They returned by train which was bombed near Wurzen, and came the rest of the way on foot. Today we can hear artillery fire in the distance.

"Monday, 16th - We take advantage of the beautiful weather to sun ourselves in the air-shelter trenches, there is a continuous air-raid alarm. Continual explosions. No sign of German planes. Lücka and Stolz angry that everyone waves at the low flying planes.

"Tuesday 17th - News that a massive Soviet offensive started on the front Frankfurt-on-Elbe to Oderbruch north-east of Berlin. Fortunately, not near us! Americans approaching the river Mülde. Leipzig nearly surrounded. Nürnberg taken. One of the guards told me that Americans only 30 km away. In the camp they are preparing to greet the Allies. Col. Strehl appointed me his interpreter. From the east we hear the rumble of artillery.

"18th - Yesterday the Russians started an offensive along the front Forst-Rothenburg, they'll be heading towards us. Street fighting in Leipzig, Halle occupied by the Americans. They are close to us!

"Thursday 19th - Leipzig taken. No more artillery fire to the west of us but in the east the Bolsheviks are advancing, they took Cottbus and approach Bautzen. Why aren't the Americans moving faster? I'm afraid the Russians'll get here first. I've packed a knapsack.

"Friday - Heavy bombing around the camp under beautiful clear skies. Squadrons of 4 engine bombers flying high, and smaller ones with twin tails dive bombing against targets in Riesa and finally the stores by our camp. Explosions of the ammunition dumps cause many of our windows to break and things drop off our shelves. In the evening we hear artillery to the east and even machinegun fire. From the west silence, what does that mean? What should we do?

"Saturday - All day refugees trailing along the road just beyond our camp fence, just like in Poland in 1939. Thin horses pulling carts loaded with luggage and household goods, women and children trudging along the road tired and scared. Small groups of German soldiers, unshaven, dirty, dragging their feet. A sad sight -a group of emaciated women from a concentration camp guarded by SS men - so thin, barely able to drag their feet, they keep stumbling. The beasts in black uniforms scream at them and beat them with their rifles. We stand along the barbed wire clenching our hands, wishing we could help - we feel so helpless."

Saturday 21 April is a date I will remember for ever. Very early in the morning, while it was still dark, a German guard came with a flashlight searching for Major Nizankowski, our camp liaison officer. He was woken up and told to dress. After he left the hut we all start talking, wondering what is happening. Those of us belonging to the group that had decided to leave the camp, got dressed quickly ready for action. Three quarters of an hour later, Nizankowski returned and in a voice choked with emotion he shouted, "We are free!"

Quickly he related what had happened. At the Commandant's headquarters, the liaison officers from the Italian, French and the two Polish Compounds had been assembled — no Russians. Colonel Stachel addressed them, "*Meine Herren*, Soviet troops are only a few kilometers away. I and my staff are leaving. Here are the keys to the camp stores." He stood at attention, saluted and continued, "I wish you well," and strode out the door, got in a staff car with his officers and drove away.

Before day break the entire camp was up. The watch towers around the camp perimeter were deserted. Our senior officer, Colonel Strehl, immediately organized a Polish camp guard armed with rifles. He consulted with the other national commanders. They listened to the radio which was repeatedly broadcasting a message from General Eisenhower, saying in effect:

".. do not impede the movement of the Allied Armies, stay in your camps until army units reach you.."

A message well meant, but certainly not applicable to our situation. Nevertheless Col. Strehl issued an order:

"In compliance with General Eisenhower's instructions, I forbid anyone to leave the camp."

Lichomski and DuChateau pleaded with him In vain, insisting that they had received instructions by radio from the Polish Command at Allied Headquarters to the effect that all Polish prisoners of war should avoid being taken by the Soviet Army. Even our own organized group that had been so determined to leave, wavered and was unwilling to disobey Colonel Strehl.

In the end only Lili and I, together with Jerzy Deren and his wife, agreed to go with the three Polish officers from the French camp. The gates were guarded, so we cut a hole in the barbed wire fence and left the camp at 10 a.m., watched by a group of our undecided friends. A few minutes later, another of our group, Jan Thomas came through the same hole and caught up with us. We were overjoyed to be free again, although we were also nervous not knowing what we would run into on our way across the narrow strip of land over which the swastika still flew.

FREE!

Our first obstacle was the broad River Elbe. We were certain that the closest bridge, in the small town of Strehla, would be heavily guarded. We met up with a convoy of British POWs that were being marched westward under army escort. Deren was fluent in German and talked to the sergeant in charge and convinced him, with the help of some American cigarettes, to let us join the group. At the same time I explained our dilemma to the English. Quickly, they let us into the middle of the ranks so that we were surrounded by the tallest of the prisoners. This way we crossed the pontoon bridge guarded by SS troops. Fortunately, they had more serious problems on their minds and didn't pay any attention to the prisoners guarded by German soldiers. Once we were safely past the town, we thanked our hosts and left them to continue at our own pace.

We were very tired and sat down in the shade of some trees by a farmhouse. As fortune would have it, some Poles were working on the farm as slave laborers. When they recognized that we were also Polish, they quickly took us to a barn, in which we could rest peacefully. They brought us some food and fruit and then we went to sleep. In the evening we were aroused by the sound of shells exploding not far away. The Russians had already reached the river.

Refreshed by our rest, we scrambled to our feet and continued on our way. We passed groups of German soldiers hastily digging foxholes and preparing a defense line. We thought it might be dangerous to be wandering at night through an area being prepared for a last ditch defense. So we repeated our tactics of that morning and joined up with a another POW group marching westward under guard. These were Americans who were in much worse physical condition than the British had been. All night we marched past gun emplacements and barricades, all facing east. In the morning, on the outskirts of the village Oschatz, we left the group. We took a side road into a forest and, exhausted, lay down to rest. After a few hours we continued over a hill and along a deserted forest path until, in the afternoon, we reached the outskirts of a small town called Warmsdorf.

Large red lettered signs said that the town had been declared an "open hospital city" and passage by armed troops was prohibited. Indeed, enormous Red Crosses had been painted on all the roofs. A large convoy of ambulances, furniture vans and other vehicles was assembled in the town square. Deren approached an officer wearing the insignia of the Medical Corps and learned that the hospitals were being evacuated to the American lines to escape from the Bolsheviks. He suggested that it would be helpful if they had some Polish officers with them when they reached the Americans. The Germans agreed and loaded us into vehicles. They decided that I, who spoke English, should be at the head of the convoy directly behind the staff car. I rode in the cab of an ambulance squeezed between an Army nurse and the driver. The nurse was very frightened and asked me whether it was true that American soldiers were raping German women (rumors spread by Goebbel's *Propaganda-amt*). I assured her that American soldiers were very courteous to women, not sure whether that was true or not. Anyway, she cheered up. Unfortunately, we did not get very far. At the next town the road was barricaded, and the officer commanding the army unit in the town, would not permit the convoy to proceed any further.

We disembarked quietly and walked into the center of the small town, Mützchen. The defeatist attitude of the Germans made us much bolder. We calmly entered the inn situated in the town square, sat down at a table and demanded food, even though a group of army officers was sitting at another table close by. They glowered at us but made no move. The waiter brought some soup and while we were eating this the town mayor came in, stood in front of us, clicked his heels and bowed, welcoming us, "*Meine Herren, Ich grüsse euch* (Gentleman, I greet you)," he ignored the two women, "I have hoisted the white flag on the town hall tower. We await the Americans. They will enter the town tonight."

In effect he was surrendering the town to this ragged group of ex-prisoners! Only a couple of days earlier he would have been summarily arrested. Now the German officers at the table in the corner, turned their heads away and pretended they had not witnessed this extraordinary event. Shortly afterwards, some Polish farm workers came in and invited us to spend the night at "their" farm. We accompanied them to the farm house. The farmer and his wife looked at us sullenly, but did not react at all while their "slaves" calmly gave us beds with clean linen. For the first time in nine months we slept in luxury in soft beds, our heads on goose-down filled pillows. Lili and I were astounded at this amazing turn of events, but our weariness quickly overcame our excitement and we fell into a deep sleep.

Morning came but no Americans. The white flag was still flying over the town hall but there was no sign of any military activity. We wolfed down a substantial breakfast, served by the downcast and frightened farmer's wife. Then, we decided that, as the Americans did not want to come to us, we would have to go and look for them. We learned that the Americans were still near Grimma, ten miles away, and apparently had made no move for several days. We trudged along the country road and shortly encountered a German patrol of about ten men, marching in the opposite direction on the other side of the road. We eyed one another but not a word was said. When they were behind us we heard the command, "Halt!"

We stopped and turned around. The sergeant, leading the patrol, came back to us and said, "When you get to the Americans, tell them to hurry up! They have been sitting there in Grimma for a week, while we wait for them."

He did not use the treasonous word "surrender" but the implication was clear, they were anxious to have the opportunity to surrender to Americans and were scared of the Bolsheviks.

A farm tractor pulling a cart came up from behind. We hitched a ride. The sun was shining from a clear blue sky. It was quiet as if the entire world were at peace, the only sound the song of some larks flying above us. Finally, we came over a slight rise and saw three partially wrecked farm buildings and nearby a crowd of people and vehicles. The vehicles were all German, but most of the people were workers and prisoners of war of various nationalities. We were told that an American outpost was positioned a few hundred yards further down the road and was not permitting anyone to pass.

I set off down the road by myself, dressed in my German army gray-green trousers, dirty black jack-boots, black leather jacket with a worn red and white armband on the left sleeve, on my head a Polish officer's four-cornered cap, called a *rogatywka*, on the cap a Polish crowned eagle and a second lieutenant's silver star. I noticed two tanks with white stars on their turrets, dug in on either side of the road. When I got closer a sergeant and two GIs, arose out of their foxholes and stood with their guns at the ready.

"I am very glad to see you," I said, "I am Lieutenant Biega of the Polish Underground Army. I and my seven comrades have been walking for three days from a prison camp on the other side of the Elbe river."

"Where are the Ruskies?" asked the sergeant. "We have been waiting for them for a week"

"The last I heard they were still at the Elbe. If you hadn't sat here waiting, you would be meeting them there, and we wouldn't have had to walk so far," I said. "Any way we are tired, hungry and thirsty and want to come through."

"Wait here, I'll get the captain," the sergeant responded.

In a few minutes a jeep drove up with the captain. He explained that they had orders not to let anyone through except surrendering German soldiers, because the town was already overcrowded with refugees. I told him that most of the people back at the farmhouses were all allied people, some civilians, the rest prisoners of war trying to reach freedom. He said that they couldn't tell one from the other and they can't talk to anyone, because none of those people spoke English.

"Could you get things organized back there, split all the allies into groups, civilian and soldiers. Tell all the German civilians to go back home?"

I agreed and he promised to return shortly. I walked back to my group who were waiting anxiously on the edge of the noisy throng. Quickly, we got the groups organized as requested, and in about half an hour, the jeep drove up with the captain and a major. The major greeted us and then made a statement to the assembled people, which we translated into various languages. Then the captain escorted us to the badly damaged bridge over the Mülde River. We noticed a small monument with the Polish and Saxon eagles and an inscription honoring August, King of Poland and Saxony (in the early 18th century). I pointed this out to the captain and some photos were taken.

After crossing the bridge, the Americans guided us to a German army *Kaserne* (barracks). The barracks had been turned into a camp housing refugees awaiting the availability of transportation to return them to their native countries. The camp was run by an ad-hoc committee of inmates. Food was provided to the kitchens by the U.S. Army. We were assigned a couple of rooms and, because we were exhausted, we quickly ate the food that we were given and went to sleep. In the morning we decided that we should try to get better living quarters and also find out what we could do to get in touch with Polish Army authorities.

I went to the center of Grimma and soon found the headquarters of the infantry division stationed there. I learned that G-5 was the section dealing with refugee matters and local civilian affairs and that it was installed in the town hall. I found Captain Newman, the officer in charge of G-5. When I explained who we were, he was delighted to hear that we spoke several languages and could help him understand the complex problems presented by the thousands of refugees of many nationalities.

He already had a secretary, a very attractive, blonde German woman. All three of us got into a jeep and, guided by the girl, he drove out to the area of homes used by officers of the German garrison. They all appeared to be deserted. We stopped in front of one of the larger red brick houses, Captain Newman got out, knocked on the door and, when nobody answered, pulled out his Colt and shot through the lock. We entered the nicely furnished home.

He looked around and said, "I think your people'll be comfortable here. Move in and as soon as you have settled down come and see me." The captain drove me back to the barracks and I gave my friends the good news. It didn't take us long to settle in our new home. There were enough rooms and beds for us all. It must have belonged to a high ranking officer, because the furnishings were of good quality. For the first time in many months we enjoyed the luxury of good beds and the amenities of a well-appointed house. We found a good selection of clothing in the wardrobes and quickly selected clean underwear. The two girls spent hours soaking in warm baths and trying out the cosmetics they found. The captain didn't forget about food for us. Shortly after we moved in, a GI drove up and brought us several cartons with a variety of C rations. The girls found some vegetables in the pantry and started cooking our first home meals.

We spent the next few days organizing the civilian camp under Captain Newman's instructions. A little further from the center of town there was a second camp run directly by the U.S. Army, which was used for the returning POW's. At first the majority of its inmates were American, British, French, Dutch, Belgian. They generally stayed only two or three days before being transported to an airfield in the rear and then flown home. The number of Polish ex-prisoners continually increased, the majority coming from Stalag IV-A in Muhlberg, and then many of our colleagues started arriving in small groups from Zeithain.

In the meantime, two days after our arrival in Grimma, the Russians finally linked up with the Americans at Torgau on the Elbe river 30 miles north-east; the following day they finally reached the River Mulde at Grimma. During the next few days the Russians did little to prevent a continual stream of Polish POW's from crossing over to the American side, from Zeithain and other camps east of the demarcation line. Likewise, large numbers of civilian men and women continued to cross over the river from the various farms and factories where they had been slave laborers. They were housed in the camp under our care until a small UNRRA team finally arrived and took over the responsibility for them. Transportation was arranged to take the west Europeans back to their homes.

To the consternation of the American officers, the Poles refused to consider being repatriated, but there were no instructions from higher authorities what to do with them. By the beginning of May, Poles were the only occupants of the military camp. In the civilian camp there was also a number of Ukrainians, Lithuanians, Latvians, Czechs and Yugoslavs. I spent many hours explaining to the Americans why these people did not want to go home. They did not understand that the east Europeans were very afraid of the Bolsheviks and of the communist totalitarian governments that the Soviet army was installing in their homelands. I asked for help to contact Polish Army representatives somewhere in western Europe or in London. However the war had not yet ended and army field phone lines were still the sole means of communication.

Then, on May 3rd, Lt.Col. Szyleyko, a Polish liaison officer attached to SHAEF* in Paris, arrived in Grimma. He brought the information that this part of Germany was to be surrendered to the Russians in accordance with the Yalta Agreement between Roosevelt (who had died just three weeks earlier) and Stalin. He had specific instructions from SHAEF that the freed Polish prisoners of war were to be evacuated to camps in West Germany before the Russians took over.

I took Szylejko to meet the staff of the infantry division and acted as his interpreter because, unfortunately, he spoke very poor English. The American officers appeared to be stunned by his revelations, for which he had supporting documents. It seemed that they had not been able to understand why they had been forced, by orders from above, to stand idle at the River Mulde during the several days before the Russians arrived. General Patton was the only American commander to disobey these orders and in early May some units of the Third Army advanced almost to the outskirts of Prague in Czechoslovakia.

To my dismay, I soon discovered that the caliber of many of the men assigned as Polish liaison officers was very poor. Presumably, these were officers who did not meet the requirements for command positions in the fighting units or for headquarters staff. Many of them

---

* SHAEF - Supreme Headquarters of the Allied Expeditionary Forces.

had learned very little English during the four or five years they had been sitting in camps in England, possessed little initiative to get things done, and sat around with chips on their shoulder complaining that nobody paid any attention to them. Unfortunately, Col. Szylejko was also of this type, though not as bad as many. He had managed to get to Grimma somehow, although he had lost his car and driver somewhere along the way. He now asked me, a second lieutenant from the Polish underground, if I knew how he could get back to Paris. I took the matter up with Captain Newman. It was decided that it would be best to take the colonel to First Army Headquarters in Weimar, from where transportation on to Paris should be available. He assigned me a German car from the town's motor pool, and gave passes for me, the colonel, Lichomski and a cadet officer from the Polish camp, to proceed to Leipzig, which was as far as the jurisdiction of the division extended. On May 7, the day that the German surrender was signed, we set off early in the morning.

This was still a war zone, so every few miles we had to pass a road-block. I was dressed a little better than when we arrived in Grimma. I still wore my Polish army cap, German trousers and jack-boots. But Krystek had given me his French officers tunic and shirt with tie, so I looked reasonably presentable. Lichomski was in French uniform and Szylejko in British battle dress with black beret, with his colonel's bar and stars on epaulets. The poor GIs manning these posts were thoroughly confused to see officers in strange uniforms, bristling with stars like American generals, and with much saluting and presenting arms let us pass.

We covered the 30 miles to Leipzig in about an hour. I had been given instructions where to go, and had no trouble obtaining new passes from the army headquarters to take us on to Weimar, 75 miles further on. It was beautiful sunny, hot weather and the drive through the peaceful countryside was very pleasant. Unfortunately, the German automobile had seen better days and started making ominous noises. Finally, the drive shaft fell out of the transmission and we came to a screeching halt about a mile from the First Army compound.

We walked the rest of the way. The gates to the *Kaserne* were barricaded and guarded by a Sherman tank. I marched up to the MPs on guard, showed the pass from Leipzig, explained that we were

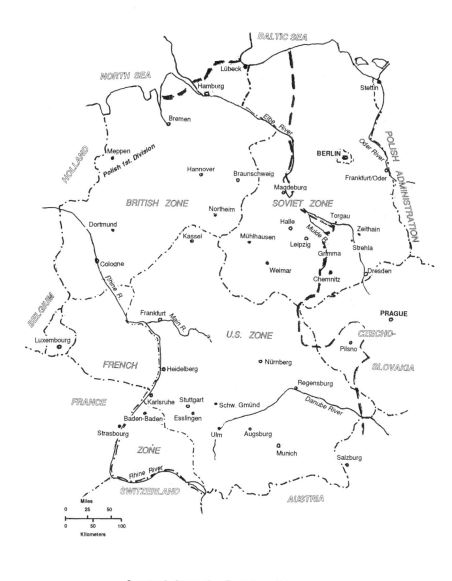

Germany 1945-1946

accompanying the Polish liaison officer Lt.Col. Szylejko and that our vehicle had broken down. The MP, in his immaculate uniform, white gloves, shining helmet and boots, looked at me in my strange uniform and asked for identification. Of course I had none except for my metal POW tag, which he examined with curiosity. The colonel showed his credentials, upon which the MP guard briskly saluted and let us pass. Szyleyko knew the name of the Polish liaison officer at First Army. After making several inquiries we located him sitting in a sparsely furnished room on the fourth floor of one of the *Kaserne* buildings.

He wore British battle dress with red POLAND shoulder patches and three stars indicating the rank of captain in the Polish army. I didn't notice the tiny triangular flags on his lapel which indicate a cavalry regiment. I saluted smartly and presented myself in Polish, "Captain, I am Lieutenant Biega of the Polish Home Army, Sir."

"Young man, don't you see that I am a *rotmistrz* (Cavalry Captain)." he growled, not even returning my salute.

Then he ignored the rest of us, sat down with the colonel and started a long tale of woe - how the Americans are badly disposed towards the Poles, how he could not visit any Polish camps because they would not provide him with transportation, that it would not be possible to transport Poles to West Germany, on the contrary the Americans wanted to get rid of them, that is send them back to Poland. He droned on and on, one complaint after another. We listened to this for several minutes.

Then, I interrupted and said, "Cavalry Captain, Sir, it is getting late, we have not eaten since breakfast this morning and are all very hungry. Also, we should make some arrangements where to stay for the night."

"You are all ex-prisoners. You have no right to be here at all. I am surprised that you were allowed to come through the gate. You will have to go back to your camp. There is nothing I can do for you," and he dismissed us.

The three of us went down the stairs, leaving Colonel Szylejko with the captain. A short distance away we found the Officers' Mess and entered. The MP asked for our passes. I explained that we had just arrived and were in transit. He directed us to the office upstairs. There a very sympathetic master-sergeant wrote out passes for the three of us to use the Officers' Mess. Then he made arrangements for us to have accommodations in the Transient Officers' Quarters for two days. He gave each of us a pack of cigarettes. With this we returned downstairs and had our first introduction to an American army chow line. We passed down the line and had our trays filled to the brim with food. Then we sat down at one of the long tables.

Some officers, who had just finished their dinner, asked who we were. After I had explained that we were from a POW camp, and that I and the cadet were from the Warsaw Uprising, several officers moved over to our table and started plying us with questions. When we finished our food, two of the officers went to bring us seconds. Others brought us cartons of cigarettes and candy bars. While this was going on the Polish captain entered with the colonel. His face turned purple, I thought he would have a stroke.

In the course of this pow-wow I mentioned the fact that we had come to Weimar by car which had broken down. After we finished our dinner, one of the officers took us to the Armored Division in a neighboring barracks, up the hill. An enormous tank recovery vehicle was dispatched and our tiny car hauled into the repair yard. Mechanics examined it with curiosity but shook their heads, they couldn't do anything to it.

After a good nights rest in comfortable quarters, we met the colonel at breakfast. He had spent the night on a cot in the Polish captain's room. He asked me for help in finding some way to return to Paris. Within a couple of hours I discovered that such matters were arranged through Department G-3 at Army headquarters and had obtained space for him on an Air Transport Command plane going to Paris the following morning. I had also found out that First Army was being deactivated in preparation for its imminent departure to the Pacific. The command of the whole area was to be transferred to the Ninth Army. Therefore I was unable to get transportation for myself and Lichomski to return to Grimma. They sent me to the military government detachment in the town of Weimar. They were unwilling to give me a car. Instead the Transportation Officer at M.G. assigned a car from the Motor Pool, with a German driver, to take us to Leipzig the following morning.

That afternoon another friendly officer took the colonel, Lichomski and me to the Buchenwald concentration camp, located a few miles away. This was the one of the first of the infamous Nazi camps and was established in 1936. The officer told me that all the Germans, living in the vicinity, claimed that they knew nothing about what was happening in it. This was the camp in which a German woman SS officer had lamp-shades made out of human skin.

In the morning we saw Colonel Szylejko off to his plane, then Lichomski and I were taken by the German driver to Leipzig. The cadet decided not to return with us, but to find his own way to the Polish Forces in northern Germany. Upon arrival in Leipzig, we went to the headquarters of the VII Corps, located in a large downtown bank building. Now I knew the routine. I presented our pass to the MP on duty and asked to be directed to G-5. He called another MP who escorted us up the stairs to an office. Here we were greeted by Major Gardiner.

After talking to us he introduced us to Lt.Col. Hardin who was Chief of Section G-5 of VII Corps. The American officers were pleased to see us because they had responsibility for all civilian affairs within the area of VII Corps (basically all of Saxony and Thüringen), including the care and repatriation of refugees. The problem of east European displaced persons was one for which they were totally unprepared and needed help. They arranged for us to stay in the elegant hotel across the square, which was being used as officers' quarters. Although Leipzig had suffered considerable damage from the Allied air raids, the area around this square was almost untouched.

That evening Lichomski and I were enjoying our dinner in the restaurant, while an orchestra played light music. Suddenly Major Gardiner appeared with a tall officer in British battle-dress and with POLAND slashes on his shoulders.

"What luck that you are here today," he exclaimed, "this is Captain Stocker, Polish liaison officer, who has just arrived from Ninth Army Headquarters. He has instructions for solving the problem we were discussing this afternoon. I will leave you to get acquainted and we will meet again in my office in the morning."

Captain Andrew Stocker was quite different from the Polish liaison officers that we had met up till now. He was tall and slim with slightly stooped shoulders. He face was gaunt and deeply lined and he looked tired. He turned out to be very energetic, made quick decisions and spoke excellent English. He talked quickly, explaining the political situation, making rapid gestures with his hands. Apparently, Captain Hempel, the senior Polish liaison officer at Ninth Army, was also of the same type and had taken immediate action when Ninth was instructed to replace First Army in the area. He had dispatched Stocker to find out what was happening and to prepare for evacuation of Poles from the area before the Russians took it over. This move had already been approved by SHAEF.

Stocker appointed us as temporary liaison officers to work under him in the VII Corps area. This was approved by Major Gardiner the next morning. We were issued passes to use the Officers Mess, to use the PX and to obtain uniforms and other articles of clothing. It was agreed that our assignment was to make a survey of all DP (Displaced Persons) camps in the areas of the 104th and 69th Infantry Divisions (the eastern part of the Corps area) and prepare lists of Poles and other DP's who requested evacuation from the area. We were also assigned a Mercedes car from the local Military Government motor pool.

First we went back to Grimma to run the survey there and at the same time close down the house. We recommended to our friends that they leave for west Germany with the Polish POW's. In particular I asked Lili to go with the other women to the camp for Polish ex-POW's in Northeim, just inside the British Occupation Zone, as I would be very busy the next few weeks and I was worried by the close proximity of the Russians just across the small river.

Lichomski and I split up in order to work faster. We got a second car, a black Opel, and we co-opted a couple of young men from the DP Camp to act as our drivers. My driver, Stasz Krygier, turned out to be very resourceful (a desirable attribute to maintain a car in post-war Germany) and dependable. He stayed with me until I left Germany over a year later. Our method of operation was as follows:

Upon arrival in a garrison town, the first step was to locate the American officer responsible for civilian and DP matters in the local army unit or military government. Then, I had to explain the circumstances, that the area was to be taken over by the Russians (always a surprise, this information was not yet general knowledge in the U.S.

Army) and that most of the east European and specifically Polish DPs were afraid and did not wish to be repatriated at the present time. Then, I went to the camp, usually, accompanied by the American officer.

All camp inmates were called to a meeting in whatever place was suitable for such an assembly. I made a speech outlining the existing political situation, and telling them that those who wished would be evacuated to another camp in western Germany until the situation became clearer. The senior person or leader in the camp (there nearly always was one, either elected by the inmates or self appointed by virtue of being an energetic person getting things done) was then instructed to make a list with the names of those who wanted to be evacuated.

I stressed that those who wanted to go home to their families in Poland quickly should not be entered in the lists. As soon as the Russians came they would, most likely, be allowed to go home. I also explained who was possibly endangered by staying —anyone who had been in the Polish police or any government positions before or during the war and members of the underground army. Then on to the next place, returning two or three days later to pick up the lists and discuss the preparations for evacuation with both the camp leader and the American officer who would have to carry it out.

In ten days we had completed the first part of the program, then moved on to other areas out to the western borders of the region to be occupied. By the end of May we, and two other Polish ex-POW officers that Stocker added to our group, had surveyed the entire area of about 10.000 square miles with close to 40 camps and almost 80,000 inmates. Half way through this work, VII Corps was pulled out and replaced with XXI Corps. The new Chief of G-5 was Colonel White and his assistant Captain Lehman Lewis, who were just as helpful as Major Gardiner had been. We did run into a couple of army officers who were uncooperative, but they were the exception. Early in the campaign Lichomski discovered that the commander of an American army unit on the border of the Soviet zone decided to solve his DP problem on his own by packing everyone, men, women and children into trucks and driving them across the demarcation line. Fortunately,

Lichomski was close by and found out while there was still time to sound the alarm at Corps headquarters and the action was stopped before it had proceeded very far.

I was able to visit Lili in Northeim twice during this period. The first time I rented a room in the town, but the female Duty Officer at the camp refused to give Lili an overnight pass! After an amorous night Lili had to return to her quarters early in the morning by climbing over a fence. The next time I visited, it was to take Lili back to Leipzig. Here she became part of the evacuation effort. Her assignment was to go through all the hospitals in the major cities to find sick DP's and to arrange for their evacuation, if requested. She only found a few, but most important this assignment made it possible for us to be together again and to ensure that we would not become separated when the time came to leave Leipzig.

The final step was to make sure that the evacuation had been carried out. I was assigned the area of the 5th Armored Division which included large concentrations of Polish and Baltic DPs in Erfurt, Muhlhausen and Nordhausen. By June 27 all who wished had been evacuated, a total of close to 68,000 from the entire area, including POWs who were evacuated by another team reporting to Colonel Szylejko. Most of the American officers cooperated completely and energetically. In one case they were too enthusiastic. In the camp at Muhlhausen about 800 out of a total camp population of 8,000 did not wish to go. When I arrived at the camp for a last minute check I found the *Kaserne* completely deserted. I hastened to the station, where two long trains were still standing. As soon as I arrived, some women came running up to me.

"Mr. *Leftenant!* The *Amerykanski* are taking us away," they cried. "We want to stay! We want to go back to our families in Poland"

After about an hour of checking through all the cars, about 600 men, women and children were extricated with their bundles and returned to the camp, to await the arrival of the Russians. Then the trains pulled out on their way to Ulm in Bavaria.

I had one other interesting experience. In the middle of June one of my American friends took me to Nordhausen to view the secret underground factory in which the Nazis had built the V-1 and V-2 rockets used to terrorize London in the last months of the war. Two several hundred yard long parallel tunnels had been dug through a mountain. They were spaced about a hundred yards apart. They varied in diameter from about 20 feet to 40 feet. They were connected by over a dozen chambers, the largest of which was high enough for V-2 rockets to stand upright during testing. A complete rocket was still standing in one of these five-story high test bays. At the southeast end of the tunnels camouflage netting covered a railroad yard.

At the time of my visit the yard was full of trucks and railroad cars into which American, British and French technical teams were busily loading rocket assemblies, parts, machine tools and documents to be evacuated before the Soviets take over. This entire underground facility had been built by concentration camp inmates, thousands of whom had died from accidents, malnutrition and brutal treatment. This camp was situated at the northwest end of the tunnels. Some of the inmates were still in the camp being nursed back to health by UNRRA doctors and nurses. The west European nationals had already been repatriated and Jewish survivors had been evacuated to better facilities in the American occupation zone. Those that remained were mostly Germans or east Europeans who wished to return to their homelands as quickly as possible.

Satisfied that the task was completed, I returned to Leipzig. On July 1 our team stood at the windows of the second floor of XXI Corps headquarters watching the entrance of the Soviet Army into the city. We were all astounded by the ragtag appearance of the soldiers, many of them carrying their rifles secured with pieces of string, horse drawn carts carrying supplies. Early in the afternoon, we and the Headquarters Company embarked in our vehicles and drove out of the city. As we left the city we saw Russian soldiers breaking into stores and terrorizing groups of civilians. No wonder the Germans had been scared of the Russians.

Soon we caught up with the columns of trucks, artillery and tanks of the XXI Corps. All convoys move at a slow pace with many stops. We drove all night, Staszek and I taking turns. In the morning we reached Augsburg in Bavaria. After a long stop there, the Headquarters Staff was directed to continue on to Schwabisch Gmund, a charming small town in the hills about 50 miles east of Stuttgart.

LIAISON OFFICER

A s soon as we arrived in Schwabisch Gmund and had found suitable living quarters in the home of a German woman, my efforts turned towards getting away to London. From Leipzig I had written to Baba in London, to tell her that I had survived the war and where I was. I received a letter back giving me the address of Bill Murray-Lawes's new home near Cranbrook in Kent and all the family news. While we were in the middle of the evacuation, an official request came through Ninth Army channels, to send me to London. Col. White had discussed this with me and I had agreed to stay till the end of the evacuation.

I went to Col. White now and asked him to make arrangements so that I could go to London as promised. He was very apologetic when he explained that XXI Corps had just been deactivated and was no longer part of Ninth Army. He and all the other staff were awaiting new assignments. Therefore, he no longer was able to provide me with travel orders, but he would send me to Seventh Army HQ in Heidelberg, where G-5 would certainly help me.

I returned to our house to find Major Koziebrodzki, the senior Polish liaison officer at Seventh Army, waiting for me. He had come specifically to see who were these "irregular" Polish liaison officers that had suddenly turned up in his area of responsibility. He ordered us to proceed immediately to the Displaced Persons Camp in Karlsruhe, where we were to work under Lt. Kempinski who was officially assigned there. I explained my circumstances, but he was adamant that first we move to Karlsruhe; then I should come to see him in Heidelberg. Lili and I together with our driver, Stasz Krygier, moved to Karlsruhe on July 6. Lichomski did not go with us and went off on his own. He was still an active officer in the French Army, he should return to France. We were assigned two rooms in the Karlsruhe camp, but I was not given any duties.

The next day we drove to Heidelberg. Major Koziebrodzki informed me that the British authorities had put a freeze on the count of the Polish Army under their command. This prevented any more Poles, released from POW camps, from joining the Polish Army. Without any official army papers it would be very difficult to enter England. He said, "It's too bad that you've been busy working, while others were looking after themselves, and joining Polish Army units whether in Germany*, or in Italy**. Sorry, but there's nothing I can do. Why don't you go to Frankfurt to the Polish Mission and try to get some help there?"

So Lili and I drove the extra 50 miles to Frankfurt. We found the Polish Mission, which was housed in a large villa in a residential district, which had been taken over by the various staffs associated with SHAEF. When we walked in, we were embraced by our friend from Warsaw, Nina Reszkowna, who was working there. We excitedly recounted our adventures since we had last seen each other a year before. Then she introduced us to Colonel Malhomme, who was the Deputy Chief of Mission. He listened to my story then said that I should talk directly to the Chief, Colonel Kaczmarek.

The Supreme Headquarters were located in the large I.G.Farben office complex which had been virtually untouched although Frankfurt had been heavily bombed. I found Kaczmarek at his desk in the

---

* Polish First Corps and Armored Division had taken part in the defeat of Germany as part of the British Army and were part of the occupation force north of Hannover.

** The Polish Second Corps, formed in the Middle East from Poles pulled out of Russia after Hitler attacked, had played a major role in the capture of Italy and were stationed along the Adriatic coast.

large room at SHAEF, where each of the Heads of Missions had a desk. I explained my problem to him; showed him all my supporting documentation.

He shrugged his shoulders, and said, "The British will not allow us to add any more people to the Polish Army payroll. You will just have to go to a camp like all the other ex-POW and wait."

"But the British are reasonable people." I argued, "If I had not been working for you, helping to extricate Poles from Saxony and Thuringen, I would have been in England three weeks ago."

"Unfortunately, there is nothing I can do. I have many more important problems to deal with. There is nothing more to be said. Go back to a camp and present your case through proper channels," the colonel said impatiently.

"What is the problem?" asked an American officer who had come up, hearing the argument.

"Oh, it's nothing important. This young man imagines we can bend rules for him." The colonel tried to pass the matter off.

The American, Captain Andersen, didn't let the matter drop so easily. "Lieutenant, I don't understand Polish, but I see that you are very agitated. What is your problem?"

I started to give him a brief synopsis of my situation, when the colonel again interrupted, "Captain, please don't worry about it. I will take care of this young man."

By now the American was intrigued and told me to follow him into his office. We passed through the door into another big office which was labeled "U.S. Army Liaison with Allied Liaison Missions." He sat me down next to his desk, offered me coffee. He studied all my papers, asked me for a detailed account of my activities during the previous weeks.

Finally, he said, "We made a commitment to you when we asked you to stay at your job in Leipzig. Don't worry, I will find a way to get around the red tape. Come back directly to me in two weeks."

Feeling much happier, Lili and I returned to Karlsruhe. My Guardian Angel was still with me, putting me in the right place at exactly the right moment. Just as I had been in Leipzig and talked to Major Gardiner the same day that Stocker had come; now I had my altercation with Kaczmarek at precisely the moment that a sympathetic American officer happened to be walking by.

It took a little longer than two weeks, but on August 6 I received a special order cut for:

" 2nd. Lt. Boleslaw Biega, detached Supreme Headquarters Allied Expeditionary Force for special duty as courier to carry dispatches to Headquarters Polish Army, London.

By order of General Dwight D. Eisenhower"

I was assigned space on an Air Transport Command plane leaving the next day for London from the military airfield at Hanau. Captain Andersen admonished me, "I did what I promised. We are getting you to London. Once you have seen your family and straightened out your affairs, I expect you to come back. We need people like you here in Germany."

"Thank you Captain. I promise you I'll be back."

Then he accompanied me to the desk of Colonel Kaczmarek.

"Colonel, do you remember Lieutenant Biega? Well, we've arranged everything so he can fly to London. He is going as your courier to the Polish Staff. Would you please give him some papers to take with him."

"I don't need any one to take papers for me," Kaczmarek replied with annoyance, "I am going myself the day after tomorrow."

"Colonel, you don't understand," the American insisted, "We have arranged everything for Biega to go to London. But his travel orders say that he is a courier, so you must give him some papers to carry, that should not be too difficult for you to do!"

Captain Andersen was getting a little angry. Officers at the neighboring desks were looking at us. Finally Kaczmarek opened his file drawer, took out some papers and put them in an envelope and handed them to me.

"Here you have some papers."

Captain Andersen was not satisfied. "Please address the envelope and put your seal on it. These are official papers!"

Kaczmarek shrugged his shoulders, annoyed. He took the envelope back from me, addressed it to someone at the Polish Staff, lit a lighter, melted some wax and dripped it on the flap and put his seal on it, then he handed it back to me.

"OK," said Andersen, "Now you are all set. Have a good trip, Lieutenant, and come to see me when you return."

I thanked him, saluted them both and left the room.

The next afternoon, Lili drove out with me to the Air Transport Command airfield. I checked in my dufflebag, but there was still plenty of time, or so I thought. I retired with Lili to the car for a few last minute caresses and kisses. When I returned to the terminal the plane had gone! It had left ahead of schedule because of worsening weather. I tried to get on the Paris plane that was supposed to leave half-an-hour later, but it had already been canceled because of the threatening conditions. There was nothing left to do but wait till the morning. Lili had already left with Staszek, our driver.

I got accommodation in the transient quarters at the ATC headquarters. In the morning the cloud cover was low and it rained continually. No ATC planes were leaving. I dashed over to the bomber command on the other side of the field. They were flying returning veterans back home via Paris or London.

"No," they shook their heads, "The war is over. We are not going to risk our necks flying in bad weather!"

Back at the ATC terminal, in the afternoon, suddenly it was announced, "One plane will leave to Paris as soon as the cloud cover lifts."

A mad rush to the desk, because of canceled flights there were dozens of stranded officers. My orders specified that I was a courier - this gave me the second highest priority. When the plane finally started boarding passengers, a Polish second lieutenant joined the generals and full colonels that had managed to get on the plane. A ray of sunshine came out past the hovering clouds, the plane took off. It was an army DC-3 with normal passenger seats. This was the first time I had ever flown in an airplane.

We landed in Paris, at Le Bourget airfield, about five o'clock. The weather was still bad, all military transport flights to London had been canceled. I was given a bunk in the transit quarters at the airport. I had a few dollars and took the bus into Paris, where I wandered around in the rain along the almost deserted streets. The only people in the streets were GIs walking around with their girls. I reached the bus stop just in time to catch the last bus back to the air base. I checked again, all flights canceled. An English colonel was making a big fuss because the sheets on his bed in the transit quarters weren't fresh. He should have been happy to have any at all. In the morning no change, it was still raining.

" There will be no flights this morning. Come back after two o'clock, it might clear then. "

I had no toilet things, everything had gone in my dufflebag direct from Hanau to London. All I had with me was a shoulder bag with my papers, a book, and some cigarettes. A young English lieutenant, on his way home from Italy, lent me his razor. We had breakfast together, then took the bus into Paris. We wandered around together, then he took me to the British NAAFI* Club near Champs Elysees. We read magazines, had a few martinis, ate an excellent lunch, before returning to Le Bourget. My "Priority 2" got me on the first U.S. plane that left about 4 o'clock. It landed at the American base at Bovingdon. The British Security Police were suspicious but could do nothing considering the type of travel orders that I had. I explained that I had no luggage because my dispatches were so urgent I hadn't time to collect my duffel bag from my quarters. I had my "urgent dispatches" in my shoulder bag. They hesitated to break the official red seals to check them. Finally, I reached the ATC terminal in the Cumberland Hotel at the Marble Arch. It was 7 o'clock. I took a taxi to the Polish Headquarters in Queens Gate to deliver my dispatches, but it was closed, nobody was there.

I called Baba in the country, she was very surprised to hear from me so suddenly. When she finally understood that I was in London, she told me to call her husband, at their London flat in Cranmer Court. Bill, whom I had last seen at his boat club in Maidenhead in 1938, greeted me most affectionately. Now he was a colonel in the Grenadier Guards, performing some kind of staff function. In the morning he took me to his office, got me a driver with a car to take care of my affairs. I went to Queens Gate where I met Colonel Bystram, who explained to me all the steps I had to go through for my status as a Polish officer to be verified. Then I collected my dufflebag from ATC. My clothes were saturated with schnapps. The bottle I had packed so carefully had been broken.

After lunch with Bill and his chief at the Army-Navy Club, we both took the Saturday afternoon train to Robertsbridge in Kent, where we

---

* The British equivalent of the American USO Clubs for servicemen.

were met by Baba. Baba was very happy to see me for the first time in six years. She hugged and kissed me and cried with joy, but was shocked to learn that her "little Bill" was now a married man. I enjoyed the weekend of luxury in the beautiful old Elizabethan house at Old Standen. Bill still had a good stock of prewar French wines. Living in the country they were also able to get some extra eggs and butter, that were unobtainable in London under the strict food rationing in force in England. On Sunday evening Bill and I returned by train to London, where I stayed in the flat at Cranmer Court, which had survived the bombings without any significant damage.

All that week, I was busy with my verification. I also looked into possibilities of going to America, or getting into permanent American Army employment. Neither of these were possible. I was also interested in any chance for Lili to continue her medical studies, and for me to obtain a British engineering degree or equivalent. I learned that my cousin Janek had reached England and at the moment was in Scotland. The following weekend, I went again to Old Standen with Bill. The news of the surrender of Japan was followed by celebrations of VJ-Day, the end of the terrible war that had devastated the entire world. For everyone this was a moment of relief, that finally the privations and family separations would end, that, slowly, but, surely life would return to normal.

But peace did not mean return to normality for us Poles. Our country was now occupied by the Soviet Army and the future was very uncertain for us. Bill took me to lunch with some of his fellow officers. They did not share my pessimism that Russia would not leave Poland. I brought up the massacre of the Polish officers at Katyn. They still believed the Soviet version of this tragic affair, that this crime had been committed by the Nazis. I gave them the facts that had been uncovered by the Polish and Swiss Red Cross, such as diaries found on the bodies, in which the final entries had been made months before the Germans entered the area. This gave them some food for thought, but the whole subject was a touchy one. Nobody in England was willing to believe that their Soviet allies had committed atrocities just as shocking as those of the Nazis.

My verification was completed at last. My rank of Second Lieutenant, given to me during the last days of the Warsaw Uprising was confirmed. I received my British Army Pay-book and was given the temporary rank of First Lieutenant and orders transferring me to duty as a liaison officer attached to the Polish Mission at U.S. Army Headquarters in Frankfurt. After spending another weekend with Baba and Bill in the country and procuring some gifts for Lili and my driver, I flew back to Frankfurt with these important papers.

Lili greeted me joyfully in Frankfurt. I reported to Col. Malhomme, Kaczmarek's assistant, who provided me with the necessary orders to return to Karlsruhe. He indicated that I would be transferred as soon as possible to a more important post. All the official papers arrived within the next five weeks, and I was officially assigned to the Headquarters of the Seventh U.S. Army together with my driver. On October 18 I was reassigned to the U.S. Military Government of Wurttemberg in Stuttgart to work under Captain Stanislaw Kowalski. He was responsible for the Polish DP Camps in the entire territory of Wurttemberg (all of the U.S. Occupation Zone in southwest Germany).

Kowalski was a very pleasant man. He was older, not as tall and of a heavier build than me. His hair was already becoming grey, his face was rounded and gentle and rather jolly looking. I always thought of him as a lovable teddy bear. His English was reasonably good and he had none of the personality problems so common among Polish liaison officers. Consequently, he had a good rapport with his American contacts. He assigned the southwest part of the Wurttemberg area to me. This included the large DP Camp in the old German army barracks in Böblingen and a number of smaller groups of Polish DPs in the towns of Esslingen and other smaller communities.

For the time being, we all shared the villa that had been assigned to Kowalski, in Degerloch — a residential suburb in the hills south of Stuttgart. The city, which lay in a valley surrounded by wooded hills, had been severely damaged by Allied bombs, but the suburbs were virtually unscathed. We ate in the Military Government Officers' Mess located in a palatial residence on the slopes of the hill overlooking the city. Kowalski had engaged an older DP woman to take care of the house who resented the presence of another woman in the house and was very unpleasant.

In November, Lili discovered that she was pregnant. I was not very pleased, mainly because of the uncertainty of the future, and the fear that the problems of looking after a baby would be an additional burden. However, Lili was so happy that I put aside my concern. Part of the reason for her joy was that she had been afraid that she might be sterile because of being a twin girl. I don't know whether this fear was founded on any medical fact, the important thing for us was that, in our case it was unfounded. Unfortunately, she was extremely weak and continually sick for the next two months and the hostile attitude of the housekeeper added to her discomfort.

Fortunately, on January 4, 1946, I received new orders transferring me to the First Armored Division in Esslingen. We took over a comfortable modern house at 52 Hasenrainweg, up on the hill overlooking the town of Esslingen. The owners, an elderly couple, left in tears, but I permitted them to take all their personal belongings. I told them that they were fortunate, the Germans had only allowed us to take one suitcase when we were evicted from our home in Warsaw. Furthermore I assured them we would take good care of the house and the furniture, and unlike the German occupiers in Poland, we would not steal anything. We allowed the housekeeper, who occupied an attic flat with her small daughter, to stay. Stasz had acquired a girl friend during his sojourn in Karlsruhe and I allowed her to join us.

With such a large household to care for, I made arrangements to receive our rations in bulk, rather than eat in an army mess. We received such ample quantities for the two of us that we were able to feed the whole household quite satisfactorily.

I was still responsible for the same territory. The duties of the Polish liaison officers were to take care of any problems that might exist in the Displaced Persons camps, such as complaints regarding treatment or rations. I discussed any such problems with the appropriate officers in Military Government. If satisfactory solutions could not be found, then the matters were reported to the Polish Mission in Frankfurt, who would try to get a resolution at higher U.S. Army echelons. Fortunately, I had a very good rapport with all the appropriate officers at the local levels, who were generally cooperative. Conversely, if the army or military government had problems with DPs, they were supposed to bring them to our attention so that we could take proper steps to correct the problems. One of our responsibilities was assisting in getting the people resettled in some other countries.

A new problem now faced us. Shortly after VJ Day the American government had withdrawn its recognition of the Polish government-in-exile in London and transferred it to the communist government in Lublin. Early in November, the first communist liaison officers arrived from Poland. Their function was to get as many Polish displaced persons to return to Poland as they could persuade or coerce. The euphoria of friendship that had developed in the last few days of the war in Europe had already evaporated, and the U.S. Army was looking askance at this new influx of communist officers, who they feared would add to the problems they were already encountering with Soviet liaison staffs. They designated the new arrivals as Polish liaison officers (Repatriation). To us they assigned the designation Polish liaison officers (Welfare). Very few of the new arrivals from Poland spoke any English and had no understanding of the way of life in western occupied zones or of American military etiquette. Ironically, they frequently came to us to ask for assistance in the simplest tasks, such as getting medical assistance (one of the new arrivals had to be hospitalized a few weeks after arrival).

Many of the Polish displaced persons were, by now, getting discouraged living in crowded living quarters in army barracks, and many of those from central and western Poland were anxious to go home. The Russians, under pressure from the United States, had agreed to holding elections and to permit Prime Minister Mikolajczyk (of the Polish government-in-exile in London) to return to Poland, so it seemed that perhaps the situation was improving. Others had received news from Poland that were discouraging. I, myself, had learned that my father had been arrested by the Russians and had disappeared.

The first repatriation train was leaving from the Stuttgart area. I went to the station to check the situation. No Polish Repatririation officer was there. Obviously, they did not care what happened. I discovered that insufficient food and blankets had been provided and no heating for the freight cars was available, even though this was winter time. The train was no better than those used by the Nazis for transporting people to concentration camps, or by the Soviets for carrying millions to exile in Siberia. The only improvement — no more than forty people were loaded into a single car. I sounded the alarm with my U.S. Army contacts and the departure of the train was held up, until UNRRA had provided the essential supplies and stoves with fuel had been installed in the cars. I also insisted that adequate medical personnel be assigned to take care of the transport.

From then on I checked each repatriation train, but never saw a Repatriation liaison officer. They didn't care whether babies had milk and warm clothes, however they were busy visiting the camps and spreading communist propaganda. During October, November and December several more repatriation trains left from my area. According to my reports 3,009 people left on four trains from the Stuttgart area alone. A similar number left on other trains from camps elsewhere in Captain Kowalski's area of responsibility, Wurttemberg.

At the end of January, 1946 there were still 48,174 displaced persons in camps in the area, 87% Polish, the remainder Ukrainians and a few from the Baltic countries. All of them were awaiting opportunities to go to other countries, not wishing to return to their homes under Communist domination.

One of my greatest concerns was the Polish Technical School in Esslingen. The camp commandant was Captain Florian Szczepanski, We managed to get sufficient financial and material support from Military Government to turn it into a fully fledged Technical School. The school used the premises of a German technical school which had been closed since the spring. The office building of a factory was transformed into dormitories to house the students who came from DP camps in the American and British Occupation Zones. We recruited teachers from DP Camps all over western Germany. Among them were Witold Skuba and Konstanty Okon, both prominent engineers in pre-war Poland. We brought them to Esslingen with their families and established them in comfortable houses. By the summer of 1946 there were over 200 students and 20 teachers. The class rooms and laboratories were equipped to a reasonably satisfactory level and the curriculum was as close to that of a technical high school as circumstances permitted. Many of the students graduated during the two years of the school's existence and others went on to complete their studies in the United States or Canada.

Some DPs got into legal trouble. As allied citizens they were not brought before local German courts but to Military Government courts. Every time there was a case in my area in which Polish nationals were involved I was called to be present. It turned out that in most cases I acted as advisor to the judge, as interpreter and as defense counsel. Sometimes I would get mixed up in my triple role, and started talking to the judge in Polish and the prisoner in English! Whenever Germans were involved, for example to complain that the Pole had stolen some chickens, German lawyers and interpreters participated as well. Then the situation got very complicated with all the proceedings being translated into three languages. The judges were American army officers who, usually, had no legal background, but had been given a hasty four week course in basic law.

After hearing all the witnesses and arguments the judge and I retired "to chambers" and the judge would ask me for my opinion. In many cases, particularly those in which the accused had been arrested by Military Police and accused of possession of U.S. Army property, I managed to get the defendants declared "not guilty" and released. UNRRA had been distributing clothing, utensils, food, and cigarettes from Army surplus stores. In other cases were it seemed evident that the accused had in fact stolen property or beaten somebody, I managed to get the sentence reduced to a few days, which meant the immediate release of the prisoner, taking into account the time already spent in jail.

The most troublesome case arose in July. A new unit, the 9th Infantry Division, had recently taken over occupation responsibility in the area, with headquarters near Böblingen. The officer responsible for local security, Colonel Smith decided to show everyone that he meant business. In the middle of the night he surrounded the Böblingen camp with troops, and then had MPs go through the personal possessions of all 1,250 people. 38 men and women were arrested and carted off to a German prison in Schwabisch Hall, 50 miles away.

I was awakened at 6 a.m. by a phone call from the Polish camp chief and within 45 minutes I was at the scene. After listening to all the tales of woe I went to Military Government. The M.G. officer, responsible for DP affairs, was also angry because he had not been consulted nor even informed of the raid. The next day I drove to the prison and interviewed all the prisoners. As usual the reason for arrest had been possession of American army rations, cigarettes or clothing. A couple of those arrested admitted that they also had knives or bayonets. It was obviously useless to take the matter up with the local American authorities, so I went directly to the Polish Mission in Frankfurt, who referred the complaint to U.S. Army headquarters. The following day I received a phone call from the Adjutant General's office to verify some of the details. Three days later a court was set up in the Böblingen county court room. Three legal officers arrived from the Judge Advocates office in Frankfurt, a judge and a defense lawyer. All 38 defendants were tried within a single day's session and were all found not guilty and released immediately. Colonel Smith was furious!

Once we had settled down in our own quarters in Esslingen daily life became more relaxed. Lili was now her fourth month of pregnancy and was feeling much better. Our housekeeper, Mrs. Schirm, took care of all the house work. Stasz's' girlfriend did most of the cooking under Lili's tutelage. The cooking was not complicated. We received our rations twice a week. They were ample in quantity but very limited in variety. The best items never reached us. The meat was mostly canned hamburger and Spam. When spring arrived, we were able to obtain some fresh produce in exchange for coffee and cigarettes. Cigarettes, candy, toilet soaps and some other similar items were purchased for cash from the Army PX Store. In the spring the PX started operating an ice cream factory in Stuttgart, producing American type vanilla ice cream. About once a week Stas would make the trip to get a gallon of ice cream. As we had no good way of storing it, it was quickly eaten up. Our friends, the Skuba and Okon families helped us out!

We had limited social activities. Our only close friendship was with the Skubas and Okons. We maintained friendly relations with others of the staff at the Technical school and with an American, captain Tubbs. During the week I was always busy visiting the various camps and Military Government offices, or making frequent official trips to Heidelberg or Frankfurt. For entertainment we had the army cinema and the officer's club. At the former we could see quite recent releases. The main film was always preceded by a Sing-along and the Movietone News. During weekends we did some sightseeing in the beautiful countryside of southern Germany. The mountains along the Austrian border were only a few hours away. We visited Lili's aunt Hania quite frequently. She had been transferred with other DPs from Halle to a camp in Ulm less than three hours away.

American officers, who had decided to stay on for a year or more, were bringing their families over. Therefore there was more activity at the Officer's Club, including weekend dances. Lili and I were astounded by the dancing styles unfamiliar to us, such as Boogie-Woogie. In particular the Mess Officer had an attractive wife, a slender brunette. Their renditions of the more acrobatic versions of the new dances provided great entertainment.

The German economy was in ruins and the money virtually worthless. Because of the shortage of everything, a black-market existed for items like auto parts, cigarettes, real coffee (Germans had been drinking a coffee made from grain for years), gasoline, clothing, soap. It was possible to acquire items such as works of art, cameras, jewelry for bargain prices, using commodities in payment. The occupation armies were being paid in a script money, "Occupation dollars," to avoid real currency making its way into the black market and to make it more difficult for army black market operators to transfer their gains back home. The script money was not easily convertible back into real money. The German cities were also in ruins, as a result of the intense bombing particularly during the last two years of the war. The center of Stuttgart was badly damaged, as were the eastern suburbs in which important industries, such as Mercedes-Benz and major railroad installations, were located. However the residential suburbs in the woods around the city were largely undisturbed.

Esslingen, an ancient and picturesque city in the deep valley of the Neckar river, was also untouched except for a few damaged buildings close to the main railway line. Every noon the bells chimed and a parade of figures marched around the clock in the tower of the 15th century town hall as they had for the last 400 years, as if the cataclysmic events of the last six years had never occurred. The only anachronism in the ancient town square was the American Red Cross center in the base of the town hall at which coffee and donuts were served to the GIs who were off duty.

Just before Christmas 1945, I received news that my father had returned to Warsaw from Siberia, where he had been taken after being arrested in Piotrkow by the Russians in March. Up to that moment all I knew was that he had disappeared. On March 27 1945, 16 leaders of the Polish underground government during the war against Nazi Germany, who had remained in hiding after the collapse of the Warsaw Uprising, went to Piotrkow to meet with General Ivanov of the Soviet Army. They had been guaranteed safe conduct and transportation to London for discussions with the Polish government-in-exile preparatory to the setting up of a new government in Poland in accordance with the provisions of the Yalta Conference. Instead of the promised transportation, they were all arrested and transported to Lubianka Prison in Moscow. Later they were tried and given long prison sentences. Two of them died in prison. Protests of the British Government were ignored by the Soviets.

My father was arrested two days earlier at the railway station in Piotrkow and transported with several other Poles to a camp on the north eastern slopes of the Ural mountains in Siberia. Somehow Dad managed to conceal his identity and was never brought to trial with the other sixteen. At the labor camp in Siberia he somehow convinced the camp officials that he was a German. In November 1945 together with a group of other Germans he was transported to East Germany. On November 22 he crossed back into Poland arriving in Warsaw November 27, almost exactly eight months after being arrested. He appeared at the flat of his previous secretary, Janka Mazurkiewicz, early in the morning, gaunt and hungry in ragged clothes, with no money, no documents. He had been lucky in his misfortune: first, that he had avoided imprisonment and trial, secondly, he managed to get out of the camp before the Siberian winter started.

Lili was receiving news from her mother and sister on a fairly regular basis. There was still no regular postal service, but people were traveling back and forth and carrying messages for friends. Eventually, we also learned that Aunt Jadwiga and her daughter Marysia had survived the upheavals and were back in the ruins of Warsaw. I had been searching for my cousin Staszek who had been in one of the guerrilla units fighting in the Swietokrzyskie Mountains in southern Poland. Some elements had fought their way through

Czechoslovakia and had reached the Third Army of General Patton in May of 1945. These formations were now serving as guard units at U.S. Army installations. One morning a young man turned up at my office in Esslingen. His name was also Stanislaw Biega. Because of my enquiries, he had been sent to me by his commanding officer. But it was the wrong Biega, obviously a very distant cousin, his family home had been near Sanok. We gave him a good dinner, chatted a while, then sent him back to his unit. My cousin had already made his way to the Polish Second Corps in Italy and we finally met again in England over a year later.

Although elections were scheduled to take place in Poland in 1946, which were supposed to be free and democratic, the situation at the present time in Poland were most disturbing. The country was firmly in the hands of so-called Government of National Unity created in Moscow in June, 1945 which consisted almost entirely of communists. The waves of arrests of all people that had been active in any way in the underground continued. Few of the members of the Polish Armed Forces in exile were willing to return to Poland under these conditions. Those who had close families in Poland tried to smuggle them out. Several organizations had been set up to do that. I had made contact with such a group in Nürnberg in the spring of 1946 to get Hala out of Poland. Unfortunately, something went wrong and arrests were made, luckily, before Hala got involved. Eventually she made her way to Sweden hidden under the bunk of the captain of a Swedish vessel. Captain Kowalski's wife was more fortunate and arrived safely in Stuttgart in the late summer.

On June 16, about two weeks earlier than expected, Lili started having labor pains. I took her to the Kennenberg Hospital which was only a few blocks away. A few hours later Mark was born, a tiny red, wrinkled baby, weighing only five and a half pounds. Unfortunately, the doctor who attended the birth had been careless and some remnants of the afterbirth had remained in the womb. Suddenly, four days after Mark was born, while I was away from home, Lili had pains and started bleeding. Fortunately, her aunt Hania had been visiting us and had the same blood type and was available for immediate blood transfusions. This averted a possible tragedy such as had happened to my own mother. Lili stayed in the hospital about a week regaining her strength.

Finally, Lili came home with the baby. Mark was pampered by all the womenfolk and quickly gained weight. Very soon Lili also returned to her normal slim form and was able to put on her uniform once more and travel with me. For the only time in her life she did not have to worry about babies. Mrs. Schirm was there all the time and Irena Skuba and her daughters spent many hours helping to look after Mark, who was an ideal baby. He slept well, had a good appetite, and grew rapidly.

During 1946, the efforts of various organizations working on the problem of resettling the many thousands of Poles in DP Camps and in the Army Work Battalions started to bear fruit. The immigration laws of the U.S.A had been liberalized by Congress to allow a larger number of DPs of east European origin to enter the country. Various churches and fraternal societies organized sponsors who agreed to be financially responsible for the first year to meet the requirements of the immigration law. A transit camp was set up in the port city, Bremen and gradually DPs started moving out of the camps on the way to a new life, mainly in the United States and Canada. Other opportunities opened up in Venezuela, Brazil, Argentina and Australia. European countries had their own severe economic problems and were unwilling to take in more refugees. Some temporary opportunities opened up for students to attend universities in Belgium. Belgium also needed workers for the coal mines. England was already faced with the obligation to care for the 200,000 Polish soldiers who had served in the Polish I and II Corps of the British army, and their families.

Naturally, we were also discussing our own future. I had no problem going to England as I was an established member of the Polish Forces in Britain with a British Army pay-book. I could expect to get help from Baba and Bill Murray-Lawes. However I had been completely charmed by my very positive relationships with many American officers who discussed all the opportunities available in America and told me many intriguing details of their own lives. Their directness and openness, and my own experiences with the ease of cutting through the inevitable red tape, convinced me that we should start our new life in the United States. I had no doubt that life in England would be much more difficult economically, and knowing how insular many Britons are, I foresaw big difficulties in realizing a meaningful career.

Unfortunately, my inquires revealed that, as I was not a Displaced Person but a member of the Allied Armed Forces, the new special immigration quotas were not available to me. The normal U.S. immigration quota of some 2000 per year for persons born in Poland was filled for many years ahead. Therefore I had no alternative but to go to England with my family, and then register at the American Embassy and await my turn.

Matters suddenly came to a head in August. The army Military Government officers were going home and were being replaced to a large extent by young officers trained specifically for M.G. duty, who had not seen any combat and to a large degree were politically very liberally oriented and still believed in the good intentions of the Soviet Union, many of them children of German Jews who had fled to America in the early 1930s. They were outraged that thousands of east Europeans were refusing to go home. They considered the Polish officers from London to be fascists who were maligning the "democratic" Polish government and encouraging the Polish DPs to refuse repatriation. A committee of Democratic congressmen came out to investigate the situation. As soon as they returned to Washington, the Army withdrew its recognition of the Polish Mission for Welfare and all of its staff. On August 26 orders were issued for us to return to our "proper station," a few days later this ambiguous statement was revised to read "return to London, England."

Suddenly, I was faced with a formidable problem. These orders made no provisions for my family. I had to quickly find a way of getting Lili and the baby into England. Initial inquiries to the Polish Mission and the British Mission brought the response:

"Send them to a camp in the area of the Polish Armored Division in north Germany. In due course arrangements will be made to transport families of Polish Army personnel to the UK."

This was unacceptable to me. I knew that it could take months before anything happened, and I certainly wasn't going to send Lili back into a camp with the baby. Lili and I drove to the British Zone to visit the headquarters of the Polish First Division in Meppen and to the British Occupation Forces Headquarters near Hannover. I was hopeful that somehow, with personal visits, we might be able to find a solution. The trip gave us the opportunity to visit north Germany but otherwise was fruitless. All I learned was that there was no way a British entry visa could be obtained in Germany. Also, it would be necessary to obtain an exit permit issued by the Combined Travel Security Board in Berlin, as no civilian personnel were allowed to leave Germany without it.

Disheartened, we returned to Frankfurt. Colonel Weytko in the Polish Military Mission turned out to be most helpful, he knew my father. He made arrangements with his counterpart in the French Military Mission to provide Lili with a transit visa with permission for a stopover in France. The French officer gave me a letter to the French Consul in Baden-Baden in the French Occupation Zone in southwest Germany. However it was still necessary to obtain the Exit Permit. My American friends helped me out and pulled all the necessary strings to get this permit as quickly as possible. Even with this help, it still took nearly three weeks. Without help it would have taken months. I included Captain Kowalski's wife, who had arrived from Poland a few weeks earlier, in all these steps.

Now we had to stall for time. My friends at headquarters arranged an extension of one month in the date of our travel orders. Lili was obliged to go back to the hospital for a minor surgical procedure which provided a legitimate excuse for the delay. An intelligence officer actually visited her in hospital to verify that she was ill.

I also had to figure out transportation. Several months earlier I had obtained a 1939 German built Ford car in very good condition, which had all the legal papers and registration plates issued by the American Army for families of service personnel. One option was to drive the car to France and sell it there. This could get very complicated, how would I take the money out of France? All currency transactions were tightly controlled in most European countries at that time. There was a daily military train that ran from Vienna to Paris, via Munich and Stuttgart. I was able to get additional orders stating that I and Capt. Kowalski would be accompanied by our wives and that travel by military transport was authorized. American officers, assigned to occupation duties, were anxious to obtain civilian registered cars for the use of their families, and they were in very short supply. I had no difficulty selling the Ford for five hundred dollars and a Swiss gold watch. Now I had a good watch and some spare cash.

On October 16 I received the exit permits for Lili and for Helen Kowalski with the proper stamps of all four occupation powers. On the 22nd, I got the French Visas from the consul in Baden-Baden and on October 27th, we all got on the train together. All our friends had gathered in front of the station to see us off. The Skuba and Okon families already had sponsors for their immigration to the U.S. and were scheduled to go to Bremen to await a ship. My driver wanted to go to America. Technically, he was always a DP, I had made him my driver, but he had never really been in the army. So he and his girl friend returned to a DP camp to await their turn.

The train journey to Paris took about 16 hours with many long stops (major track and bridge repairs were being made). Little Mark, now 4 months old, traveled well and slept most of the time. The train commander came to visit us in our compartment. As there was no dining car, nor any facilities for heating a bottle, in the morning he stopped the train at a station in France, so that I could go to the station restaurant and heat the bottle. GIs hung out of the windows of the train and cheered me on.

Our orders entitled us to stay in officers' quarters while in transit. Upon arrival at the Gare de l'Est we took taxis to the prestigious Hotel George V, which was being used as transient quarters for U.S. Army officers. Unfortunately, there was no room for us, and the other American transient hotel was far away from the center. We proceeded to a hotel in Montparnasse which was being used as a hotel for Polish officers, however we took advantage of our privilege to eat in the exceptional restaurant of the George V for the next couple of days. American officer's families were moving to Europe in large numbers and we met American children for the first time. We were astounded by the lack of discipline and the way the young children were allowed to run all over the elegant dining room!

The day after we arrived in Paris, an amazing coincidence occurred. Stasz Kowalski had a brother whom he had not seen since 1940. When the Germans marched into France, Stasz had managed to get to England with the Polish forces, but his brother had remained in France. Stasz knew his address in southern France. The morning after our arrival, we were all walking down the Champs Elysees on the way to a post office to send a telegram to this brother. A man in civilian clothes, wearing a beret, passed us walking in the opposite direction. Almost simultaneously, Stasz and the other man stopped and turned around to look at each other. The man in the beret was Stasz's brother! My immediate concern was to locate Lili and Mark somewhere, where they could stay for a few weeks, while I went on to England to arrange to get a visa for her. Stefan DuChateau, our companion on the march from Zeithain to Grimma, helped us find a place for Lili to live with Mark. This was a room on the 4th. floor of a building at 39 rue La Bruyere, just off rue de Clichy. Stefan lived quite close and would be able to help Lili. It turned out that all the neighbors in the building were ladies of the night. They were fascinated with the baby boy, cuddled him and were very helpful to Lili. Before leaving for London we spent a few days enjoying the fun life of Paris, including an evening at *Moulin Rouge* and another at the famous night club *Bal Tabarin*. Stefan accompanied us also to the palace at Versailles and the Louvre Museum to make sure we saw not only the gay life, but also the culture of France. Food was still rationed so it was essential to obtain a ration card for Lili. The baby was entitled to a special milk ration. There was of course no refrigeration in the room, but as the weather was already cool Lili kept the milk bottle on the window ledge.

After a week in Paris I hurried off by overnight train to London. Baba had arranged to get me acquainted with my mother's sisters, Lady Maizie Fisher and Lady Ada Mary Heath. Another sister, now dead, had been married to Colonel Couchman, retired from the British Army in India and living with his second wife in a house in East Grinstead in Surrey, about 45 miles south of London. They had ample room and agreed to put us up until we were able to get settled. It was more convenient than Bill's residence of Old Standen, because East Grinstead was located on a main line with fast and frequent train service to Victoria Station in London. Having found a place to live and with some help from Bill Murray-Lawes, within 2 weeks I obtained the necessary entry permit for Lili from the Home Office.

On the November 18 I returned to Paris. Just as I reached the house in rue la Bruyere, Lili reached out of the window for the milk bottle and knocked it off the ledge. It fell four stories to the street and broke right in front of me. My guardian angel was still looking after me, if I had been there one second sooner the bottle would have fallen right on my head. What a welcome — Lili was mortified.

The Allied Exit Permit from Germany was no longer a suitable passport. It was necessary to get a French travel document. This was obtained on the 20th. On the 21st the British Consulate stamped a British Entry Visa into this new document. That same evening we boarded the night train to Dieppe. The train was full, most of the passengers military personnel. The fellows in our compartment looked askance at the small baby, I am sure they were cursing silently that they would have a crying baby all night. However, Mark slept soundly and in the morning we were complimented on our lovely baby. The channel crossing the following morning was very rough. Poor Lili had to stay below in a cabin with baby Mark. It was so rough the portholes were leaking water. Some woman kept shrieking that she was dying. I sat up in the bar on the upper deck sipping cognac thinking about my good fortune. Lili and baby Mark survived the six hour crossing and we entered the United Kingdom together on November 22. We had a new future ahead of us. We were young and happy and felt confident that we would never again have to endure such hardships and dangers as those we had overcome during the last few years.

LIFE IN
POST-WAR LONDON

B
aba and Bill Murray-Lawes met the boat train at Victoria Station. Bill and Baba were, I think, pleasantly surprised by Lili. I don't know what they expected. Baby Mark was angelic at the time and they adored him immediately. After a couple of days in London we moved on to East Grinstead to the house of the Couchmans who were very nice to us. Couchman's daughter, my cousin Aileen Hopkins and her husband, an executive at Shell Petroleum, came down from London several times at weekends and we got along very well together.

My status at the moment was still that of an officer in the Liaison Section of the Polish Army, on temporary extended leave, with permission to live in private quarters. However, as this was at my own request, I did not receive any additional housing allowance, only my normal army pay which amounted to some 35 pounds sterling a month (about $170 at that time). I had a fair amount of cash from the sale of the car and had saved some money while in Germany, where our out of pocket expenses had been minimal. We bought some clothes and went to London several times and then realized that our funds were dwindling rapidly. It would be necessary to cut back sharply on our expenditures to live on my army pay.

I had decided that I should get out of the army as soon as possible. Naturally I wanted to find a job as an electrical engineer. This is what

I had trained to be, and this is where my interests lay. However I did not have a single piece of paper to prove that I had any qualifications or had finished any school. While still in Germany I had ascertained that in England I could obtain this certification by passing examinations given by the Institution of Electrical Engineers. I had started taking correspondence courses to prepare for these examinations, which were in two parts taken at intervals of at least six months. However, in order to be admitted to the examinations it was necessary to become a Student Member of the Institution. This required the sponsorship of at least two senior members of the Institution, who would certify that I had the necessary educational qualifications and was of satisfactory moral character*.

I discovered that several Polish engineers were members of the IEE. Naturally, they were also army officers and there was an organization at the Polish Army headquarters, which had the purpose of providing assistance to would-be professional candidates, whether to become engineers, lawyers, doctors or whatever. I went there but ran up against a brick wall. No one was willing to assist me. Even though I had witnesses who could testify that I had graduated from the school in Warsaw, all the engineers were older men who had graduated from the prewar Technical University, the Politechnika. They were unwilling to acknowledge that any system of underground schooling in war-time Poland had any value. Their only recommendation was that I start from scratch and enroll in the new Polish University then being organized in London.

This was quite unacceptable to me, it would mean that I would not be able to start my career for at least another three years. I took my problem to Bill Murray-Lawes, once more I asked him for help. He was a professional army officer and knew nothing about engineering, but he found some friends who did. He introduced me to them. Each asked me a number of questions which I answered to their satisfaction and then, purely, on the basis that a friend had recommended me to them, they sponsored me for Student Membership in the IEE.

---

* This sounds like a complicated procedure, however it would be simple for a student at one of the accredited colleges.

The Sulkowski castle in Rydzyna. Site of famous school in 1930's. (1936 photo)

Wedding of Bill and Lili Biega during Warsaw Uprising–August 13, 1944.
(film clip)

The Main Post Office in Warsaw (center left) after capture on second day.
(film clip)

Bishop Adamski celebrates Mass on August 15 in courtyard of Main Post Office.
(film clip)

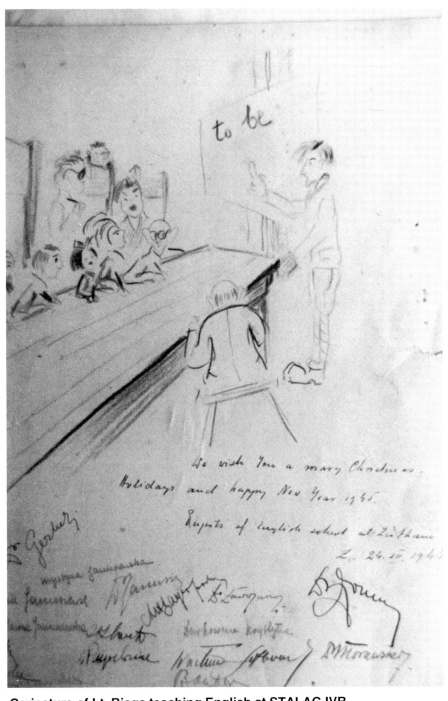

Caricature of Lt. Biega teaching English at STALAG IVB.
(Christmas 1944)

Bill and Lili in Grimma. Bill is wearing uniform made up of German trousers and boots and French officer's jacket. (May 1945)

Bill Biega in front of his headquarters in Esslingen. (July 1946)

This is how engineers worked before electronic calculators and personal computers. (1953)

General David Sarnoff, Chairman of RCA, presented with medal by the Assembly of Captive European Nations, 1967. From left to right: Alexander Kutt (Estonia), Boleslaw Biega (Poland), David Sarnoff, Chairman of ACEN Vasil Germenji (Albania), V. Sidzikauskas (Lithuania). (Fragment of press release photo)

The Biega family in 1965.

In January of 1946 I was accepted by the Institution and was scheduled to take the first part of the examination in the spring of that year. Christmas came, we were invited to Old Standen. We spent a very pleasant ten days in luxury. Old Standen was an old country estate dating back to the XVI Century, which had been modernized to the extent that there was central heating, electricity and indoor plumbing. Granny and Grandpa Seely, with whom I had lived as a child, were now living in a small modern cottage on the estate. This was the first time that they had met Lili and baby Mark and they took them both to their hearts. Baba had borrowed an antique wooden cradle for Mark to sleep in. During the day it was brought down to the enormous drawing room with its beamed ceilings and large, ancient brick fireplace.

In English upper class style we had to dress for dinner every evening. Fortunately, in Germany, I had bought Lili a very elegant, black, velvet evening dress which had belonged to some actress and which had a hundred tiny buttons down the back. Every evening after our baths, I had to button Lili up and then unbutton her again before going to bed. Lili looked very beautiful and glamorous in this dress, with her blonde hair worn long and curled up in page-boy style. Bill and Grandpa wore tuxedos for dinner and I wore my best American style uniform. Everything was very elegant, the table laid out with early Georgian silver, candles flickering in tall Georgian, silver candlesticks, the wine poured into crystal goblets, logs blazing in the fireplace throwing flickering light on to the beamed ceiling.

After this luxurious interlude we had to return to reality. Our sojourn at the Couchmans was intended to be only temporary to give us a chance to get ourselves organized. Lady Couchman was already showing signs of impatience with her unaccustomed guests. Also I wanted to look for a job and it would be better to live closer to London. I could ill afford the fare for constant journeys from East Grinstead to London and back. At the end of January we moved into rooms in a large Victorian house in Strawberry Hill Road, just west of Twickenham. This house belonged to a professional army officer who was stationed in Germany. His daughter lived by herself in the large house. For ten pounds a month we had the front drawing room, a large bedroom upstairs and use of the kitchen and bathroom.

This arrangement would probably have been fine under normal circumstances. But this winter was one of the coldest in memory. Coal was rationed. A cast iron stove had been inserted into the drawing room fireplace, but it was hardly able to heat the room. In our bedroom there was a gas fire but the pressure was so low that the pale, anemic, flame barely gave off any heat. One morning, I had to leave early to catch a train to Liverpool for a job interview. I made some coffee to drink while I was dressing, but did not finish it. When Lili woke up a few hours later ice had formed in the coffee cup on the dressing table. Mark slept in a bassinet, wrapped in woolen garments with a knit cap on his head and gloves on his hands, his face barely visible under the layers of blankets.

A few days later, we woke up in the middle of the night to hear water running down the stairs. The water storage tank in the attic had frozen and burst. We were alone because our landlady had gone away and I had no idea how to shut off the water. In the morning, in response to urgent phone calls, an old man arrived on a bicycle with a long tool over his shoulder. With my help he dug through the snow to find the valve cover in the street and, finally, he shut off the water valve. It was impossible to get a plumber because pipes were bursting all over London. In English houses, all the water pipes were mounted on the outside wall at the back of the house, completely exposed to the elements. The train into London ran behind houses and it was an amazing sight to see all the frozen waterfalls, created by water cascading from burst pipes. We were without any water for more than two weeks, but fortunately our next door neighbors had done something to protect their pipes and I was able to carry water in buckets from their house. I was reminded of my days in the forestry in Ceglow during the first war-time winter, bringing water from the well every morning.

To add to the problems, everything was still rationed in England, food, clothing, shoes, fuel, coal. Meat was rationed by price, we were receiving about two shillings and sixpence worth (less than $1) per person per week. Therefore we bought the cheapest grades to obtain larger quantities. Only rabbits (imported from Australia), chickens and offal, like kidneys and liver were unrationed, if you were lucky enough to find a butcher who had any. Fish was plentiful and not rationed, but better kinds were hard to find and more expensive than we could afford. Whale steaks were eaten by some to replace meat, but we never found them very palatable. We received two eggs a week per person, small portions of butter and other cooking fat, 16 ounces of sugar a month. Tea, the traditional beverage of the British, was rationed, coffee was not. Although the sizes of rations gradually improved, the system was still in effect at the end of 1950 when we left England. In fact England was the last country in Western Europe to drop this tedious and costly system, which was intended to ensure that all levels of the population were equally fed at the expense of an enormous bureaucracy needed to maintain and enforce it. This kind of egalitarianism was a mainstay of the political program of the socialist Labour Party that was in power from the end of the war until the late 1950s. Only the inborn self-discipline of Britons enabled rationing to be sustained as long as it was.

Finally, spring came. Trees and flowers bloomed and in spite of food shortages life became much more pleasant. We were able to take Mark for walks in his pram. We went to Hampton Court and visited the Botanical Gardens in nearby Kew. Janek visited us several times and one day Staszek came to see us just before departing to Australia to work as a contract laborer building power dams. Stefan DuChateau visited us from Paris and caused consternation by the amount of scarce sugar he put in his tea. Our most wonderful surprise was the unexpected visit of my father who was working for the Polish Ministry of Foreign Trade and had been sent to Holland to negotiate the sale of Polish coal.

The British Government was faced with the problem of absorbing approximately 200,000 Polish soldiers and dependents who refused to return to Poland under the conditions then existing. The elections had been held January 19, 1947, in accordance with the provisions of the Yalta Conference. However the communist government installed by Moscow made it virtually impossible for the noncommunist parties to campaign or even to put up candidates. 118 leaders of the Polish Peasant Party were murdered. The counting of votes took days and predictably, when the results were finally announced, none of the opposition candidates were elected. There were continual reports that opposition party members were being arrested as were many of the officers and soldiers of the Polish Army who had returned home. Members of the wartime underground and the AK were also being arrested and imprisoned, many of them died from beatings they received, or from malnutrition and exposure. Vice-premier Mikolajczyk fled from Poland, as did Baginski and Korbonski in October and November 1947.

The British government organized the Polish Resettlement Corps with the purpose of retraining the Polish soldiers for civilian life and to gradually find jobs for them within the British economy. Over a period of a few months in 1947 all the Polish units were demobilized and the personnel transferred to the P.R.C. At the same time members of the P.R.C were encouraged to emigrate to other countries with promises that passage for them and their dependents would be paid to any destination in the world. I did not wait for the P.R.C. to find employment for me, I was already actively seeking a job. For me this was easier than for most of my compatriots as I spoke English fluently.

At the end of June I officially enrolled in the Polish Resettlement Corps. But I was already working, and was demobilized the day after I registered. On May 19 1947, I had started work as a draftsman at a small company manufacturing transformers and voltage regulators - Brentford Transformers Ltd. - located on an industrial estate in suburban Kidbrooke in northern Kent. This company had been established in 1939 by a German Jew, Rosenfeld, who had managed to leave Germany with his family in 1938. He was an electrical engineer and had developed a unique type of voltage regulator, a device to provide power at a constant level to a load even while the supply voltage was varying. This invention had been successful and had been purchased in substantial quantities by the government during the war. Now operations of the company were being expanded to include power transformers.

It became necessary to move from Strawberry Hill, because the journey, all the way into London and then an equal distance eastward out of London, took too much time and I could not afford the cost of the train tickets out of my 5 pound a week salary (about $25). Lili was pregnant once more and it was very difficult to find rental rooms at an affordable price, if at all. Bill Murray-Lawes agreed to loan me the necessary money for the down payment on a house and to provide references to enable me to obtain a mortgage. We found our first house at 10 Further Green Road, in the suburb of Catford, which was still in Greater London, but on the border of Kent. It was the end unit of a row house in a working class district, with three small bedrooms upstairs, a living room and dining room and kitchen downstairs. There was a small garden in front and behind. The house was in good condition because it had been built just before the war and had not suffered any damage during the bombing. The price was about 2,000 pounds (at that time equal to $10,000).

We moved in on August 21, a hot summer night. Our entire furniture at the time consisted of a mattress, a kitchen table with four chairs and Mark's crib. We were exhausted with all the rushing around we had done and sank down on our mattress at about 10:30. The main line from London to southeast England ran on an embankment 300 yards away, the other side of a vegetable garden across the street. We lay on the mattress, tossing and turning in the unusual heat, listening to the trains rushing by. We knew that the last train passed at about 11:30 and after that we expected peace. The last train did pass and then, it started. *Chuff- chuff-chuff; bang -bang - bang*. Unknown to us, a marshaling yard for freight trains was situated on the other side of the embankment. This noise continued all night. Worse, from time to time one of the locomotives stopped and let off a blast of steam from its safety valve. We didn't sleep very well that night. But it's amazing how quickly one gets accustomed to various noises. After a few days we never noticed the locomotives any more.

I bought a second-hand bicycle to ride to work. This normally took me about 25 minutes, riding through Lee Green, crossing the Eltham Road and the Dover Road. The plant was a new one, a one story steel frame building with the offices along the front. I was one of six draftsmen (one of them a woman). There were two design engineers, Ted Levy, who designed the regulators and who had been with the company for some time, and John Palmer, who had recently been hired from the British subsidiary of the Swedish company ASEA, to design the oil-filled power transformers. Old man Rosenfeld was the president and still did development work on new regulator designs.

I quickly learned the mechanical design of the regulators as well as of the simpler power transformers. The regulators were all fairly well standardized, and customized features were drawn quickly by making copies of existing drawings and then modifying the copies using carbon paper to produce an additional file copy. The original went to the shop and from it the transformer was fabricated. Special parts were drawn almost free hand in a book with two carbon copies. This was a simple system with minimum paperwork. A new transformer design was whipped out in two days, often less. I was able to complete drawings for at least two fairly standard designs a day. One of the peculiarities of the work at Brentford Transformers was that all the electrical designs were in the metric system, for example coil and core dimensions were all in millimeters. However the mechanical design was in English units (England did not formally adopt the metric system until ten years later). This caused some problems in matching the two.

The general shortage of materials caused another problem. Before completing a design I had to go into the shop and check what material was available. Having selected the material I needed, I marked the Job Number on it using chalk. Nevertheless, when the time came that this unit was to be manufactured, perhaps three weeks later, the reserved pieces had mysteriously disappeared. If the desired size of steel was no longer available, it was unthinkable to delay manufacture for the several weeks that would be needed to procure the specified material. So I searched the stores for a piece of the closest size. Then I went back to the drawing board to modify the drawings accordingly. There was complete cooperation between the production and design people. Everybody understood the economic problems of the day and all workers wanted to get the job done as best as possible under the difficult circumstances. Needless to say, there was no union at Brentford Transformers; if there had been, the situation might have been different.

October 17th was the day of the final examination for the Chartered Electrical Engineer certificate. I had been studying the subject material by correspondence course and felt quite confident that I would pass. However Lili was also approaching the day of birth, in fact it was already overdue.

That night, in the early morning hours, Lili started having labor pains. We had no telephone, I dashed off to the phone booth on the corner of Lee Green Road. An ambulance came to take Lili to the hospital. I arranged with our next door neighbor to look after Mark and, then, I walked to the station to catch the train to London. I couldn't allow myself to be distracted, the examination was so important to our plans. Although I was worried, I resolutely pushed any thoughts about Lili out of my mind. Finally, I had answered all the questions, quickly I rechecked, then turned my papers in an hour early. I rushed to the station and hurried to Lewisham Hospital.

Peter had already arrived and I was able to see him and then enjoy a short visit with Lili, who was in a general ward containing about twenty new mothers. One of the benefits of socialized medicine was immediately evident — the birth of a baby cost us nothing. However the food was so poor in the hospital, that during each of the visiting hours, which were one hour only, each evening, I brought tasty little items of food. Five days later Lili came home with the baby. Mark accepted the new brother without any overt expression of jealousy; he just looked at him with a surprised expression.

After a few weeks it became obvious that Peter had a problem. An eczema had developed on his face and arms. His hands had to be restrained to prevent him from continually scratching his face. Visits to various doctors resulted in special milk and diet being prescribed, and various ointments to relieve the itching. None of these measures provided any substantial improvement in his misery. A cure was not affected until we moved to Deerfield twelve years later. The poor baby was miserable and cried frequently, and for the next two or three years neither of us ever had a full night's sleep. We each took turns getting up to try to soothe Peter. After he was a year old and started to eat various baby foods, we discovered that he was allergic to anything that contained eggs, milk, peas, fish and many other foods. Several times during the next few years he had to be rushed to hospital to have his stomach pumped out, because inadvertently he had eaten something which caused severe reactions. One of the problems was that even the smell of cooking fish caused distress. As fish was one of the few foods that were not rationed, we ate it at least once a week and Lili had to take all kinds of precautions in cooking it to avoid causing an asthma attack.

Our house had three bedrooms upstairs, one of them so small it could really only be used for storage. The bathroom and separate toilet and a closet completed the upstairs. The closet contained an electric hot water heater. This heater was of the storage type with a clock which allowed it to be switched on only in "off-peak" hours. Downstairs the entrance hall opened onto the front room, which would normally be the living room, and the rear room which had large french windows opening into the back garden. Under the stairs there was a broom closet and behind it the kitchen which also had a separate entrance to the outside. All the rooms had fireplaces, but, of course, the supply of coal was limited, so most of the time we used radiant space heaters to provide warmth. The cooking stove was also electric.

The back garden was half paved with irregular shaped stones (so-called crazy paving). The remaining half was a vegetable garden, in which we grew some vegetables, mint, rhubarb, dill. I quickly discovered that mint grows like a weed and I was forever digging up the spreading roots. In the end, I contained them by digging a twelve inch deep trench all around the mint patch and filling it with cement. The small front garden, separated from the street by a waist high wall, was also partly paved, the rest devoted to a rock garden in which I planted perennials.

Along the side of the house a narrow passage led to an alley which ran along the backs of all the houses. A six foot high wooden fence enclosed the back garden, through which a door opened to this passageway. All the services were underground, but, of course, all the water pipes were on the outside of the back wall of the house. We had no telephone. For many years after the war it was virtually impossible to get a telephone unless one could get a certificate of priority. These were given only to doctors, nurses and policemen. There was a coin call box on the main road about 300 yards away. Our next door neighbors had a telephone that was installed before the war, but we did not like to bother them except in an emergency, for example, when Peter had one of his attacks.

In order to meet our expenses, we decided to rent out the front room as a "bed-sitting-room" and provide an evening meal. I installed a couple of extra electric outlets, put linoleum on the floor, and purchased some reasonably comfortable furniture: a bed, easy chair, small table and chair, wardrobe with a mirror, a radiant heater and a standing lamp. Our first lodger moved in shortly after Peter was born. He was a red haired Welshman, who was a school teacher in one of the Catford schools, a happy man with great sense of humor with whom we got along very well. He didn't mind the children and was always interested in any new dishes that Lili managed to cook for the evening meal. He stayed about a year until he changed jobs and moved away.

Our next tenant was Mr. Mulholland, a tall, thin, elderly bachelor who worked as a carpet salesman in a department store in Lewisham. He was very correct in his behavior but was humorless and not very friendly. He was very particular about his food. Previously, he had lived with his mother, who came frequently to check on his living conditions. She told Lili what he liked and what he disliked. She explained that he had a delicate stomach and the only green vegetable he could eat was green peas. In spite of the disturbances caused by the children, he lived with us until the end of our stay in England.

About a month after the examination, I was notified that I had passed and henceforth had the right to append the letters AMIEE after my name and to call myself a Chartered Electrical Engineer. At Brentford Transformers I was given a raise but no change in job classification. However, the two design engineers, tutored me in the electrical design of transformers and voltage regulators and gave me new designs to work on. I did this work in my own free time at home. They made any necessary corrections and gave me comments; then, they issued the designs to the shop after signing their own names. This didn't seem fair, but I was happy to be given the opportunity to learn new skills.

When I realized that, at least in the foreseeable future, Mr. Rosenfeld had no intention of increasing the design engineering staff and therefore I would be stuck as a draftsman, I started looking for another job. This was not an easy task, because I had little experience yet and on top of that I was a foreigner. In addition, the job had to be in a location that was easily reachable from our present house. I answered many ads in the trade magazines and got no replies. Finally, I was invited to come to an interview at a small company in the Strand, close to Charing Cross Station. The location was ideal because most of the trains from Hither Green Station, five minutes walk from home, ran to this London terminus. Fortunately, they had no prejudices and hired me to be the understudy for their electrical engineer who was approaching retirement age.

After giving suitable notice to Mr. Rosenfeld, I started my new job at Equipment & Engineering Company Limited on May 24, 1948. Normally, I caught the 8:15 train from Hither Green which ran non-stop to London Bridge, then continued to Waterloo and across the Thames to Charing Cross. In fine weather, I walked through the gardens along the Thames embankment and then up Norfolk Street to the office, which was on the corner of the Strand. Otherwise, I walked along the Strand where the buildings gave some protection from wind and rain. The offices occupied the fourth floor of the corner building and offered an excellent view of the processions which proceeded down this main route connecting Westminster and Buckingham Palace with the City and St. Paul's Cathedral. The Lord Mayor's procession was an annual event every November. Guests were always invited to the offices to view these ceremonial occasions.

The company manufactured two specific ranges of products at a dingy factory in the East End. One range included the signs on buses and trains that indicated route number and destination, as well as other devices used by the transportation industry. Philip Fearon was responsible for the design and sales of these products. I was hired for the design and application engineering of the other product line — a range of crack detectors used in the testing of automotive and aircraft parts such as crankshafts, pistons, valves, suspensions, springs to ensure that they were free of stress cracks. The Magnaflux Company in the United States was our only important competitor. In addition, a major source of income was the trading company operation, importing as well as exporting a variety of products. We were the exclusive agents for the Simplex Company of Philadelphia, not only for the UK, but also for the British Crown Colonies. Their product line included mechanical lifting jacks for the mining and automobile service industries.

About a dozen people worked at the Norfolk Street offices: the two directors Daglish and Lorkin and their personal secretary; P.V. Fearon and a draftsman that worked on the automotive products; my boss, who had originally designed the magnetic crack detectors which were patented, and myself. The commercial office consisted of a sales director, an assistant and three girls who typed all the quotations and correspondence. Relationships with all the people in the company were very friendly, although no after hours social relationships developed. The main social events were the annual summer outing and a Christmas party. The company chartered a river steamer for the summer outing which everyone enjoyed. They dropped their typical English reticence and by evening, after a quantity of drinks, the mood was mellow. Lili was always invited but it was difficult for her to leave home because of Peter's problems. It was very difficult to get a responsible babysitter, especially during a week-end. One of the office girls liked swimming and every so often we went together to one of the public indoor swimming pools during lunch time.

Quickly, I learned the principles of magnetic crack detection and the design procedures for which there were no text books. My boss was already a sick man, so within weeks I was already being sent to visit customers in England, to discuss new applications or to train operators of a machine purchased from us. By the end of the year he became bed-ridden and I had to take on the full design responsibility for the electrical products. I was still learning and had to go to his home in South London to obtain advise how to solve a specific problem. Early in 1949 he died. Shortly after that, I was promoted to the position of chief electrical engineer with an increase in salary to the princely sum of 50 pounds a month (then equivalent to $250).

Within the next few months I made some design improvements, designed two new crack detector products with more modern appearance and improved performance, and I rewrote the manual. After this was all done, I had a lot of free time and started learning the commercial side of the business and, particularly, the intricacies of international quotations. I was traveling in England, at least once a month, and made two trips to Holland, the first to make a presentation to the Netherlands Air Force, the second to train operating personnel after the order had been obtained.

I was very happy and enjoyed my work. I had the ideal position with considerable responsibility and freedom to explore new fields, try out new ideas, to take the initiative. The commercial aspect of the business opened new horizons and gave me the opportunity to meet new people and see the country. Within two years I knew about as much as could be learned at this small company and started looking for other opportunities. I responded to a job opening that I thought would be interesting and was invited to an interview at a fairly large company in the south of London. It was obvious that they thought I was British. The interview proceeded very well, my prior experience was very appropriate for the job opening. Finally, we got to the point of discussing salary and the date when I could start work. Once that matter was settled, they gave me a form to fill out. Only then did they discover that I was not British.

"We will get in touch with you," they said. They never did.

My lifestyle had changed. I no longer rode to work by bicycle but commuted to London by train. So I dressed more formally and was away from home for longer hours. Financially we were a little better off, particularly after my promotion. With the added income from our lodger it became possible to put aside some money in a savings account. Fortunately, Peter's sickness was not a financial strain, because the health service was socialized and all medical services and prescription medicines were free. However our family doctor was overworked and every visit required long hours of waiting. He referred us to a specialist, a Jamaican, in the neighboring suburb of Beckenham. Medical knowledge about allergies was still limited and this doctor's knowledge of the subject was even more so and, unfortunately, he was able to do little to alleviate Peter's problems.

When Mark was about four, and Peter two and a half, Mark learned how to open the garden gate. Lili was busy doing house work confident that they were safe in the back yard. When she called them in for supper, they were gone. Lili was frantic, she dashed up and down the street and over to the little shopping center on the main road, no sign of them. She found a policeman who was on a bicycle. He finally tracked the boys down at the station. They had gone to meet daddy's train!

One of the characteristic features of life in London in those days was the effect on the environment of burning coal in open fireplaces. In particular, this caused the fogs, which occurred frequently during the winter months, to be much denser and darker than normal. This was such a prevalent factor in life in those days, that "fog-service" in the transit systems was a normal feature. Under "fog service" all normal timetables and routes were abandoned. Trains proceeded as often as possible, making stops at all stations.

The fog was frequently so dense that the driver could not even see the brightly lit electric signals. Men were stationed at the signals with a device to place detonators on the track when the signal was red. The first wheels exploded the device with a loud bang and the driver halted the train. Then he stuck his head out of the window and awaited verbal permission to go ahead. This was given when the man standing under the signal could detect that the loom of light above him changed from red to green or yellow. Buses also abandoned their normal routes and drove slowly along the streets, often with the conductor walking in front holding a flare. Needless to say, under these conditions a twenty minute journey could take an hour or two, if at all possible. Whenever a fog alert was announced over the radio, one of the managing directors would come into the office to announce, "Everybody go home, while you can!"

Everyone rushed to get their coats and ran out the door to catch their trains or buses. This happened four or five times each year.

Another effect of this condition was that all the buildings were grimy and required frequent repainting. During the war this had not been possible so that all London buildings looked dark and dirty. Window-washing services enjoyed a booming business. Ours came once a month. This condition was not good for Peter and every time it was foggy he breathed much worse. A few years after we left England, the burning of coal was banned in London. Although fogs still occur because of weather conditions, they are no longer as bad or so disruptive.

Our social life was limited, not only because it was difficult to arrange baby sitters due to Peter's problems, but because we just couldn't afford it. Once in a while we managed to go to a local cinema together, but generally we took turns to go separately. The Lewisham Gaumont was an old style theater, built in the twenties. Vaudeville acts on the large stage and organ music preceded the main film. Other cinemas were cheaper and offered double features for a shilling (about 25 cents), but on Friday and Saturday nights one had to wait in a long queue.

We did have a few outings with the children during our four years in England. Bill and Baba invited us several times for dinner at their London flat in Cranmer Court near Sloane Square. Bill or friends of theirs took us by car to Old Standen for long weekends and summer holidays. One of these friends was the Belgian Military Attache, Andy Bigwood, who drove a big American car at fast speeds along the narrow, twisting, hedge lined country roads. Once we had a real night on the town. We spent the weekend at the house of another of Baba's friends in Chelsea. She had a daughter of the same age as Mark and a nanny who looked after the children while we went dancing to a night club.

Occasionally, we took the boys and went to London to visit Polish friends, most of whom lived in furnished rooms in the Earls Court area. Sometimes friends would visit us, but it always seemed to be very difficult for any of them to make the trip by train to Catford. The Derens and my cousin Janek were the most frequent visitors, particularly, at holidays such as Christmas and Easter, which we tried to celebrate in the Polish fashion as much as we were able.

Most of our Polish friends were still in the army, and studying, or if they had left the P.R.C. they only had low paying jobs and were having a hard time. We were relatively wealthy, we owned our own house and I earned 50 pounds a month, two to three times the wages of our Polish friends. The general attitude of the Poles in England was dispirited. They felt betrayed by the Allies. The West had gone to war in defense of Poland's freedom. The war had been won but Poland was still not free. In fact, Poland had been sold down the river by Roosevelt and Churchill at Yalta. We were well aware that the Allies had been in the position to take Berlin and most of Germany before the Soviets got there. They had waited at the Elbe and Mulde Rivers for nearly two weeks, because of the agreements made at Yalta.

The fact that, realistically, the Allies could not have stopped the Soviets from occupying Poland was not taken into accounts in all these discussions. The bitterness persisted and was also directed at the British. This was not fair, I pointed out to my friends, the British were in no position to change very much in the last year of the war. They had supported the Polish position as far as it was possible. As was later revealed in his books, Churchill had been afraid of the Russians gaining hegemony in Europe and in 1943 had pleaded in vain with Roosevelt for a strike through the Balkans at the "soft underbelly" of Europe.

Now my father was also in exile in Sweden. After his return from Siberia he had worked for the State Foreign Trade company, Polimex, and at the same time was involved politically in the Polish Labor Party (*Partia Pracy*), a social-democratic party with some connections to the Catholic church. After the fraudulent elections in 1947, in which the Communist Party and a couple of its allies won all the seats, vice-premier Mikolajczyk and most of the other opposition leaders fled the country. My father's days were also numbered. He lasted as long as he did, only because the government needed his foreign trade expertise. Nevertheless, at the end of April 1948, upon his return from a trade mission to Sweden, a friend warned him that the police were going to arrest him on some trumped up charge. He still had not turned in his passport (which had to be done after each trip) so he took the next plane back to Stockholm.

When I went on my first trip to Amsterdam in February 1949, he also came there on a business trip from Sweden, and we spent a couple of evenings together. We went to restaurants and ate the excellent Dutch food which was already abundant. Later in 1949 he received permission from the French Government to settle in Paris. There he entered the Polish National Committee as a representative of the Polish Labor Party. From there it was easy for him to visit us in England. His political contact in London was a group associated with the Liberal Party, called Liberal International. The director of this organization was MacCullum Scott. I got involved with this organization and did some work and participated in some meetings. But I did not have any real political interests, nor did I have the time to get deeply involved.

We had not given up on our desire to go to the United States. I had no hope that the economic situation in England would improve significantly in the next few years. This, together with the difficulty for a foreigner to obtain a better paying position in any major British company, made the prospects of improving our economic well-being look very bleak. Almost immediately after our arrival in England, I had registered at the U.S. Embassy to be put on the list for an immigration visa. But there appeared to be little hope of accomplishing this goal in the near future. The quota of immigration visas for Poles, under then existing American law, had been filled for years to come by the displaced persons from German camps. The fact that the quotas for people born in England, France and other west European countries had never been utilized had no bearing on the situation. The rigid quota system set up by Congress in the 1920's was still in effect. In the meantime, we had looked at other possibilities such as Australia, Argentina, Canada. Several of our friends had already emigrated to these countries. However, except for collecting information from various embassies, I had not yet taken any further steps.

On Easter Saturday, April 8, 1950, we were both lying in bed, taking it easy and listening to the news on the radio. Suddenly, our attention was caught by a news item stating that the United States Congress had just passed new legislation which would give 20,000 immigration visas, outside the quota system, to Polish soldiers who had served in the Allied Forces and their families, and who were presently resident in England,

We jumped out of bed and danced with joy and then collapsed back on the bed in an embrace. Immediately, after the three day Easter holiday, I dashed to Grosvenor Square, to find out what exactly I had to do. Although, it was too early for the embassy staff to have any details of the new law, they were aware of the efforts that were being made to pass such legislation. I verified that our name was still on the list of Polish applicants, and had been assigned a serial number. The friendly consular assistant advised me to start searching for a sponsor who must be an American citizen.

Without delay, I wrote to our friends the Skubas. Witold had received a job with the research department of Ford Motor Company in Dearborn soon after their arrival in 1947 from the DP camp in Germany. Fortunately for us, they had just returned to Detroit from Brazil and were able to start looking for an American citizen who would sponsor us. They also started to send us various information that would help us get oriented in the job situation, costs of living, etc. They sent us the advertising sections of the Detroit newspapers and a complete Sears catalog. We studied the latter with fascination. It gave us a very good idea of the range of products to be bought in America and of the prices we could expect to pay. We discovered that many of the prices were somewhat higher than in England, but the range of products and features was very much greater. We quickly found out that the higher prices didn't mean anything because I could expect to earn a higher salary too.

Early in the summer, we received an official notification from the United States Embassy that we were on the list to receive visas. The necessary forms were enclosed for our sponsors to fill out as well as forms for me to complete. We soon received the forms back from The Skubas' landlords, who had come to Detroit from Poland prior to World War I, and agreed to sponsor us and returned the completed forms. Then we went to the Embassy for interviews and medical examinations. In the middle of September we received our immigration visas and started to get our affairs in order for departure. Under the terms of the Polish Resettlement Act transportation was paid by the British Government to anywhere in the world within five years of entering the Corps. Sometime in December we were advised that we would receive space on the Queen Mary leaving right after Christmas. I gave Fearon, Lorkin and Daglish advance warning that I was planning to leave. They were genuinely sorry to see me go, but realized that I would have greater opportunities in America and did not try to dissuade me.

We sold the house and made a modest profit. After paying off the mortgage and repaying Bill's loan we still had a few hundred pounds left over. After four years of skimping and saving this seemed like a fortune. The problem was that exportation of currency was restricted and we would have to leave most of the money in England until later. We bought clothes and shoes for all of us. My father came for a visit and suggested that I buy Lili a fur coat. A small Polish furrier in London made her a beautiful coat from sleek, dark Canadian squirrel skins. It was so well made and the skins were of such good quality that it was often mistaken for ermine. We also went to see all the things in London that, normally, only tourists visit, like the British Museum and the Tower. During his visit Daddy baby-sat for us, while we went sight-seeing and shopping. One evening we came home to find him fast asleep in his chair, with his reading glasses balanced on the end of his nose. The boys were having a ball. Newspapers were torn and thrown all over the room.

Baba and Bill were sorry to see us go, but they also realized that we would have more opportunity in America than in England. The socialist government had made it very difficult for the old gentry and people with inherited money. High taxation made it almost impossible to accumulate any new money. Father came over from Paris to see us off. The day after Christmas we moved out of the house at 10 Further Green Road to the Strand Palace Hotel in London. Baba had a party for us at Cranmer Court to which various friends came for drinks and to wish us well, then we had dinner together.

In the morning, the hotel forgot to give us a call, but fortunately, Daddy woke up just in time. We had a hurried breakfast then we dashed to Waterloo Station to board the boat train to Southampton. We were seen off by Baba, Bill, my father and Janek. Peter and Mark each got a teddy bear from Baba. My good luck omen was still with us. I counted our luggage, there were exactly 13 pieces!

In Southampton, we boarded the liner Queen Mary which had just been converted back to passenger ship service after serving as a troopship throughout the war. She was the largest civilian ship in the world at the time. We traveled in third class and our cabins were down near the water line. The class was crowded with emigrants, most of them Poles. Lili and the two boys had a tiny cabin with upper and lower berths and a cot for Peter. I shared a four-berth cabin with three other Poles. However, even in Third Class the service was impeccable and the food excellent, in quantities that we had not seen for years. We spent as much time as possible on the promenade decks walking, playing games or lying in deck-chairs bundled in blankets.

There was an excellent play-room supervised by a nurse. We hoped that the boys would spend some of their time there and allow us more freedom to do other adult things. Unfortunately, they, particularly Peter, did not want to be separated from us. When we tried to take him to the playroom, he lay on the floor and screamed, having a tantrum.

A woman passing by said, "Poor little boy, he has lost his mother." Lili, embarrassed, stood a short distance away waiting for him to calm down and didn't admit she was the mother.

We were very fortunate to have a superb calm crossing. The stewards said it was the finest winter-time Atlantic crossing they had ever experienced. We put the boys to bed early, right after tea, so that we could enjoy the evening entertainment in peace. For us this crossing was a vacation. All our previous hard times had passed and we looked forward to the future with confidence.

On Sunday we attended Mass, which was held in the gorgeous two story high First Class Lounge. Unfortunately, the boys thought this was great fun to be able to jump up and down on the comfortable sofa and we were obliged to leave early. This was the only time we were allowed to visit this prestigious part of the ship. In the Third Class section we also had plenty of fun. Every afternoon tea was served in a spacious lounge with entertainment furnished by a live band. Peter and Mark were entranced and sat on the floor and watched the musicians play. One day Peter lost his teddy-bear and the staff searched high and low, finally finding it behind a sofa in the lounge. There was a great party for New Year's Eve. We got to toast the New Year twice, because the clocks were set back one hour at midnight to account for our passage westward through the time-zones. Dancing on the rolling floor was slightly difficult, but we had no trouble adjusting our steps to account for the motion. Perhaps the champagne helped.

Finally, early in the morning of January 2, 1951, we entered New York Harbor and, entranced, we looked at the magnificent sky line of downtown New York. Then we rushed to the port side to look at the Statue of Liberty, but we were somewhat disappointed. Seen from the perspective of an enormous ocean liner, it seemed so much smaller than we had imagined. Processing of the immigrants started after all the regular passengers had disembarked. When our turn came it was brief. the officials were courteous and welcomed us to the United States. We had some fruit from the breakfast table in a bag, we were told that we could not take it ashore, so Lili peeled the oranges and we ate them on the spot.

We had planned to stop one day in New York and were booked into a small hotel in the 50's near 6th Avenue. We were amazed to see all the rubbish in the streets and the newspapers flying around. London was much cleaner even though the buildings were blackened with soot. The weather was extremely warm for January and we did not need to wear our winter coats. We also found the temperature in the hotel and in all the stores and restaurants much too high, accustomed as we were to the cool interiors in England. We marveled at all the magnificent displays of all kinds of goods and foods in the stores, at the bustle of traffic in the streets and the crowds hurrying along the sidewalks. The boys were excited at all the wonderful new things they were seeing. Finally, tired out we retired to our hotel room for our first night in America.

Accustomed to European habits I put our shoes outside the door to be polished. Shortly there was someone knocking at the door, I opened it. A bellboy was shaking his head, "Man, what yer doing? Dis ain't Inlan, yer wanna lose em?"

"Oh, don't you polish shoes here?" I queried.

"Na, inna morning ya go to shooshine boy in de lobby," he shook his head at my naivete. Lesson number one in the many we were to learn in the next few days about our new country.

In the morning, we went to St. Patrick's Cathedral and we thanked God that He had been so merciful to us, brought us safely through all the dangers and trials, and granted us our wish to start our lives from the beginning in a new country. We prayed for His help in the days to come. We were confident that from now on our lives would be much easier, the opportunities would be there for us to build a good life for our children.

In the afternoon of our second day in America we took a taxi to Pennsylvania Station. This was still the magnificent structure that had been built at the beginning of the century, that later was torn down to be replaced by the present cramped station under Madison Square Garden. These were still the days when most people traveled by train and Penn Station was full of people departing to destinations all over the United States. We boarded the train for the 16 hour overnight journey to our new home — Detroit.

The Polish and English chapters in our lives had closed. I was 28 years old and starting a new life with Lili and my two boys. After years of living in what seemed to be a temporary state, we had reached a country that we could call our permanent home.

THIRTEEN IS MY LUCKY NUMBER

13

PART TWO

A NEW WORLD

10

STARTING AFRESH

O ur goal had finally been achieved — we had arrived in the New World. We came with great expectations, but very little in terms of worldly belongings or money. However, we were much better off than many other immigrants; we had an education and we spoke English. Beyond that, we had almost $100 in cash, two children and thirteen pieces of luggage, which included a box of pots and pans, and a folding baby chair. We also had friends who were already established and could provide us with a place to live and some support until we found a place of our own and a job.

The first few days were spent on excited meetings with our friends, dinners accompanied by traditional Polish toasts; our various stories were told over and over again. We were driven all over the city and we absorbed the sight of snow-filled streets full of people, huddled in thick winter coats, bustling to-and-fro or riding the long yellow streetcars. Our heads were filled with new information and suggestions for job hunting, where best to look for apartments,etc.

We read the thick newspapers from front to back. Lili studied the clothing and food ads, the boys pored over the comics and I studied the help wanted pages. I developed a plan; I went through the "Yellow Pages" and made a list of companies that I thought might have a need for someone with my skills. I borrowed Janek's typewriter and composed about twenty letters. To my great surprise, within a few days I received answers to fifteen of them, a great rate of return for an unsolicited job-seeking letter. About half the replies regretted that the company had no openings. Five or six more said that they had no opening but suggested names of other companies that I should contact. Finally five letters asked me to come in for an interview. I was elated with this great response.

My faith in America proved to be fully justified. In no other country in the world would it be possible for a foreigner, just arrived in the country, to get such a reaction. Of course, at the time there was a shortage of young professionals. The Korean War was in progress, many had been drafted, and industry was working overtime to satisfy the pent up demands from the long World War, to rebuild Europe, to support the new war in Korea.

I went to the interviews and ended up with two definite job offers, one from a large manufacturer of electrical equipment, Square D Company, the other from the local power utility, Detroit Edison. The latter was somewhat better initially and offered a slightly higher salary, but I felt that I would have greater possibilities for the future working for a manufacturer. Therefore, I decided to accept Square D's offer, which gave me a starting wage of $65 a week. Then we found a furnished house on Garvin Street on the north east border of Hamtramck for $85 a month. It was a bungalow, typical for the working districts of Detroit, with two bedrooms, a living room, kitchen, basement and a front porch. The owner lived next door. We had brought linen, blankets and tableware and needed to buy very little.

We were intensely interested in all aspects of everyday life in Detroit, so different from everything we had been used to before. Hamtramck was almost 100% Polish in those days, inhabited by immigrants, mostly peasants from impoverished villages, uneducated and poor, that had come from Russian and Austrian occupied Poland in the years 1890 to 1914, looking for an opportunity to better themselves. They worked hard in the lowest paying jobs in the bustling new automobile industry of Detroit. They had created a thriving community with its own government, police, fire department, churches, social clubs, newspaper and radio station, completely surrounded by the city of Detroit. In this community the language was Polish, but a Polish that we found hard to understand.

They had come from a country without streetcars, electricity, gas ranges or automobiles and many other things for which Polish words exist today. They had created new words by adding Polish word endings to English expressions. Thus a car became *kara*, and a streetcar, *stritkara*. Many of the older people still did not speak English after living 50 years in America; they dwelled in a ghetto of their own creation, just as the Irish, Italians, Swedes, Jews lived in theirs. The Polish spoken in Hamtramck was just as strange to us as the French spoken by the Quebecois is strange to Parisians.

We also discovered that many of the old-timers were resentful of the new wave of Polish immigrants who were educated and quickly got new jobs with better pay, and within a few months acquired homes, cars — things that they had only obtained after many years of hard, back-breaking work. I ran into this jealousy very quickly. I traveled to work at 6600 Rivard Street by streetcar*. I had been only two months at the new job when the drivers and conductors of the Detroit transit lines went out on strike, which lasted many weeks. I had no way to get to work, so I borrowed $400 from Lili's cousin, Janusz Zaleski, who was working for a bank in Venezuela, and bought a light blue 1946 Nash for about $600. The next warm, sunny Saturday, I was washing my new possession in front of the house. One of our neighbors, a man in his late 50's who was an assembly line worker at Packard Motor Company, strolled by, stood for a while watching me, scratched his head and said (of course, in fractured Polish):

"Well now, *pan* Biega, is this your *kara*?"

"Well yes," I said apologetically. "You know I have a long way to go to work, so I had to get a car."

"Always I ride to work on a bicycle," he declared.

"Unfortunately, I have too far to go." I defended my choice.

He shook his head, mumbled something under his breath, and walked away.

The next weekend the sun was shining again. Once more I was washing my car. My neighbor came by. He was very pleased with himself.

---

* We also quickly learned a new vocabulary. The English "tram" became a "streetcar", "lift" changed to "elevator", "football" became "soccer", and so on.

"Well, *pan* Biega," he said, "Now I have a car too. I have a new Packard. Come and look at it."

Indeed this man, who had never owned a car, had bought a brand new Packard (in those days a luxury car equal to a Cadillac) just to show off to this new Polish immigrant! The problem was he didn't know how to drive. After I had made the suitable expressions of congratulation and awe, he said, "Next Saturday my daughter will come for a visit and will take us for a ride."

Our friend Witold Skuba experienced another example of this strange resentment. Before the war he had been an automobile development engineer at the Polish Fiat Factory in Warsaw. Consequently, shortly after arriving in Detroit from Germany, he received a job at Ford as an engineer in the Research Department. Subsequently, he and the whole family had been sent by Ford to Brazil to supervise the building of an automobile manufacturing plant with its own engineering department. Two years later they returned to Detroit and were living in a rented apartment in a modern complex on Eight Mile Road, on the northern boundary of the city of Detroit. Now with a good position and considerable savings accumulated as a result of the Brazilian assignment, they wanted to buy a house. He went to one of the banks in Hamtramck to arrange for a mortgage. He was refused. The bank official, of Polish parentage, was jealous that someone who had only been in America for four years should already be able to buy a house! Witold then went to a Home Savings and Loan Company in Detroit. This bank was delighted to deal with a Ford Motor Company research engineer.

We were amazed at the abundance of everything in the stores, by the amount of packing material used on everything, by the relatively low cost of food, clothing and appliances. The number of different radio stations also was a novelty. In England, as in the rest of Europe, radio programs were provided by the government. At that time in England there were only three programs to choose from. The thick newspapers with all the advertising and continual sales and special price offers, and the weekly magazines such as *Life*, provided us with hours of study.

Our friends, the Skubas and the Thomases, took us for rides all around Detroit and the surrounding area as soon as the snow melted away. The only negative impressions we had of America were the festoons of overhead telephone wires and power cables hanging from ugly wooden poles along all the streets and the amount of trash, old newspapers and paper wrappings, lying in the streets. In England wiring was underground and the streets were comparatively clean, even in the drabbest working class districts.

Gradually we got used to the high temperatures that were maintained inside houses and offices all winter long. At the office many of the girls wore thin summer dresses or the almost transparent nylon blouses, that were were fashionable at the time. This was very distracting in my work. Then warm weather came and about May 1 the air-conditioning was turned on in the office. To my amazement the temperature was set so low that it was uncomfortably cold inside! All the girls suddenly started coming to work in woolen dresses or thick sweaters. Homes did not yet have air-conditioning, so hot weather brought more discomfort, which was only moderated by using portable electric fans to blow the hot, humid air around.

I learned a lot at work. Square D was a manufacturer of electrical control equipment. Its Detroit plant occupied a whole city block and employed close to 5,000 people. I worked in the engineering department and sat at a drawing board learning about the products, the indexing system used to facilitate fast retrieval of desired drawings and the way in which standardization permitted the same parts and subassemblies to be used in dozens of different applications. During the first week I sat for hours studying a small plastic-cased circuit breaker trying to figure out how to take it apart, so that I could look at the mechanism inside. Finally I swallowed my pride and asked for help. My neighbor, a tall Texan, whom I had difficulty understanding, placed the sharp tip of a screwdriver against the case and with two blows of a hammer cracked the housing into several pieces.

"That's how you do it," he said.

"But how do you take it apart for service and repair?" I asked, bewildered.

"We don't repair them. If they don't work, we throw them away, anyway, they usually last long enough." he said. "They only cost about $2. It'd cost more to try to repair them."

Thus I was introduced to the secret of American low cost mass production. For a European it was wasteful to throw things away if they could be fixed and reused. I soon learned that in the U.S.A. there was a limiting cost to anything, above which repair became worthwhile. For example, the larger circuit breakers, which in those days cost more than $10 to produce in quantity, were designed to be opened up for repair.

After about six weeks I had learned a great deal about the products of Square D and the organization of the engineering department and started making changes to designs for cost reduction purposes or for performance improvement.

However, I also realized that my present position was little more than a glorified drafting job with little promise for the future. I went to my boss, Ralph Kingdon, and asked about the possibilities of transfer to the Application Engineering Section.

He said, "Bill, you're doing a great job. Starting next week you'll receive a $10 raise; don't even think of transferring. Then you'd have to start from the bottom again. Anyway, I don't think they have any openings right now."

I was happy to receive a raise, but was upset at being denied the possibility of trying a position, which I felt would be more interesting and provide more opportunity. That Sunday I noticed an ad in the newspaper stating that General Electric would be interviewing candidates for engineering positions at their plants in Fort Wayne, Indiana. These interviews were being conducted at one of the downtown hotels. I absented myself from work on some excuse and went to the hotel. I filled out questionnaires and then was interviewed by a couple of people. Chuck Kronmiller, who was the Assistant Manager of Engineering of the Specialty Transformer Department, spent at least a half an hour with me and asked many questions. A few days later, I received a letter asking me to come to Fort Wayne for further interviews.

On the Monday after Easter, I took the "Wabash Cannonball[*]" from Detroit's Union Station, and an hour and a half later I was in Fort Wayne. I talked to the Engineering Manager, Tommy Thomas, and a

---

[*] The crack train of the Wabash Railroad that ran from Detroit to St.Louis, immortalized in a popular song of the 40's.

number of other people. After lunch Chuck asked if I would like to go to another of the Fort Wayne departments for more interviews.

"No," I answered. "I have transformer experience and I'm really interested in working in this Department."

"Wait a few minutes in my office. I'll talk to Tommy," Chuck said. After waiting about half an hour, he came back and offered me a job as Design Engineer with a starting salary of $400 per month. I accepted without hesitation. Unfortunately, I was not a U.S. citizen and would have to be screened as a security risk by the Armed Forces because G.E. was engaged in defense contracts. This procedure might take several weeks.

After returning home I went to the police station to be finger-printed, filled out all the necessary forms, attached photographs and sent them to Fort Wayne, then settled down to wait. In the meantime I continued at my job at Square D. Finally, in the third week of May I received a letter from Kronmiller confirming that I had been cleared and could start work at any time. I went to Ralph Kingdon and told him that I was giving him two weeks notice.

He was startled and said, "You are doing very well and you have a bright future at Square D. I know that there are small companies in Detroit that offer higher salaries than we do, but when their contracts end, they will let you go. Don't make a rash decision. Think it over and I will ignore your notice."

"That won't be necessary," I replied. "Two months ago I talked to you and inquired about getting a transfer to Application Engineering. Your response was negative. With my education and experience the job that I have now is not satisfying and the new position I have received gives me a better opportunity. My notice stands."

As soon as I returned to my drawing board, he dashed off to the administrative offices. An hour later he came back and invited me back into his office.

"There is an opening now in Application Engineering. You can start there next week with an increase in salary to $90 a week. I will forget about you giving me notice."

"I'm sorry, Ralph. I would have been pleased if you had offered that to me soon after I asked for the transfer. Now it is too late. I have made up my mind."

Ralph wouldn't give up.

"I only want to help you make the right decision for yourself and your family. As I told you earlier, there are a lot of companies that make big promises but cannot provide you with a career opportunities that we can. At least wait while I run a business check on the company that you are thinking of going to, to make sure what kind of company it is."

"Ralph," I responded, "I don't really think that is necessary. The company I have accepted a job with is General Electric Company. I'm sure you will agree that they can offer me as good a career opportunity as Square D!"

To this he had no adequate response; he wished me good luck.

On Monday, June 4, 1951, I arrived by car in Fort Wayne. I spent the first day going through the usual medical checkup and personnel department procedures. I filled out the usual forms. Place of birth: Warsaw. The clerk checked the form and added after Warsaw: Indiana. I said, "No, not Warsaw, Indiana. *Warsaw, Poland!*"

"When were you naturalized?"

"I'm not."

"Then you can't work at General Electric," she said.

I lost my patience. I had been sitting around all day.

"Lady, the F.B.I. says I can. The Army, the Air Force and the Navy say I can. Mr. Thomas says I can. You don't have anything to say in the matter!"

Obviously I didn't earn any Brownie points in the Personnel Department.

I found a room in the house of a widow, not far from the General Electric plant, and settled down at my new job. It was another period of intensive learning — new systems, new ways of doing things, new procedures, new people. I found everybody very helpful, very willing to make the newcomer feel at home. Now I was a professional, an engineer, so quickly I got acquainted not only with the technical details of the products and the production techniques, but also with other aspects of corporate life — sales, accounting, advertising, standards, and also relationships with other entities of the gigantic General Electric Company.

In Fort Wayne alone there were four divisions, each as large as many individual industrial companies. The Specialty Transformer

Department produced a wide range of products from tiny electronic transformers through fluorescent lamp ballasts to large 200 KVA units, standing six feet high and weighing a quarter of a ton. It occupied a five story building a full city block long. Just across the company street was the large Motor & Generator Department of approximately equal size. The entrance to this complex was on Broadway. The Small Motor Department was located just across the street. The Fractional Horsepower Department occupied a large factory at Winter Street across town. Further south westward was Taylor Street, a brand-new facility producing small electric motors such as those used in refrigerators. Next to it, a large wire mill manufactured all the copper wire used by all these operations and also sold it to other divisions in other cities. Altogether, General Electric was the largest employer in Fort Wayne with a total pay-roll, at that time, of close to 12,000 people.

Fort Wayne had a population of about 150,000 and was also home to a large truck plant of International Harvester, the producer of radios and television sets, Magnavox, as well as a plant of U.S. Rubber which manufactured rubber and plastic tubing. Another smaller company, Zollner, made piston rings for all the automobile manufacturers and sponsored a professional basketball team called the Zollner Pistons, which several years later became the Detroit Pistons.

The town was prosperous. As a result, there was a housing shortage and it was difficult to find rental housing that was affordable and where children would be accepted. In the meantime I drove back to Detroit every Friday evening, returning to Fort Wayne very early Monday morning. It was a tedious three hour drive. In those days there were no super-highways, only two-lane roads until close to Detroit. During my early Monday morning drive back to Fort Wayne, I listened to an all night female disk jockey, who talked soothingly to the truck drivers and insomniacs and played the latest hits. This was another innovation for me. European radio stations all close down about midnight and don't start up again until about 6 a.m.

In a few weeks I found a house that was affordable. The rent was $100 a month, but it was unfurnished; although the downstairs had new wall-to-wall carpets. It was an old house with old-fashioned heating, an enormous coal burning stove. Only the downstairs had heating ducts, openings in the floors covered by metal gratings allowed hot air to move up into the bedrooms. Mark and Peter had great fun dropping various objects through these openings!

At the end of the month we moved in and once more we started out with a double mattress and two singles for the kids, and a kitchen table with four chairs. I also invested in a washer and dryer, and then, little by little, we bought additional pieces at various used furniture outlets. One day we went to an auction sale in a small village north of Fort Wayne, expecting to pick up some bargains. We discovered that the seller was a widow. To help her, the neighbors bid up the prices of everything to a level higher than it would be possible to buy in a city store. It was an interesting experience even though we found no bargains.

An enormous old pear tree stood in the back yard. It bore a lot of fruit but it was impossible to reach the higher branches, so from them the ripe fruit fell to the ground and attracted swarms of wasps. All of our friends came over to collect fruit from the lower branches, and there was still enough for Lili to put up several dozen jars.

One day Lili put too much soap powder in the washing machine, or may be it was the wrong kind. Anyway, she came downstairs from making the beds to find the whole downstairs awash in soap suds, just like in a Doris Day movie! The carpet was soaking wet so we untacked it on two sides and put wooden boxes underneath with fans blowing to dry it off. This turned out to be a mistake because the carpet shrank. It took us weeks of shuffling back and forth from the center of the carpet out to its edges, stretching the heavy wool to get it to reach back to the walls.

When winter came we discovered that the house was not very suitable; it was cold and expensive to maintain a reasonable temperature. The work involved in keeping the furnace going and cleaning out the ashes was a nuisance, and the upstairs was always cold. The old windows were badly sealed and drafts of cold air blew through them. We started to look for another place. Finally we found a downstairs apartment in a modern house at 2211 Lynn Avenue in the pleasant north-east part of the city. It had two decent-sized bedrooms, a living room and a cheerful modern kitchen with enough room for our table and four chairs. There was a large separate basement for our use and half of the garage.

The owners, who lived upstairs, were dubious about renting to a family with children. But after I brought Lili and the children to visit them, they rather reluctantly agreed. I am sure the fact that I was an engineer at General Electric played a part in their decision. So, early in the spring we moved again. The rent was $85 a month, and the gas heating turned out to be much cheaper than the coal, so we were able to save enough money to buy some new furniture. Our relationship with our landlords, the Schirers, became friendly and there were never any problems. He was a foreman on the night shift at International Harvester and during the day he either did work on the house or worked on one of the older houses that he used to buy and then remodel for resale.

We quickly settled down in Fort Wayne and become friendly with a number of families, mostly other G.E. people, who like us had recently moved to Fort Wayne. These included Bud and Evelyn Karkoski, Dot and Lee Rademaker, Jack and Caroline Haymaker. One day I was doing something under the car and Peter brought over Henry Lojek, who with his wife Millie lived on a neighboring street. At that time Peter still spoke Polish, and wandering around the neighborhood he heard Hank, who was American born, saying something in Hamtramck style Polish to his wife and corrected him. This started a close friendship which lasted for many years. Peter also developed a friendship with Betsy Stuckey, a cute blonde girl who lived across the street. As a result, we became friendly with Dorothy Stuckey and her husband who owned an appliance store.

We joined the Newcomers' Club, which held social functions several times a year such as dances and card parties. Square Dancing was very popular then and we became quite adept and thought it was great fun. We also joined the social club of the General Electric engineers, the "Squares", which held social gatherings every few weeks and had a club room on the second floor of a downtown commercial building. I became active in the Fort Wayne Section of the AIEE[*] which also held meetings about once a month. Thus we

---

[*] American Institute of Electrical Engineers, which several years later merged with the Institute of Radio Engineers to become the IEEE. I had become a member of AIEE while still in England.

developed a lively and interesting social life. Every weekend we partied or played cards or went to dances at one or other of the social clubs. Baby sitters were not a problem, there were several teen-age girls in the neighborhood who were glad to earn some pocket-money. The going rate then was a dollar for four hours. They were able to do their homework because Mark and Peter were already in bed by the time they came. We were even able to go to a movie about twice a month, not to the first run theaters in downtown Fort Wayne, but to a small theater on the north side at which the tickets were 25 cents. TV had arrived in Fort Wayne (black and white, of course, and only one station) but we did not feel the need to be extravagant and buy a set.

Our arrival in Fort Wayne received some publicity. Illustrated articles and interviews with us appeared in the local press, the Fort Wayne *Journal-Gazette* and the G.E. weekly newspaper. Mark and I were featured in a full page ad sponsored by one of the banks on the occasion of a fund drive for the local Y.M.C.A.. The picture showed us doing exercises together in the gym, which we attended regularly for a couple of years.

In the spring of 1952 my father received an immigration visa. Shortly thereafter he arrived in New York to work with Radio Free Europe* and with the Polish National Committee in Washington. In September 1954 a new organization called the Assembly of Captive European Nations (ACEN) was organized with the financial support of Radio Free Europe. My father was a member of the Polish delegation to ACEN and served as Chairman of its Committee for Social and Economic Affairs for 16 years. It was the umbrella organization in the United States for the various emigré groups from all the countries of Eastern Europe. They prepared publications, testified before Congress upon matters relevant to the affairs of Eastern Europe, issued memoranda to the media detailing daily life in the communist occu-

---

* This organization was ostensibly supported by donations, but received most of its funds from government sources. It operated powerful radio transmitters in Western Germany and Greece broadcasting to Eastern Europe. Most of the staff was made up of emigres from Poland and other countries governed by Soviet sponsored Communist regimes. The headquarters were located in New York, but the studios were in Munich. For several years my cousin Janek read the news in Polish at the Munich studios.

pied countries, providing a counterweight to the lies spread by the governments of those countries and their sympathizers. At the same time various committees worked on plans for the day, sometime in the future, when their homelands would be free again. As bleak as prospects were during the harshest years of the Cold War, none of them lost hope that the day would come that the Communist system would be defeated. Alas, few of them lived to see the wonderful realization of their dreams in 1989 and 1990.

My father played an important part in the activities of the various Polish political organizations in exile. Until 1958 he was a member of the Polish Labor Party (*Stronnictwo Pracy*) headed at various times by Stanislaw Mikolajczyk and Karol Popiel. He was vice-president of the Christian Democratic Union and a member of the executive committee of the Polish National Committee in the United States. In 1958 there was a split in the exiled Polish organizations over policy matters. My father left the Labor Party and the Polish National Committee and joined the National Unity Camp (*Oboz Zjednoczenia Narodowego*) and the Council of Polish Unity (*Polska Rada Jednosci*) in the United States. From 1964 until 1970 he was Chairman of the Council of Polish Unity. He traveled to Europe once a year maintaining contact with Polish emigré political groups in London, Paris and Rome. He had to obtain a special travel document from the State Department for each trip until he became a United States citizen in May 1957. He discussed these matters with me every time we were together; I think he was disappointed that I did not take more interest in Polish political affairs. I was much too busy with my work and looking after the home and family to be able to afford the time, and I certainly couldn't spare the money that I would have to spend to attend meetings and conferences.

Dad visited us in Fort Wayne at least twice a year. Whenever I had a chance to go to New York, I stayed with him. At first he had a one room apartment on West 72nd Street. Later he moved to an apartment in the historic Chelsea Hotel on 23rd Street. This hotel had a long history and many famous artists had lived there. It continued to be an artist's hotel; the lobby was decorated with some unusual products of the residents, one of them a collage made up of broken hair combs. Personally, I failed to appreciate this particular work of art. Any time

I went to New York I stayed there also. Dad and I enjoyed good dinners in small French restaurants in the East 50's and 60's. I also met many of his associates in the ACEN, particularly Feliks Gadomski, who was Secretary of the organization.

In the summer of 1952 we went for our first vacation in America. We rented a small cottage at Cross Village, north of Traverse City in Michigan. It was very primitive but was affordable and was a welcome relaxation. The water of Lake Michigan was chilly, but in those days we were young and still enjoyed swimming in cool water. We had good company; Witold and Irene Skuba were there with their daughters Danka and Magda, as well as Margie Okon. Unfortunately, Peter did not have a very good time. We had expected that the pollen free cool air of the Michigan pine forests would do him good, but there was something that he was allergic to and he had an asthma attack and had to spend a night in the Traverse City hospital. An old chief came in full regalia from a close-by Indian reservation to cheer Peter up.

After our return to Fort Wayne, Mark started school at the kindergarten of St. Jude's parochial school. Our choice was influenced by the close proximity of St. Jude's church, which was only two blocks away. We had also heard that the Fort Wayne public schools were not of very high quality. The following year Peter went to the same school. Once having started at parochial schools, they continued even though after our move to Van Orman Drive the public school would have been closer. Unfortunately, once Peter started going to school he stopped using his Polish and soon forgot it even though Lili and I continued to talk Polish at home.

Our life had settled down and my career with General Electric was progressing well. Our financial situation had improved; I received two salary increases within fifteen months. Lili and I talked about having another baby, " Wouldn't it be nice to have a girl?" Very soon, just before Christmas, Lili announced she was pregnant. We were both pleased but were also concerned that we might have to move. Our landlords had been reluctant to accept two children; what would they say to three? However, they liked us and accepted the announcement that another baby was on its way with good grace. Nevertheless, we started thinking about moving into a house. This was not so simple; there was still a housing shortage in Fort Wayne. The affordable houses that we looked at were quite unsuitable for our aspirations. Any that we liked were out of our reach. We came to the conclusion that we would have to build. We started studying books of plans and saving as much money as we could.

The summer came. It was a hot one and the cicadas were in their millions; it was the eleventh , or is it the seventeenth year, of their cycle. They buzzed day and night. Lili was big and uncomfortable. We had no air conditioning, only a couple of big fans to keep the air moving through the apartment. We did not go for a vacation, just went for some day trips to Pokagan State Park, 30 miles to the north.

One weekend I took the two boys to Canada along the north shore of Lake Erie. We ran into swarms of small flies, so dense we had to stop every few minutes to clean off the windshield. I took them to a steak house for a treat. To my surprise, they didn't want any fancy stuff, just big juicy hamburgers with lots of french fries. I surprised them the following day. We stopped at a beach which was quite deserted and far away from any habitation.

I said, "What a great beach. Let's go for a swim."

"Daddy, we don't have our swim suits!" they protested.

"That's O.K. There isn't anybody around. Just strip and jump in."

I proceeded to do just that. The boys looked at me with big, astonished eyes, and just stood motionless watching me as I dashed into the water and started swimming.

"Come on," I called them. "The water's warm; it's great. You will love it. Don't be silly; nobody's looking."

They refused to budge. They had already become ingrained with American prudishness in their Catholic schools. There was no way they would take their clothes off in the open air!

On August 2 Lili woke me up early in the morning. We took a quick run downtown to the old Lutheran Hospital (the new one which would be located only a block away was still under construction). I had to return home quickly to look after the boys and only a couple of hours later the doctor called to say that a girl had been born, just as planned! In those days it was still normal for the mother and baby to remain in the hospital for at least three days. Then Annette was brought home to sleep in a crib in our bedroom. It was a little crowded, but it made feeding her in the night very easy. She was a good baby and, to our relief, cried hardly at all.

In the second half of September, with Millie Lojek's sister having agreed to look after the children, Lili and I went off for our first holiday alone together. This was our long delayed honeymoon, nine years late! We drove in our old Nash through Ohio, Kentucky and Tennessee to the Smoky Mountains, which at this time of year were a blaze of color. The weather was gorgeous and we were very happy together. We picnicked by sparkling mountain streams and took many pictures of each other. We drove across Newfound Gap to Asheville, then along the Blue Ridge Parkway to Kentucky. On the way home across Ohio, the poor old Nash started to give up the ghost, but driving slowly we to just managed to reach home.

I examined the various options and decided that it was best to buy a new car, particularly since the Dodge dealer offered a magnificent trade-in price for the old Nash. So we became the proud owners of a brand new cream and black Dodge sedan, the only young G.E. engineer to own a sparkling new car! It was interesting to note that engineers, who had their own assigned parking lot, all drove old beat-up cars. On the other hand, at least half of the cars in the factory workers' parking lot were brand new ones, not the cheapest at that, Mercuries and Oldsmobiles predominated.

11

A NEW HOUSE

I was working hard at G.E. and was also taking courses which, although held on company time, required a lot of homework. Therefore, I was always busy and had not done anything further with our intention to build a house, except we had chosen a design from one of the books we had been studying. I ordered the plans and then spent many hours with Lili redrawing them and making changes. It was a split level house with four bedrooms and a dramatic drawing room with a cathedral ceiling and an enormous window, the kind of house that really needed a sloping lot, something that was not easily attainable in the flat country surrounding Fort Wayne.

Then the bombshell dropped. In spite of all precautions, Lili suddenly became pregnant again. This had not been planned and was not particularly welcome at the moment. In those days there were no easy alternatives. We were not averse to a larger family, just the timing was wrong. We started searching for a suitable lot to fit our dream house. We found one that was suitable on the south-west side of Fort Wayne, about two miles outside the city in a sub-division called Langford Oaks. It was an old estate that belonged to two surviving spinsters, one of whom lived in the old farmhouse. A small rivulet ran down through the middle of the development. On the south side five houses had been built along Sun Valley Drive. On the north side there was just a gravel road bordered by a row of magnificent elm trees. The lot I liked had a number of large hickory trees on it and sloped down towards the creek in a southerly direction. I reasoned that, with a little grading, one could build up the upper end of the lot to fit our dream house. The enormous picture window would overlook a terrace shaded by the towering hickory trees. After a lot of dickering with the old ladies, on July 20, 1955, I bought the 3/4 acre lot for $1,900 cash. There were no services, no water, no sewers, no gas.

The lot was shoulder high in prairie grass and weeds. Mark, Peter and I burned off the grass and weeds and cleared the rubbish with rakes. We used our new property for weekend picnics and for outings of the Cub Scouts. Lili was one of several den mothers who once a month had to take care of a group of boys for a Saturday outing. One of these outings ended with a lot of excitement. We had built a fire for roasting hot dogs and marshmallows. After the meal was over, the boys went chasing each other through the long, dry grass. They discovered a nest of grass snakes and whooping Indian war cries, each of them brought a six foot long snake, wriggling on the end of a stick. The little savages proceeded to roast them live on the fire!

One day before Thanksgiving, Philip was born in the new Lutheran hospital just a block away from our apartment, which was now bursting at the seams. Fortunately, our landlords put up with all this activity without any outward signs of displeasure, but we had to move out to our new house as quickly as possible. I asked a number of contractors for bids on our plans. To my dismay, all the cost estimates exceeded what we could afford. Building a custom home turned out to be more expensive than I had imagined. Reluctantly, we abandoned our plans and started looking at other alternatives. Finally, we agreed with an Amish contractor Winfield Moses, who built ranch style homes of a basic standard design on concrete slabs.

His models could be customized within certain limits. He gave me a set of basic plans and I went back to work at the drawing board. We ended up with a four bedroom home with a living room, kitchen with breakfast nook, utility room and a two car garage. The total living area, excluding garage and storage room, was 1,350 sq.ft. All the rooms had beamed cathedral ceilings, which gave a feeling of spaciousness, and the overall result was quite pleasing. The living room had a brick fireplace and a large thermopane picture window opening on to a terrace. Winfield agreed that I could do all the interior finishing and exterior painting for which he gave me an allowance of about 10% of the total cost of the house. This and the lot constituted our down payment. After much dickering, I obtained an FHA guaranteed 20 year mortgage at 5% fixed interest. Together with the extras, which included the fireplace and a fold-back flexible wall separating the two smaller bedrooms, the total cost of the house was $19,788. After adding in the built-in appliances, landscaping, and some last minute builder's extras, the final total cost of the house, including lot, was close to $24,000.

On March 26 the equipment arrived and excavation for the foundations started. By mid-June the interior dry walls were already in place and we could start work. Every evening Lili picked me up at work with sandwiches and a thermos jug of coffee and we worked until it got dark, which was not until nearly 10 o'clock on these midsummer evenings. Lili's sister, Hala who had come form Venezuela, looked after the children and did the housework. On weekends we all came out and worked together, Peter and Mark also got little paint brushes to do their part!.

Lili and I spackled and sanded, painted and varnished, sitting on scaffolding or standing on ladders. The most tiring and dirty work was sanding the overhead beams throughout the house. My arms were perpetually sore from holding the sander above my head; the dust penetrated my hair and filled up my nose, in spite of masks and caps. We painted all the beams except in the living room. There several coats of varnish provided a luxurious appearance. We painted the outside all in one hot July weekend, with the help of our friends, the Lojeks. The asbestos sheet siding used twice as much paint as we expected. The porous surface sucked up the Swedish Red paint as fast as we could put it on. The well driller hit good water at a depth of 80 feet, well within the allowance included in the price of the house, much to our relief.

By contract we were to move in on July 19. However, the builder never expected us to finish our part of the work on time and had procrastinated with his own work. But, by God, we did our part and on July 19 we moved in with the help of numerous friends even though the electricians had not completed the hookup to the power line and the carpenters had not finished the cabinet work in the kitchen. We had promised our landlords to move out by that date, so that Mr. Schirer could use his vacation to redecorate the apartment for the next tenants. And so Lili and I celebrated our 33rd and 34th birthdays by the light of candles in our own new house!

The old craftsman who built our fireplace was one of the last of his kind. He loved the fireplaces he built and was very proud of them. When we were referred to him by our builder, he came and inspected the site. The concrete slab had already been poured, but there was still no roof or walls. Then he took us to look at some fireplaces he had built recently. We were quite embarrassed to be dragged into strangers' homes, but they didn't appear to mind. Obviously, they were accustomed to being used as showplaces. Eventually we decided exactly what we wanted and went with him to a brickyard to select the bricks. While he worked, he chewed on an old stinking cigar, which I never saw actually lit. In a few days the fireplace was completed and a fire was lit in it to check it out. Then the builder completed the roof and the walls. Needless to say, after we had moved in, the old man kept coming with new prospective customers to show them *our* fireplace. It always worked perfectly.

Another innovation in the house was an electrostatic air filter. High voltage power supplies for commercial air filters were one of General Electric's newer products and I was able to buy one for a minimal cost. The engineering model shop built for me a sheet metal enclosure to fit on top of the furnace in the space provided in my plans for future air conditioning. The idea was that the metalized fiberglass filters, energized at very high voltage, attracted dust particles and pollen. I hoped this would be helpful for Peter's asthma. The filter worked perfectly. Every once in a while you would hear the crackle of sparking over some dust particles, but it was difficult to say whether it was of any real benefit for Peter. The fuel for the furnace came from a large round propane gas tank behind the house. Piped gas didn't reach us until two years later. The hot air passed through ducts in the concrete slab to perimeter outlets keeping the floors pleasantly warm in winter.

Our house stood about 100 feet back from the gravel road. The living room and patio faced south toward a small creek which ran along the dividing line between the lots. The creek flooded occasionally but the house stood high enough to be out of any danger. A grove of tall hickory trees stood to the southeast of the house. They provided welcome shade and the nuts attracted squirrels from the entire neighborhood. At the beginning we collected the nuts too, but we soon gave up; the effort of cracking the tiny nuts was greater than the benefit. The road, Van Orman Drive, came to a dead end just beyond our house and on warm evenings was a popular parking place for young lovers. It was lined with elm trees, many of which fell victim a year later to the onslaught of the Dutch elm disease, much to my sorrow. The entire lot, except for the hickory grove, was graded and grass seed was sown. Cutting over half an acre of grass turned out to be a day's work. The following year we bought a riding mower, and then it was no problem getting Mark to take care of this chore. We planted flowering shrubs around the house and some flowers by the patio, but did no further landscaping.

One of the problems of living out in the country in those days was the lack of telephones. We had a ten party line serving everyone in the subdivision. Unfortunately one of our neighbors, Mary Duncombe, spent hours talking on the phone, and it was never possible for me to call home. When Lili wanted to call out, she had to plead with Mary.

"Mary, could you please get off the line? I have to make a call." She did, Lili made her call, then a few minutes later Mary had the line tied up again! She had six children of her own and Lili couldn't understand how she managed to find the time to gossip so much.

Although we lived two miles outside the city limits, close to state highway 24, it was very convenient for those of us who worked at the Broadway or Taylor Street plants. It took me only 10 minutes to drive from home to the plant parking lot. When Lili needed the car, she took me to work and then picked me up in the evening. Later, when the Rademakers also moved to Langford Oaks, Lee and I shared rides. At Times Corners, where we turned off Highway 24 to go into the subdivision, there was a service station and small grocery store which served well for any urgent shopping. We did all our other shopping downtown which was only 10 minute drive. Wolf and Dessauer was the big department store of Fort Wayne, a three story building occupying a quarter block on Calhoun Street. There we had an account since we first moved from Detroit. "Plastic" money didn't exist yet. You had an account at the stores where you did most of your shopping and received monthly bills from each one. This is how small grocery stores fought the chain supermarkets; they gave accounts to their regular, credit-worthy customers. The supermarkets had lower prices but were run strictly on a cash basis. There were no discount stores in those days. For small items the cheapest stores were Woolworths and Kresge, called dime stores. Back in the early 1950's nothing at a dime store cost more than a dollar.

Fort Wayne was a quiet, conservative and prosperous community in the 50's. Quiet, pollution-free electric trolley buses provided fast transportation from all the older residential neighborhoods to downtown and the major industries. Unfortunately, the increased prosperity and cheap gasoline induced more and more people to drive their cars downtown and parking was becoming a problem and traffic jams became prevalent. The downtown streets were all one-way, but the traffic lights were set so that it was necessary to stop at each intersection. Fort Wayne was one of the few cities in America to provide competing electric utility services. One was Fort Wayne Light & Power, operated by the municipality, and in those days it still ran its own power station. The other was Indiana & Michigan Electric Company. We lived outside the city and paid substantially more for electricity than city-dwellers did; we had no choice.

The residential streets were lined with old trees until the elm disease killed many of them. Opportunities for relaxation in the open air were provided by numerous parks with well maintained flower beds, picnic and sport facilities. A new covered stadium provided a venue for the popular local basketball team, the Zollner Pistons, and for a newly organized ice-hockey team. The city was served by the Pennsylvania Railroad main line from Chicago to Pittsburgh and New York with frequent trains. A new airport provided convenient plane service in all directions, including a daily non-stop to the New York area's Newark Airport. The city was expanding outward to new housing developments, and at the end of the decade the first big suburban shopping center opened up. The first ominous signs of future problems appeared in the second half of the 50's when some of the industries that sustained the prosperity started moving out.

There were no discount stores yet, but if one tried, it was possible to buy big-ticket items with a discount. A couple of mail-order companies had sprung up. One could get this catalog from the Credit Union. Later on, they would mail catalogs to registered regular customers. The discount prices were not actually printed but were coded. We bought our silverware and some other Christmas presents from one of these outlets. When it came time to buy new furniture for our new house, we discovered that a small furniture store in a tiny village about 15 miles from Fort Wayne would let you select furniture from their manufacturer's catalogs, and allow you to buy at only a few percentage points above the wholesale price. Then the furniture was delivered directly to home from the manufacturer. Strictly speaking this was illegal because archaic laws regulating retail prices were still in existence, supposedly to make it fair for everybody. These laws protected the small stores from the competition of large chains which bought in huge quantities and could therefore obtain large quantity discounts from the manufacturers.

Mark and Peter were enrolled in the closest parochial school, St. Joseph's, and were picked up by a bus on the corner of Sunset Drive. The school was not as good as St.Jude's, but they got good grades. Naturally, we had to go to church regularly every Sunday with all the children. The school also had very active Boy Scout and Cub Scout troops, and both boys participated in the activities which took place mostly during the weekends. Lee Rademaker and I both got pressed into scout activities. Lee had an active interest in scouting and had personally been a scout since a boy. For me it was more of a duty that I owed to the school and the community. For at least one year I was Assistant Cub Master, which involved me in a lot of the activities - camps, hikes and contests like building model race cars.

There were many activities for young families which cost nothing. We discovered an unused gravel pit a few miles south on Highway 24. On hot weekends we went there for the whole day to picnic and swim. It was known only to a few people so it was not crowded, the water was clean and there was a small shallow part with a sandy bottom for the children. These were still the days before the proliferation of law suits and the intrusion of local government into every aspect of people's lives. A few years later this site was surrounded by barbed wire with big NO TRESPASSING signs. We didn't like to go to Pokagon State Park; the traffic on the two lane highway was terrible during weekends. When our new neighbors, the Shrickers, built a house just up the street from us with a pool, we used it almost daily.

One major problem during the summer were the mosquitoes. Our Langford Oaks Association contracted to have the area fogged about once a month. For a few days after each fogging the situation was much better, but most of the time any outdoor activity after sunset was almost impossible. One July Fourth the Karkoskis came to us for the afternoon. Bud and I took the boys and walked over to the Fort Wayne Country Club, half a mile away, to watch their fireworks. Almost immediately, we were covered by the stinging horrors. Bud suffered most; he had neglected to take a cap and his bald head was covered with red welts. Needless to say, we retreated to our house for some stiff drinks not waiting for the end of the show.

In the winter we set up our own skating rink in the flat area near the creek. All the children learned to skate and even played hockey with the neighborhood kids. We also skated on the pond in the Maumee Park just where Highway 24 entered the city limits of Fort Wayne. The children loved it when it snowed and they used the slope of Langford Lane down to the creek for tobogganing. The entire neighborhood engaged in snow ball fights.

There was one activity which gave me a lot of personal satisfaction. The American Institute of Electrical Engineers had a very active chapter in Fort Wayne which held meetings at least once a month with speakers invited from various companies around the country. At first I attended these meetings (which were held in the "Squares" clubroom) just to listen to speakers and to meet engineers from other Fort Wayne companies. All organizations of this kind depend heavily on volunteer workers for their success. Very early I got involved in the management of the chapter, or Section as it was called in AIEE terminology, and after working on various committees, I was elected secretary in 1956, vice-chairman in 1957 and Chairman of the Fort Wayne Section in 1958. This work required a considerable expenditure of personal time and energy, which Lili resented. But I enjoyed the work and the contacts it gave me with many people I would not otherwise have met. Naturally I was also pleased with the personal recognition that it gave me. Some of the contacts that I made turned out to be very useful later in my career.

It also gave me some experience in salesmanship and organization management. The Section was financed in part by a share in the membership dues that was returned to us from AIEE headquarters. This covered some of the basic expenses such as printing programs, mailing meeting notices and meeting room rent. The participants, of course, paid for their own refreshments and meals at dinner meetings. However, we always needed additional funds to cover promotion and some of our more ambitious projects. It was necessary to raise this money by appeals to local industry and also to run membership drives to increase local membership. It was not always easy to convince engineers that they should spend their own money on membership dues; it was necessary to devote a lot of time to cajoling and arm twisting in addition to selling them on the benefits of membership.

Fortunately, professional organizations, such as AIEE, were spared the cost of speakers for the local meetings. Traditionally the employers not only gave invited speakers time off from work but also paid their travel expenses. Similarly, General Electric paid my travel expenses to attend AIEE meetings in other cities, such as New York. Of course, in each case it was necessary to justify to one's superiors why attendance at any particular meeting was necessary. In times of economic downturns managers became much more critical and would cut back on the amount of such travel. However, once I became a supervisor and also a member of the local Section's executive committee, I was almost always assured of approval. On a couple of occasions I was an invited speaker, and I also presented a paper at the annual Winter Meeting of AIEE in New York on the subject of the use of aluminum in transformer design which was published in the Institute Transactions. Subsequently, I wrote a couple of less technical versions for various trade publications for which I got paid. I even received an award from one of the magazines because my article received a record number of requests for reprints.

In 1956 I was selected to be Co-chairman of the Engineer's Week Committee. Engineer's Week, which is sponsored nationwide by the major engineering organizations, coincides with the birthday of

George Washington. For the first time I appeared on television. I was invited to take part in an interview arranged by the local station to discuss the role played by engineering in modern society.

I remember this dinner, which was held in the Van Orman Hotel, very well. We had invited an admiral, I don't remember his name, who was in charge of the Navy Vanguard program, to be the guest speaker. This program, competing with the Army's space program in Huntsville, was to launch a communications satellite into orbit around the earth. We were all enthralled by his discussion of the problems involved in bringing this project to fruition. The Vanguard was only the size of a basketball and would weigh only about four pounds. But in those days it seemed to us that the task was so difficult that we doubted that it would be achieved very quickly.

Only a year later the Russians launched Sputnik, which was considerably larger than Vanguard, which still hadn't gotten off the ground. This provoked a tremendous public outcry and a very significant increase in funds for America's space efforts and a few months later the Army launched Explorer, followed shortly by the Navy's Vanguard, just two years after this dinner speech. If anyone attending this dinner had dared to predict that only 13 years later an American astronaut would be walking on the moon, he would have been laughed at!

In May 1956 a very important event took place. We became United States citizens. A couple of months earlier we were advised that our application had been accepted, subject only to our passing the test. Lili and I studied the Constitution and basics of American history. Lili was very apprehensive; I was not concerned. We passed the test and on the appointed day we drove to South Bend with our witnesses, the Rademakers, to attend the official ceremony at the U.S. District Court. A couple of dozen other new citizens were there. We all stood up and recited the Pledge of Allegiance. I felt a great relief, after ten years of being refugees, classified as "stateless", I felt that I had reached a home, one that I was proud of. The judge congratulated us and presented our certificates of citizenship and a small American flag on a desk-top stand.

Lili's twin sister, Hala, after separating from her philandering husband in Venezuela, had come to see us on a visitor's visa, but then she decided to study with the idea of coming to the States permanently. So her visa was changed to a student visa. I was obliged to post a bond to ensure that she would leave the country after completing her studies. She went to Chicago to attend a secretarial school,which took almost a year. After completing it in 1956, she had to return to Venezuela, in order to apply for an immigration visa. Now that we had become citizens, we could sponsor her, and because she was a close relative, she received her visa quite quickly. Hala spent a couple of weeks with us in Fort Wayne, then she went to Chicago to look for a job. Her principal asset was her fluent Spanish. In a short time she got a job in the export department of the bowling alley division of Brunswick Corporation, then located in downtown Chicago.

Our financial situation had improved and we were able to enjoy life more. We went to all the dinners and dances that were organized by the social clubs that we belonged to and entertained more ourselves. When Philip was one year old, we took all the children to Niagara Falls. Dressed in waterproof coats and hats, we went along the path right under the falls. The children were fascinated. The roar of the cascading water drowned out our voices as we called out to each other in excitement. Through the spray we could see the tour boat fighting the maelstrom down below. From Niagara, we passed through Toronto to the Thousand Islands and through the Adirondacks to Fort Ticonderoga. The children posed on the ancients cannons and enjoyed the displays showing American and British soldiers in their old uniforms. The final highlight of this excursion was the drive to the top of Whiteface Mountain and climbing the rocks, looking down into the precipice. Lili had fits while I posed the kids on various rocks, some of the photos were spectacular. The return home past the Finger Lakes and along the partially completed Ohio Turnpike went quickly; the kids were getting tired. All through the trip they had behaved beautifully and we were all very pleased. Back at school in September the boys had many stories to tell their classmates.

In the spring of 1958, we took them to Brookfield Zoo and then visited Lili's cousin who looked after the children while Lili and I enjoyed Chicago's night life. We had a good time and went dancing to a night club which had sexy entertainment. This must have made us both very horny! Anyway, four weeks later Lili discovered that she was pregnant again. Now we were in a much better position to handle a new responsibility. Eileen was born the day before New Year's Eve. The following day there was an ice storm. It was so bad that the children were able to skate along the roads and it was impossible for me to drive across town to the Lutheran Hospital to visit and see my new daughter. In fact, it was even difficult to get to our neighbor's house for the party, slipping and slithering all the way over the ice. Even more difficult to get home after the party full of drinks!

We now had to deal with diapers again. Fortunately, Eileen, like Philip and Annette before her, was an ideal baby and soon was sleeping virtually through the night. When only a few weeks old, she was baptized in St. Joseph Church, the Rademakers were her godparents.

At the same time steps were in motion which would lead to us leaving the house that we had planned and built with such labor of love.

12

GENERAL ELECTRIC

The business of the Specialty Transformer Department was manufacturing a wide range of transformers. These important devices are used to change voltage from one level to another. In Fort Wayne, an astonishing variety of transformers was manufactured for use in many applications such as fluorescent lighting and neon signs, heating furnaces, all kinds of machine tools, electronic power supplies and various military applications All these were of the so-called "dry type". They were cooled by the circulation of air and only solid materials were used in their construction. By contrast all the transformers installed out of doors and connected to high voltage transmission lines are "oil-filled"; that is they are enclosed in metal tanks in which mineral oil provides cooling and insulation. We all see these transformers attached to poles that reduce the high voltage in the transmission line to the 120 volts that we use in our homes.

At General Electric my career progressed smoothly. I was assigned to the design section for the general purpose transformers normally used in the distribution of power inside buildings. At the time the section leader was Paul Vance. I worked together with Charley Derbyshire, Bob Berghoff, Stan Antalis and Harry Meeker. Harry was the oldest engineer and was approaching retirement age. He was somewhat of a maverick and consequently had never advanced beyond being a design engineer in spite of his many years with the company. He was the only person who designed the larger transformers, the so-called Type D designs, which at that time covered the range from 25 to 150 kVA[*]. He was very secretive about his design methods, kept all his knowledge in a series of personal black notebooks and refused to write any design procedures. My assignment was to be Meeker's understudy, to learn his design methods and to commit some of the rules to paper in the form of a standard design procedure. He was reticent, but gradually I pried information out of him, wrote it down and started organizing it. Much of his knowledge was empirical, learned by experience over a period of some thirty years of design work.

At the same time I was making new designs and learning as I went along. As my designs reached the manufacturing floor, I would follow them through the building process. Some of the older workers were real craftsmen. They frequently pointed out to me how the work would be easier if I made some small changes in the design. One of the older coil winders was very friendly towards me and appreciated my interest in production problems.

Often he would call me up and say, "Biega, when you have a moment come down to my machine, I want to show you something." Down I went to the coil winding shop and he would explain how a small change in the design would make it easier to wind and assemble the coils.

There were other transformer manufacturing plants in the General Electric empire. The largest and most important of these was in Pittsfield, Massachusetts. Here, at that time, all the larger transformers up to the largest ever made in the world, were designed and manufactured. Most of these were of the oil-filled type. However, in Pittsfield some dry-type transformers were also manufactured, primarily for installation inside buildings where the fire hazard that would result if oil leaked from the transformer tanks was objectionable. These transformers were considerably larger than anything built in Fort Wayne. I made several trips to Pittsfield to learn more about transformer design. Here there was a development department that had

---

[*] kVA - kilo Volt Amperes - a measure of amount of electrical energy. It is equal to the product of volts times amperes divided by 1000. A modern house requires about 10 kVA.

made serious studies to improve construction and learn more about fundamental principles. Much of this information had been documented and lengthy design procedures, so-called "Standard Practices," had been written. I brought all this information back to Fort Wayne and started writing a design manual for the types that we designed and built.

Traditionally, copper had always been used for the electrical windings in transformers and motors, as well as for the cables that carried electricity from the generating station to the users. This is because copper has the lowest electrical resistance of all commonly available metals (only silver is better, but obviously is too costly). However, as a result of the Korean War and the simultaneous political upheavals in some of the nations which produced large quantities of copper, such as the Belgian Congo and Chile, the price of copper had increased drastically. The next best conductor of electricity is aluminum. However, for the same amount of electric current a much larger cross section of wire had to be used, also it is much more difficult to connect aluminum wires — the traditional soldering and brazing techniques did not work. In Fort Wayne we were working hard to overcome these difficulties. I became involved in a major project to redesign all our units and to develop new standards.

To avoid increasing the size of all the units because of the larger wire cross-sections needed for aluminum wire, we started using new high temperature insulation materials such as asbestos paper saturated with silicone polymers to make designs that were smaller but hotter. Only recently Johns-Manville had been able to develop asbestos materials with the flexibility and strength similar to that of paper. At that time, no one had any idea that asbestos fibers were potentially hazardous and could cause lung cancer. This was not discovered until at least 15 years later. After all, this material had been widely used for insulation of hot water pipes and of buildings since before the war. I still think that in this processed form there was no danger. All the cases of cancer that came to light in later years, involved miners and those that worked in the processing plants themselves. At that time the only other material that could be used as insulation in high temperatures was cloth made from glass fibers. One of the problems with glass cloth materials was they lacked stiffness. Another problem was that workers handling it had to take special precautions to avoid dermatitis. Fragments of the glass fibers would cause severe itching and inflammation of the skin. All the workers much preferred to work with asbestos based materials than with fiber glass based materials.

My contribution to the program of developing a complete new series of transformers using aluminum magnet wire and operating at high temperatures was recognized in my third year at G.E. The size of the General Purpose Transformer Section had increased substantially due to the trend towards distribution of electric power inside factories, office buildings and even apartment buildings, at higher voltages and the increased demand for dry-type transformers, which could safely be installed indoors.

Paul Vance retired and I was promoted to Section Engineer responsible for all transformers from 20 to 500 kVA in size. Now, I had five engineers reporting to me. Myrle Marsh was Manager of General Purpose Transformer Engineering which now consisted of three sections, Charley Derbyshire was in charge of design of the so called Type M, below 20 kVA, and Stan Antalis was responsible for control transformers, the small ones used in the machine tool industry.

General Electric had an extensive educational program for all its employees that had management potential. These included courses in a variety of technical subjects, courses in public speaking, training in a wide variety of supervisory and management skills, such as accounting, cost control and budget preparation, principles of personnel supervision and general management. General Electric had developed its own management philosophy which was instilled into employees with management potential. The key factors of this philosophy were the development of incentives for employees to take responsibility, to assign clearly defined objectives to all levels of management, to measure the achievement of objectives and to assign responsibility for results.

During my eight years at General Electric I graduated from a large number of these courses. Although I never went to business school, the training provided by General Electric gave me as good, if not better, background in industrial business, than most traditional MBA courses could have done. Later on in life, I met many executives in various corporations who had also received their training at General

Electric. After completing one of these courses with a high score, I was given the job of instructor for the following year, this was a course in Principles of Statistical Analysis.

Even the factory and clerical workers were encouraged to make suggestions that reduced costs or improved efficiency, for which they were rewarded. The awards equaled 10% of the annual savings that were achieved due to their suggestions. The most famous case was that of a woman employee who recommended that her job be abolished; the work she was doing could be done better a different way. She won an award of several hundred dollars and was promoted to a supervisory position. I don't know what happened to her colleagues that were doing the same job. I imagine that the union was not pleased. As Section Engineer I had to spend several hours a week analyzing suggestions pertaining to the products for which I was responsible. No suggestion, however foolish, could be rejected without a detailed analysis and letter of explanation. Good suggestions required design changes, changes in documentation and finally a calculation of the potential annual savings. This was all very time consuming.

One of the General Electric programs, that was given strong support by top management, was called "Value Analysis". The guru and brainchild of this program was a very personable engineer in his early forties named Larry Miles. He traveled all over the country preaching the benefits of this program to all plants and offices of the company and later also to various management organizations. The key premise of Value Analysis is that any component or sub-system or even a management action has a perceivable value. Anything that causes the actual cost to be higher than that value is wasteful. Typically in his presentation he would pick up some device, for example the latch of an instrument lid and hold it up for all to see.

"How much would you be willing to pay for this?" he asked.

The perceived value is, of course, dependent upon the total function to be performed, and the desired quality level. For example, a latch for a toy box would have a lower value than one for a jewelry box. Quality was defined as that necessary to ensure that the function be performed under the environmental conditions to be expected and for the desired life of the product.

A two-day "Value Analysis" Seminar was held at the Specialty Transformer Department, with required attendance of about half of all the staff, engineers, draftsmen, accounting, salesmen, production supervisors, managers. (Similar sessions were held at all the other Departments in Fort Wayne). After the initial lectures we were split into small groups for workshop sessions, to work out solutions to problems, real or imaginary. In the preliminary session many examples were projected on the screen: specially designed and machined screws, whose function could be performed by standard screws at a tenth of the cost; expensive castings whose supporting function could be performed by a pressed sheet metal bracket with half the weight at half the cost and many, many others.

Then Larry said: "Don't think that only design engineers do such silly things. Here's an example of accounting stupidity." A photograph of a check for 30 cents, signed by a G.E. vice-president, appeared on the screen.

"This check was written to correct an accounting mistake. The accountant could have made a 5 cent phone call to verify the facts. Or even if he didn't do that, a simple payment out of petty cash should have been made. This check, including the time of a vice-president to verify the facts, cost at least $20 to process!"

The name of the payee was blacked out, but I recognized it as a check that I had received a few weeks earlier. The story behind it was as follows:

In those days in order to go to Erie, Schenectady, Pittsfield or any of the other GE locations on the New York Central mainline, it was necessary to take a bus to Waterloo, a railroad crossing on US 27, 15 miles north of Fort Wayne. Here the Chicago-Boston "New England States" express train made a flag stop to pick up, or drop off, GE passengers. The bus company had just increased the fare by 15 cents each way, but, obviously, the accountant didn't know this. When I turned in my expense account, even though it had been approved by my boss, the accountant corrected it in red ink and reduced the refund to me. The amount was negligible, but I was furious that a clerk should doubt the word of an engineer and I made a big issue of it and wrote a letter of complaint. This letter found its way through channels all the way to top management. A few weeks later I received the check for 30 cents. Incidentally, I never cashed it but stuck it up on the wall by my desk as a souvenir.

As Section Engineer I worked more closely with the Sales Department. Customer requests for special designs had to be studied, proposals and cost estimates prepared. Consequently I started traveling to participate with sales people in visits to customers, particularly to solve technical problems and to discuss special applications that required novel design solutions. One of these was the design of special transformers needed for the New York Coliseum. In the 1950's this new convention center was being built at Columbus Circle where Broadway intersects Eighth Avenue at 59th Street. The requirements for electric power for the air-conditioning, the high intensity lighting and all the outlets for the exhibits, were enormous. The best way of handling the distribution of such large blocks of power is to bring it in at a high voltage and then step down by means of transformers to 120 volts at various locations close to the point of utilization. In the past this was done using oil-filled transformers installed in fireproof vaults. This time the architects wished to accomplish this using dry-type transformers such as we made in Fort Wayne. This avoided the need for special fire proof vaults and substantially reduced the insurance premiums. However, the largest size we made was 500 KVA. Nine such units would be required to cover the power requirements of the main exhibit area.

The architects asked whether it would be possible to make three units of 1,500 KVA each, which would also be light enough to be mounted in the roof truss. The low voltage winding had to carry 4,200 amperes, which required a very large cross-section of magnet wire and very large terminals. Harry Meeker had designed a number of transformers for use in industrial furnaces which provided very high output currents, thousands of amperes at very low voltages. I discussed this application with him and he came up with a revolutionary new design for the output windings. This concept used large aluminum bars, which were formed into circles on a large press and then welded together using the new aluminum welding technique that had recently been developed in Fort Wayne. Together with Meeker and one of the industrial engineers, we developed the whole design in sketch form and prepared a cost estimate. Our design would cost considerably less than the traditional transformer made in Pittsfield or by any of the competitors, but even more important, it would weigh about 25 per cent less. The architects were enthusiastic and an order was placed.

These transformers were three times larger than anything ever built before in the Fort Wayne plant and received a lot of publicity. But when the monsters were delivered to New York and mounted high up in the trusses of the Coliseum and connected to their switchgear, problems arose. All electromagnetic equipment, such as transformers and motors, develop some noise due to the vibration of the magnetic iron cores, predominantly a low frequency hum. This was a major problem in dry-type transformers and the designers were always fighting to keep the hum down to a level at which it would not be objectionable. Noise is measured in decibels. Any noise above 55 decibels becomes noticeable because that is the ambient sound level in an office. In a quiet room noise at higher frequencies becomes very annoying, even at the relatively low energy level of 40 decibels. People often complain about appliances, such as refrigerators because any loose screw or touching metal edges will develop higher frequencies which are extremely irritating even though the absolute noise level is in the acceptable range.

When the power was first switched to these transformers, each weighing about two tons, the telephone on my desk started ringing. The sales office was being swamped with calls. First, the electric contractors called, then the architects, finally, somebody from the building owners' office, all complaining, "The noise is terrible. We won't pay until the problem is corrected."

"Bill, you'd better go to New York and take care of the matter," said the sales manager.

Off I went to New York with a noise level measuring instrument and with copies of the test reports made at the factory. The Coliseum was still unfinished. There were no interior walls yet. From the floor I could see the transformers mounted almost 100 feet above street level, from them huge copper busbars ran to the switchgear cabinets. The entire building was an echo chamber. There was no question, even with all the contractors working in the building, hammering, sawing, shouting, I could distinctly hear the characteristic buzz, down at street level. That night, with representatives of the contractors and of the architects as well as the salesman from the G.E. New York office all looking over my shoulder, I made a series of measurements. The transformer noise was at least 10 Db greater than measured at the factory[*].

I quickly pointed out the main problems. The transformers were standing on vibration absorbing pads as required in the installation instructions. But the low cost units selected by the contractor were inadequate for the weight of the units. They were squashed flat and had lost all their resilience. The heavy copper bus bars were bolted directly to the transformer terminals. Consequently the vibration of the transformers was being transmitted to the steel building structure and the busbars became antennas and radiated the hum throughout the building.

"What has happened to the flexible connecting straps that we supplied?" I asked.

"We couldn't use them," replied the electrical contractor. "The air conditioning people got there before we did and ran their duct work right where we had planned to run our busbars."

It seems that whichever contractor gets to the site first, tries to do his work the cheapest way possible, no matter what the architects plans had stipulated. Then it's too late to change and the next guy has to do the best he can (probably charging the owner for any extra costs).

The following morning, at the G.E. office, I selected suitable isolation mounts from a catalog, made sketches for new flexible busbar connections and then returned to Fort Wayne. A few days later New York was on the phone again.

"We have done everything you told us to do. The sound level readings are much lower where you said they should be. But the customer is unhappy; you can still hear the transformers all through the building."

"Have the interior walls been built?"

"No, not yet."

---

[*] Every 3 decibels represents a doubling of the noise energy level.

"Well then, there is nothing to worry about. You are the salesman. Your job is to convince the customer that when the walls are finished and an exhibition is in progress, with all the noise of people walking around and talking, and music playing, nobody will be able to hear the transformers," I explained.

A few weeks later the Coliseum was finished. The day before the official opening of the annual Automobile Show I was back again. Once more we toured the building with the customer's representatives. The exhibitors were putting the finishing touches on their exhibits. The overall noise level varied from 60 to 65 dB. Even on the highest exhibition floor which was closest to the transformers, where various vendors of parts and accessories had their booths, the transformer hum was unnoticeable in the general hubbub. The customers were satisfied. The problem had been solved.

Two years later I was once more involved in solving a major problem with a customer. About this time epoxy molding compounds had become generally available to the electrical industry and promised to revolutionize the manufacture of products that either required sealing for protection against the elements or which needed excellent insulation for high voltages. Epoxy castings had already been successfully applied to small transformers used in military applications. We decided to try to use this technology to improve the windings of our dry-type transformers operating at high voltages. If successful, we would be able to make them smaller and more reliable.

However, it was not easy to make the large epoxy castings. Meeker spent several months making models and always the castings would develop cracks as they cooled down. Finally, we succeeded in solving the problems and produced some units which passed all the tests and were installed in some test installations. At the time these transformers were much more expensive than those produced using conventional techniques. But we were convinced that eventually we could get the costs down and realize the benefits of reduced size high voltage transformers, which would at the same time be more reliable because they would be less susceptible to the damaging effects of moisture, dust and transients such as lightning.

A manufacturer of high frequency heating machines, Girdler Corporation, heard about this development and was interested in the smaller size which would improve their machines, which also used high voltages. They ordered about a dozen special transformers for a contract which they had obtained from the Ford Motor Company. We designed, built and delivered the transformers to their factory in Louisville. The equipment passed all its tests and finally was delivered to Detroit to the assembly line.

A few weeks later one of the transformers failed and was returned to us and replaced under warranty. At this time nobody was concerned; it was assumed that, in spite of all precautions, a crack must have developed in the casting, an annoying random failure, such as can always happen, particularly in a new technology. The coil was sawn apart and analyzed, but the burn damage resulting from the failure made it difficult to determine the actual cause. A couple of weeks later two more failures occurred.

Now Ford was angry with Girdler, Girdler, in turn, with General Electric. The chief engineer of Girdler and his aides came to Fort Wayne. We also brought in Dr. Harold Lord from the Research Department of General Electric in Schenectady. The designs, both of our transformer as well as Girdler's equipment, were thoroughly analyzed. We came to the conclusion that, somehow, transient voltages far in excess of what we expected were occurring. But no one could figure out how or why they were induced. It was decided to run some exhaustive tests right on site at the Ford Motor Company plant to try to understand what was happening.

A few days later I drove to Detroit with a car full of instruments and with two technicians. In Detroit I was met by the chief engineer of Girdler with several of his people. We spent two days, from early morning until late in the evening running tests on the equipment right on the Ford assembly line, making hundreds of oscillograms looking for some peculiar conditions that were causing the problem. At the end of the first day, being the senior General Electric man on the spot, I took everyone out to dinner. The following day Girdler's chief engineer reciprocated.

Later when I submitted my expense report, I had difficulty getting it approved. The reason was I had not obtained prior approval to take the customer's people out to dinner! According to company policy, only sales people were authorized to spend money on customers, not engineers. For a long time I had been thinking about moving into a more people-oriented engineering career, such as sales or marketing. I enjoyed dealing with customers and field situations, solving people problems rather than strictly design problems. This incident was the straw that broke the camel's back and convinced me that I should make my move as quickly as possible.

I started looking for opportunities. I thought that international sales would be especially interesting, and that my personal experience and knowledge of languages gave me an advantage. I contacted International General Electric in New York, but got no where. General Electric had got me typed as being a design engineer advancing towards a career in engineering management. They were unwilling to give me an opportunity to change directions.

Shortly after the New Year of 1958, I got involved in another sales project which changed my life. Fansteel Corporation of North Chicago needed some transformers and control devices to control heat treating processes in the manufacture of special alloy steels. After some initial telephone discussions, their chief engineer came to Fort Wayne. I remember the incident well. It was bitterly cold but he arrived without an overcoat; he never wore one! When we went out for lunch everyone turned around to stare at this strange man walking along the street in a suit, no overcoat, no gloves, no hat. Anyway, we discussed the application, I made the designs both for the transformers as well as for the saturable reactors to control them. Meeker had just retired so now it was all my work. The first set was shipped to North Chicago early in the spring and I supervised the testing of the installation. All the results were excellent and the customer was very pleased, the new designs would materially improve their production. Immediately we received an order for two more sets.

Shortly afterwards I was contacted by Lee Butter, who was vice president of a small transformer manufacturing company in Chicago, Precision Transformers Inc. He had tried to get the Fansteel business, but the company did not possess the know-how to solve the control problems. He wanted to induce me to join his company to be in charge of dry-type transformer engineering. I was not interested. During a subsequent visit to North Chicago, I did stop and have dinner with him in a restaurant. I told him that I was not interested in a design engineering career, only in sales and marketing. During the next several months he contacted me several times and failed to change my mind.

Finally, just before Christmas 1958, he offered me the position of sales manager with responsibility for the industrial market. Now I indicated some interest, but we were still miles apart on the question of salary. However, I did agree to come to Chicago one weekend in January to talk to the president, a young businessman named Mel Adler, and to take a test at an industrial psychologist. I was not very impressed with the company nor the manufacturing facilities which were located in some old buildings on Lake Street, just east of Western Avenue. However, I took the tests, which, as I discovered later, gave me a very high overall score, but indicated that I was not very suitable for a salesman's job. I guess that the tests assumed that a successful salesman must be full of *chutzpah* and hype. This may be true for selling most commodities or insurance or real estate. My experience with salesmen that called on me at G.E. was that the hyper sales types left me cold and never sold me a thing. Those that knew their products well and could make a good presentation, factually discussing advantages of their products, and were also able to discuss possible problems and how to handle them, always received a good hearing, and frequently could make a sale. I assume that this psychologist wasn't able to differentiate between the different selling approaches to different markets. Anyway my subsequent career has, I think, proved him wrong.

A few days later Lee Butter called again, very enthusiastic; Adler had agreed to improve the offer. He offered me the job of industrial sales manager with a salary equal to what I was then earning at G.E. (approx. $12,000) plus an override on all sales to industrial customers with a guaranteed minimum which would amount to about 25% of base salary. In spite of my reservations about the company, this offer gave me the opportunity I had been looking for to get out of engineering into sales and marketing. After considerable discussion with Lili, I decided to accept. To my astonishment, on the Monday morning at the end of February when I gave a month's notice to G.E., I was told to take my personal things, hand over all company property and to leave the premises the same day. I was told that they took this attitude because I was going to work for a competitor. On this somewhat sour note, my career at General Electric came to an end.

13

DEERFIELD

In February of 1959 I departed to take up my new career in Chicago. I stayed a few days with Lee and Ina Butter, in their comfortable house in Glenview, then I found a room in a nice home on Chicago's west side. Naturally, I had to buy a second car. I found a red and cream Plymouth station wagon which was only about a year old and started the routine of leaving Fort Wayne very early Monday morning, driving directly to the plant on Lake Street. I stayed in Chicago all week and returned to Fort Wayne late Friday evening, sometimes Saturday afternoon.

As soon as I was satisfied that the job was going to work out all right, I started to look for a house. During April and May, I looked at homes in the northern and western suburbs almost every evening. After I had compiled a short list of houses that I considered acceptable, Lili came by train one weekend in May to look over my selection. I liked one house in Glenview because it had a cathedral ceiling over the living room with a large picture window looking out into a nicely landscaped garden. It reminded me of the dream house I had spent so many hours designing a few years earlier. Lili took one look at the wall paper which depicted trees with flowers and at the balcony leading to the four bedrooms which overlooked the living room.

"Can you imagine the children playing with crayons adding fruit to the trees?" she asked. "And then if we have a party the children will be running back and forth along the balcony in their pajamas. No, it's no good."

There were a couple that she considered acceptable, but only one house that she really liked. Lili didn't expect me to buy it because it's price was beyond our budget. It had originally been shown to me by a very enterprising broker. He had read a short news item that Precision Transformer's PR people had inserted in the business section of the *Chicago Tribune*. This article gave some details about me, including the statement that I had five children and was moving from Fort Wayne. One afternoon my telephone rang and an unknown voice announced, "I have just found the house that will suit you perfectly; when can you come and see it?"

I arranged to meet him at lunchtime the next day at a restaurant at the end of Edens Expressway.

"I'll wait for you in the parking lot. I'll be in a dark green Buick Riviera," he said.

When I arrived he was waiting for me. To my surprise, it was a man I hadn't met before, but I assumed he was from one of the realtors that I had been dealing with. I liked the house, but it was priced well above the top limit that I had set for myself. I told him this, but he insisted that this was the right house for a man in my position.

"Show it to your wife," he said. "I am sure that something can be worked out. Give me a call as soon as your wife can come to Chicago." He gave me his card.

"I have never dealt with your company," I said. "How do you know so much about me?"

"I always read the business news," he explained. "That's how I find the majority of my clients."

He certainly had a good sense for matching property with clients and their wives! After Lili had returned to Fort Wayne, I went back to him and did some negotiating. The house was vacant; it had been built only a little over two years earlier by a couple who subsequently had divorced. I made an offer of $32,500, including the carpets in the living and dining rooms. The offer was accepted; the listing realtor paid for the carpets just to conclude the deal and I paid the deposit. Then I called Lili to tell her that I had bought the house she liked so much. She was very surprised and happy, but she immediately started worrying how we would pay for it.

We put our house in Fort Wayne on the market. Unfortunately, the situation had changed since we had come there. Several of the large companies had moved out, including U.S. Rubber and Magnavox. International Harvester had also cut its operations back. Consequently, there many more houses on the market than there were buyers. Nevertheless, I borrowed some money for the down payment and we started packing.

On a very hot day at the beginning of July, Mayflower Van Lines loaded all our furniture and belongings. I packed all the suitcases and odds and ends into the station wagon and drove off with Mark and Peter. Lili followed in the Dodge with her sister Hala and the three youngest. The van would not arrive until the morning, so the two oldest boys and I spent the first night in our new home sleeping on the floor.

But we were not yet through with Fort Wayne. The housing market was so slow that our realtor recommended that we lease the house out for a year or two in the hope that the situation would improve. He was very helpful; he found us a tenant, collected the rent and generally kept an eye on the property and didn't charge us anything for the service. After a few months the first tenants moved out and for a month the house stood empty. Then new ones moved in with children. Immediately problems started. The septic tank backed up; the woman was flushing diapers down the toilet. Then they were late in paying rent and had to be evicted. Our realtor became pessimistic about the market improving in a reasonable time and suggested that we should consider selling at a loss and getting rid of the problem. With these difficulties we certainly were not making any money; the mortgage had to be paid and maintenance costs were mounting.

Reluctantly, I agreed that we should cut our losses. The realtor found a young G.E. engineer, who offered to buy the house for $18,000. He knew we were pretty desperate and would not budge any higher. It was hard for me to accept the fact that the house into which we had put so much love and labor was worth so little. I spent several sleepless nights trying to think of some other solution. Finally, unhappily, we accepted and at the end of August 1960 we finalized the deal. The only saving grace was that the house had been rented for more than a year and so the $6,000 loss was a deduction on our income tax that year.

The Biega family quickly became well known in the emergency room of Highland Park Hospital. Every one of us was there more than once during the subsequent years. It started shortly after our arrival. The weather was hot and we went to the beach regularly every weekend. Residents of Deerfield received beach passes to the Highland Park beaches for a very small fee. The swimming pools hadn't yet been built. The beach at Central Avenue was still large with nice sand; the water was fairly clean and quite warm after a long period of hot weather. There were also swings and slides for the children to play on.

One Saturday afternoon in late July we were all at the beach. Lili, Hala and I were lying on our towels after swimming. Suddenly Peter came running up, crying, "Annette has hurt herself!"

We rushed over to the slide. Annette was lying in the sand crying. It was obvious from the crooked angle of her arm that it was broken. I picked her up and jumped in the car with Lili. We drove to the hospital, just as we were, in our bathing suits all covered in sand. X-rays were taken. Fortunately it was a clean break. But in order to set the arm properly they wanted to give her an anesthetic and had to wait until she had digested the food she had eaten. She had to stay in the hospital overnight. She was crying more from fear than pain. Our neighbors across the street had a daughter, who, because of a genital defect, had only a stub for one arm. Annette was afraid that she also would lose her arm. It took a lot of cuddling and persuasion to convince her that everything would be all right. For the next three weeks Annette had her arm in a cast, but, otherwise, was none the worse for the scary experience.

Gradually we settled down in our new surroundings. The children established new friends; we too got to know all our neighbors. In those days it was a friendly community. Deerfield was still a small town, just beginning its growth. Most of the houses near the center of town, either side of Deerfield Road, had been built between the two World Wars. Tall trees lined all the quiet streets, shading the lawns in front of pleasant houses of various shapes and sizes. Some were large but most of them were of modest size, a typical mid-western middle class town.

We established a bank account in the Deerfield State Bank, which then was a tiny locally owned village bank in cramped quarters on Waukegan Road with only two teller windows. We also established passbook savings accounts in the recently established Deerfield Savings Bank, which occupied a new three story brick building, the largest in town. Ford's was the only drugstore and let us establish an account. Most people still did their shopping in Highland Park although Deerfield Commons was under construction. Jewel was the only supermarket. The area where we lived, Garand Drive and its neighboring streets, was one of the first new developments just built within the last two years, and was surrounded by open fields.

The local public schools had a much better reputation than in Fort Wayne, and were so much more convenient, within walking distance, that we decided not to continue sending the children to parochial school. In September the three oldest children started walking to Wilmot School on the corner of Wilmot Road and Deerfield Road, which had all grades from kindergarten to 8th. For religious instruction they were enrolled in Sunday morning classes at the church.

Most of the residents commuted to Chicago. They took the Milwaukee Road train to Chicago Union Station, or drove along the recently completed extension of Edens Expressway which ended at County Line Road. Another convenient way of getting to the city was by the North Shore Electric line which paralleled the tracks of the Chicago & North Western freight line from Waukegan through Skokie to Howard Street and then continued on the elevated tracks of the Chicago transit system to the Loop around downtown Chicago. This last suburban electric line did not close down in bankruptcy until the end of the 60's. During the first few months I drove daily to my office on Lake Street, leaving early in the morning to avoid the worst traffic. Occasionally, I shared a ride with John Hogan, a salesman who had recently bought a home in Deerfield Park, another new development a mile south of us. I rarely got home before 6.30 in the evening. Our office was close to Western Avenue where Milwaukee Road suburban trains stopped. As winter approached, Lee Butter bought an old car which he kept at this station. Then we both rode the train and used his old jalopy to go the remaining few blocks. It was difficult to park at Deerfield station, so usually Lili drove me there in the morning and picked me up again in the evening.

During the first few years in Deerfield, we enjoyed a lively social life. A neighborhood bowling league was organized. Every Friday night in winter we met at the bowling alley on the Waukegan Road where we occupied five lanes. It was more of a social event than serious bowling, although there were some very good bowlers among the crowd. Drinks flowed freely and after the session most of us continued partying for quite a while at the pizza place on the corner of Skokie Highway and County Line Road. There was a jukebox and enough space for those of us who were still energetic enough to dance. Our next door neighbors, Bea and Carl Wittbold, were always at the center of things. They were older than the rest of us, but they loved to party, particularly Bea. When Carl was tired, she often wandered off to whatever house was lit up, walked in for a chat and drinks, carrying her glass with her. Another lively couple that added much to the general Bohemian tone of the neighborhood were the Scaselattis who lived in the cul-de-sac. She was a striking blonde who wore bold colored dresses and drove a light blue convertible with her hair blowing in the wind.

There were frequent parties, at one house or another, some of the largest at our next-door neighbors. Once Bea organized a fancy-dress party to which Lili and I came in Polish costume that we had rented from a theatrical costume company in the Polish district. One summer weekend they arranged with the local police to close off the cul-de-sac, hired a Country & Western band and we spent the night square dancing in the street, pepped up by the lavish assortment of drinks available from the bar in their driveway.

The Eckerlings were another family that lived in the cul-de-sac. They were Jewish but did not adhere to strict Jewish dietary laws and always served excellent food, including Virginia ham and various sausages, at their parties. One of these parties was on a Friday night. In those days strict Catholics were not allowed to eat meat on Fridays. Joe Eckerling knew that one of our neighbors was very strict and purposely arranged to provide several fish dishes, smoked salmon, trout and other good things. The Catholic neighbor was heard to remark to another friend, "What a shame, there's such good food, and I went specially to the priest to get dispensation. But now I have to eat the fish!"

After three or four years things started quieting down. There were a couple of divorces, several of the original couples moved away, the new arrivals didn't seem to want to join in and it became difficult to get enough people interested in bowling any more. However, Bea never gave up; she continued to walk around the street in the evenings looking for company to drink with.

There were also many children in the neighborhood. During the day our doors were never locked, even if we were away from home. There was not much crime in those days anyway, but no petty thieves would dare to try an entry with so many children running in and out of each house all day long. Philip was friendly with the Sandberg boy behind us and they moved back and forth climbing over the fence. The Sandbergs had a big dog, an Alaskan Husky, which reveled outside in the snow all winter long, but in summertime hid in the recreation room next to the outlet of the air conditioning. They were one of the first to install central air conditioning.

We rarely suffered from the heat in Deerfield. If an oppressive heat wave developed, electric fans kept the air moving, but such hot weather never lasted for long; soon cool air moved in from the north. We were close enough to Lake Michigan to enjoy its moderating influence; however, the western and southern suburbs of Chicago had much hotter weather in summer but also lower temperatures in wintertime.

When we moved in there was no high school, Deerfield teenagers had to go to Highland Park. But that year construction of the new school started on Waukegan Road, just north of the town. Mark was in the first freshman class of the new Deerfield High School, and, consequently, in the first full graduation class. Mark played on the basketball team and in intramural football. Peter followed him a year later. Because of his asthma problem he was never able to play on any of the teams, but became team manager for the school basketball team. As a result, he got to go to all the games, both home and away. For a few years I took an active apart in the PTA activities at both the high school and at Wilmot school, but later the pressure of other activities became too much and I dropped out.

During the years that we lived in Deerfield the town expanded rapidly in population from its initial 5,000 to 20,000. Wilmot school could not keep up with the population explosion, and a new four year primary school was built on the Busse farm, just north of Greenfield Road. By the time Philip and Eileen were old enough to go to school they became students of the Woodland School, as it was called. Philip still went to Wilmot Junior High and graduated from it, but Eileen was one of the first students of the new junior high school built a few blocks away from Wilmot, closer to the toll road. A move was afoot to raise funds through another bond issue to build still another high school. However, the voters had enough of continually increasing taxes and voted it down. It was fortunate that they did because Deerfield High peaked at about 2,200 students, then the "baby boom" of the 60's was over and virtually all vacant land within the township had been built on. Beginning in the mid 70's enrollment started to decline. Today many of the classrooms have been closed off and stand vacant. Similarly Wilmot School has been closed down and has become a synagogue.

When we moved in there was no industry and few commercial offices. Hard pressed to pay for all the newly needed facilities, the town council actively sought ways to expand the tax base and courted industries. The first major industry to move into Deerfield was Sara Lee, a manufacturer of high quality frozen cakes and other foods. A group of older inhabitants vigorously opposed this move away from a sleepy village, but the votes of the newer inhabitants crushed the opposition. In 1963 the modern factory in a park-like setting started operations. The pleasant odors of baking cakes wafted over the village. This factory provided employment for hundreds of women and men from the surrounding communities. Sara Lee Industries was one of the first factories of its kind to be completely computer controlled and it became the destination of many tourist groups from all over the country. It also radically changed the habits of local housewives. Any product that failed to meet the exacting standards of quality control (for example, the label was crooked, the packaging was slightly dented, or it was slightly underweight) was sold at considerably reduced prices in an outlet store. The products were excellent in quality and at these reduced prices nobody could bake cakes any cheaper. So women from miles away, even from Wisconsin, flocked to the outlet store to buy not only cakes and rolls, but also other products such as lasagna and mousses, which were made under contract for hotel chains and airlines.

The open fields around us slowly gave way to the onslaughts of developers. In 1964 the growling roar of enormous earth-moving machines in the fields north of the creek which bounded our area made us aware of another large project taking shape. An artificial lake was carved out of the fields and around them expensive new homes were being built with prices considerably higher then any of the existing houses in western Deerfield. Unfortunately, this project upset the drainage of the entire area, and in following years, during the torrential rains that frequently accompanied summertime storms, the lower lying houses in our area suffered flooding. Fortunately, we were high enough to suffer only minor damage. Once we had a foot of water in our recreation room, the other time, about three inches. Our neighbors closer to the new lake suffered more frequent and more severe damage.

About 1970 a series of office buildings were constructed in the old tree nurseries along Wilmot Road south of us. The headquarters of several corporations such as Abbott Laboratories and Walgreens moved into this new office park. Then County Line Road was widened to four lanes and more office buildings and shopping centers were built along it. These developments made it possible for people to live comfortably in the suburbs and at the same time be close to their work. Bruce Malloy was one of the first new executives that walked from home to their offices.

He and his family bought the Scasselati house in the cul-de-sac next to the Eckerlings. We became friendly with them as soon as they moved in and often played bridge with them. Nancy was very conservative in her personal outlook and did a lot of volunteer work for the Republican Party. Also she was involved in various other local volunteer work such as the Red Cross. She got Lili involved in a program to take care of various spastic children, taking them to physical therapy activities, including a swimming program in the swimming pool at Lake Forest school. The Malloys had three children. The oldest daughter, Cathy, was away at a university in New England, but the two youngest were the same ages as Philip and Eileen. One late summer weekend the Malloys had a big neighborhood party around their swimming pool. It was chilly so there were no volunteers to go swimming, but somehow Bea and I ended up in the pool; as I recall, both fully clothed! Obviously, we all had a lot to drink and were enjoying ourselves. In fact we were having such a good time that nobody noticed that the ambulance had arrived to take Bruce Jr. to hospital. He, with some of his friends, had climbed up into a tree to watch the grown-ups making fools of themselves. Somehow he managed to fall out of the tree, fortunately his injury was nothing worse than a broken collarbone.

For a couple of years we had a lot of excitement. In the mid 60's the farmland on the east side of Wilmot Road became available for sale. The village wanted to buy the land for a park, swimming pool and a sports complex. A bond issue was floated but had to be approved by the voters. At the November election the Bond issue was voted down by the older residents who still commanded a majority. The farmland stayed vacant. But some out-of-town corporation prepared plans for a housing development with about one hundred homes in the 30 to 40 thousand bracket. The plans were presented at a village council meeting for approval and, in spite of opposition from those who still wanted the swimming pool and park, they were approved.

Suddenly a bombshell burst on the community. The corporation had inserted a secret covenant into the property deeds which required that the majority of the houses had to be purchased by blacks. I learned about this from our neighbor from across the street, Mort Siegel. He came over to our house to complain about the perfidy of the democrats (he was one himself), who secretly were carrying out a plot to bring blacks into pristine white Deerfield. I listened to the whole story, which was news to me.

Then I got angry with him and exclaimed, "Mort! You should be ashamed of yourself. Only a few years ago, you, a Jew, would not have been allowed to buy a property in Deerfield. Now you want to deny some people whose skin happens to be black the right to buy a house here?"

"We have to worry about the value of our property," he parried.

"Mort, the only person that can reduce the value of your property is you yourself, and others like you, if you create a panic. Remember, the houses they are planning to build are not slums; they are houses equal in value and size to what we have now. Who is going to buy them? Only black professionals who can afford this kind of house."

"But," he argued, "how do we know that they won't change the zoning to allow small, cheap housing on tiny lots to be built right in our backyard?"

"O.K., Mort," I said, "that is what we have to fight for, not to allow the zoning laws to be changed. Forget the color of the skin or the religion or nationality of the people who will buy the houses. But I don't think we have to worry about it. Hasn't the zoning for the development already been approved by the village council? They have already started construction on three houses along Wilmot Road, just north of the Episcopalian church."

"Well, yes, that's how the scheme came to light," he explained. "The pastor of some church on the south side of Chicago was chosen to be the first to move into one of these three houses. Apparently he wasn't very excited about moving into a house in Deerfield, 40 miles away from his church and congregation. He came to visit the pastor of the Episcopalian church and talked about the whole project."

As it turned out, Mort worried unnecessarily. The Episcopalian pastor, in turn, told somebody on the village council. Within a few days a special meeting of the village council was called, then a special election to approve the bond issue to purchase the property. This time the bond issue was approved overwhelmingly. I am not sure of the details, but I believe that the original option to buy the farmer's property had not yet expired. In any case, within weeks the entire property was purchased by the Parks Department of the Village of Deerfield.

The Development Corporation (the principal officers were rumored to be Eleanor Roosevelt and Senator Adlai Stevenson) immediately went to the courts. The matter dragged on for a couple of years, going as far as the Supreme Court. The same courts that had ruled just a couple of years earlier that it was illegal to have restrictive covenants to prevent property from being sold to a black or a Jew, now ruled it to be equally illegal to have restrictions that permitted only blacks to buy a property.

The end result was that Deerfield finally gained a beautiful swimming pool, tennis courts and playing fields. This came too late for Mark and Peter, but Annette, Philip and Eileen enjoyed them all through the summer. A ritual that became established was that on Labor Day, the last day of the swimming season, in the afternoon the pool was cleared. All the little kids were given cups. Then hundreds of goldfish were dumped into the pool. All the kids jumped in too and tried to catch as many fish as possible. This was great fun for all concerned. A couple of these goldfish, caught by Eileen, survived in a big glass bowl until we left Deerfield.

Unfortunately poor Mort Siegel didn't live to see this happen. The following year, during a cocktail party in their home, he suddenly slumped to the floor and died almost instantly. It was a heart attack and he was only about 40 years old. Henrietta carried on working for a while as a hostess in a local restaurant, then running a boutique in her basement. Finally she moved with her children to Southern California.

In addition to the neighborhood social life, we gained something which we had lacked in Fort Wayne — a circle of Polish friends. Chicago always was a large Polish center; in fact its population of ethnic Poles, counting both first and second generation, was the largest of any metropolitan area in the United States, even larger than any city in Poland outside Warsaw. There were two areas of Chicago in which Polish names predominated: one was along Milwaukee Avenue from Ashland to the city limits on the near north side, and a smaller one on the industrial south side between Archer and Cermak. Although the majority were pre-World War I immigrants and their descendants, a large and growing group were those who had come, like us, as refugees after the Communist take over of Poland. All had come to Chicago either directly from displaced persons camps in Germany or from England. Little by little we got to know more and more people from this latter group. We attended parties, typically on the occasion of someone's namesday - *imieniny*. The more parties we attended, the wider became our Polish group of friends. In turn we had parties at home to which we invited those to whom we felt closest. Many of them, as their finances improved, moved out of the small apartments of the Polish neighborhood to better apartments or homes in the extreme north side of the city or in the suburbs.

We did not join any of the Polish organizations or clubs. They were all in the downtown Polish district, and we had little time to spend on such activities. Our only Polish social activity that we engaged in outside the parties in private homes was a monthly outing to a Polish Social Club, which was held in the building of the Swedish Club. This was an inexpensive affair with dancing downstairs and bridge upstairs. As was usual in those days, almost everyone smoked and by the end of one of these evenings the air was blue with the haze of smoke.

Some of our Polish friends criticized us for not sending our kids to the Polish language classes on Saturday mornings. This would have been another big effort to drive them into the city every Saturday morning. In effect this would have occupied half of Saturday. Frequently, I had to work on Saturday so it was impossible for me; Lili already had her hands full with household chores and the younger children. It was easy for our friends that had one or two children at the most and who lived within 10 to 15 minutes of the churches where these classes were held.

We had other family activities. My father visited us regularly, every Christmas and most years during the summer. Christmas Eve was always a festive occasion for the family celebrated in the traditional Polish way. On Christmas Day we were joined by many of our friends for dinner. New Year's Eve was another occasion for a party. In all the years, except one, we greeted the New Year at a party in a private home. Several times we had the party at our house, with the festivities all over the house, but the main revelry and dancing in the recreation room downstairs. The children enjoyed sitting on the stairs (although they were supposed to be in bed) watching the grown-ups making fools of themselves! At our house we tried to have a mixture of American and Polish friends. Other years we were at parties in Polish friends' homes, or at one of the parties in the neighborhood.

In the summer of 1960 all of us, except baby Eileen who stayed with friends, went camping in the Porcupine Mountains of Upper Michigan, making a couple of stops at other lakes in state forests of Wisconsin on the way. We had two tents which had to be pitched at each stop, not the easiest thing to accomplish in spite of the training Mark and Peter had received in the Boy Scouts. Maybe I expected too much from them; I was anxious to get camp set up quickly. Mark and Peter were only 12 and 14 and were more interested in exploring around than in the hard work of unloading the Plymouth station wagon, driving in stakes and raising the tents. Anyway I got angry, which momentarily upset the atmosphere. But once the camp-site was arranged and Lili had cooked us a meal, we were all happy together again.

When we reached the camping ground on Lake Superior, we pitched the tents on a small headland overlooking a cove and stayed there several days. The soil was very red in color due to the high copper content, and the dust got into everything. Many years later Annette admitted that she got her socks so dirty that she was scared that Lili would be angry with her and just buried them! The water in Lake Superior is always very cold, but in the shallow cove it got just warm enough in the rays of the July sun for me and the boys to splash around. Fortunately, we had beautiful weather and hiked to the top of the mountain to enjoy the lovely views of the wild country and the lakes. On the way home we had a scare. We had just set up camp and were all sitting around the table enjoying our meal when a skunk slunk out of the undergrowth towards us, its bushy striped tail erect.

Annette cried out, "What a lovely kitty!"

"Hush! Don't any of you move," Lili admonished. "It's not a kitty, it's a skunk which makes a horrible smell if it gets frightened."

We sat there mesmerized watching the skunk. It looked at us, then turned around and slowly walked back into the bushes. We gasped a sigh of relief. Lili was not really the outdoors type and this was our last camping trip together, although later I made a couple of short weekend trips with some of the children. As a matter of fact we did not have any more vacations for the next four years, only short trips to visit friends in Fort Wayne or Detroit.

A HARD
MARKETING SCHOOL

The original factory of Precision Transformer at 2218 West Lake Street in Chicago was not a place to inspire confidence. It was a dirty, dark, old factory building, in the shadow of the El. The manufacturing operations were crowded together and poorly lit. The office space was reached up a rickety staircase and was also very crowded. To add to the overall gloomy appearance on the cold, cloudy, February day of my arrival, was added the aroma of burnt wood and paper. The previous week, during the night, there had been a fire. Fortunately, the damage had been confined to a small storage area. None of this was very good for morale nor did it encourage trust in the quality of the product.

I quickly got to learn the routine and the people. To my astonishment, the chief engineer was another Pole, Leon Szorc. He had come, like me, from the Polish army in England, and for several years had worked as a design engineer for Moloney Transformers in St. Louis and had been hired by Mel Adler to start up the design and production of liquid-filled power transformers. He had a wife who was the absolute epitome of a dainty Englishwoman. John Wozniak, who was of Polish origin but did not speak Polish, was the engineer who designed the dry-type transformers which were the major part of Precision Transformer's production.

Lee Butter was the technical driving force of the company. Being an electrical engineer but without transformer experience, he had strong sales experience in electrical products. Mel Adler, the president of the company, knew little about technical matters but was energetic and ambitious. Initially sales were primarily in the Midwest, but Lee was anxious to expand nationwide and already had signed up electrical sales representatives throughout the country. In the Chicago area, however, sales were made directly to the customers or through electrical distributors. John Hogan and Jim Bonner were the two local salesmen, the first, handling the north half and the other, the south half of the area.

My job was ostensibly to generate sales to industrial customers for which task a strong technical background with specific knowledge was a major asset. My secondary function was to provide technical backup for the design and production departments, specifically for the dry-type transformers, utilizing my General Electric experience. Leon had no background at all in dry-types and John Wozniak was a young engineer with very little experience. At that time there was very little supervisory expertise in the production department. I was appalled by the lack of quality control and the generally poor quality of the designs, and spent almost as much time instilling knowledge both in design and production as I did on the job I was hired for — sales. Within a year the quality of the Precision dry-type transformers had improved significantly.

In one respect I had to delve much further back in my experience, back to the days of Brentford Transformers in England. We no longer had at our disposal the wealth of resources I had enjoyed at G.E.. Particularly in the supply of materials such as insulation and magnet wire, we were limited to that available from routine suppliers and because of the cost of obtaining any special materials in small quantities, had to improvise a great deal. I also missed being able to call on the advice of specialists in many fields by simply placing a phone call to any one of the various General Electric departments and specifically the Engineering Development and Research Laboratories in Schenectady. I spent many hours writing Procedures and Standards for design engineering as well as for production. Danny Prystash was the technician responsible for production testing and he appreciated all the advice I gave him and learned quickly to apply the more rigorous test procedures that I insisted on.

Lee Butter had joined the company a couple of years before. He had considerable experience in the electrical contracting field and had many excellent contacts with consulting engineers and architects in the Midwest. He had hired Hogan and Bonner for sales in the metropolitan Chicago area and developed a network of sales representatives, initially through the Midwest. Input from consulting engineers had resulted in the design of two types of dry-type transformers that were unique with Precision, although later copied by competitors.

The first of these were outdoor transformers mounted on concrete pads, complete with circuit breakers. They were unique in that they were not oil-filled, as most outdoor transformers were in those days. A major installation had been made in the Old Orchard Shopping Center parking lot, in Skokie, Illinois. Several smaller installations were made elsewhere in the Midwest. Substantial savings resulted from distribution of power throughout the parking lots at 480 volts. The transformers provided the 120 volts required by the lighting fixtures installed on the decorative poles. Of course the whole power distribution was underground, which in the 1950's was also a novelty in America. This type of design was later widely used by other manufacturers in similar situations, although the use of high voltage oil-cooled transformers was the normal practice. Twenty years later I visited Old Orchard and found that these transformers were still working.

The other Precision Transformer innovation was specially designed transformers that could be mounted directly in walls, rather than in special closets, as was the usual practice. They had been dubbed "Hush Flush." They were aimed particularly at the growing high rise office building market. The concept was interesting and a number of installations was made, but the difficulty of reducing the level of the transformer hum below what was perceived to be a problem turned out to be unsolvable within the cost constraints established by the competitive nature of this market.

Mel and Lee observed that the market for oil-filled transformers was considerably greater than for dry-type. The market for the distribution transformers mounted on poles was huge, but also the number of competitors was correspondingly large and the per-unit profits low. Therefore they decided initially to concentrate production on the so called "small power transformers" ranging in size from about 150 to 1,000 kVA, with input voltages up to 35,000 volts. Leon Szorc had been hired to design this new product. The major customers for this type of transformer were the electric power utilities, but they were unwilling to buy from small unknown manufacturers.

However, large industrial companies, commercial area developers, military installations and other large users of electric power bought electricity in bulk at high voltage at much lower rates. The contractors involved in building, expanding or renovating electric systems for such customers were always willing to increase their profits by buying from small manufacturers at lower prices, provided the architects and consultants would allow them to do so. The key to developing sales for these products was: first, to have a price that was lower than that of the major transformer manufacturers (General Electric, Westinghouse, Allis Chalmers) and second, to convince the architects and consultants that they could risk their reputation and agree to the substitution of Precision Transformer for the usual ".....manufactured by General Electric, Westinghouse or equivalent...." clause in the specifications and drawings. Lee Butter was masterful at convincing reluctant engineers to acquiesce. Now this also became part of my job. As we successfully completed more installations at various job-sites and developed a User's List with good names, this became easier. Nevertheless, we never succeeded with some of the largest consulting firms in which individual engineers, even if they were willing to take the risk of accepting a little known supplier, could not override their bosses who were firmly entrenched in the camp of the big manufacturers.

Another target for our sales of these products were the small municipal and state-owned power utilities and REA's[*]. These were bound to accept the lowest price bids, unless the responsible engineer specifically rejected the supplier on the grounds of unsuitability.

---

[*] Rural Electricity Authorities - small federally subsidized utilities distributing power in rural areas.

This was more difficult to do, because he was obliged to give reasons for rejection, and it was not sufficient to say "quality is inferior because the manufacturer is small and unknown." One by one the user list became larger as more small power transformers were shipped, predominantly in the Midwest, but gradually the customer list expanded to the eastern and southern states. Although the number of units shipped grew, there was little profit for the company because to gain the initial sales, the prices quoted were much too low. Even though our overhead costs were much lower than those of the large manufacturers, the actual cost of materials bought was greater because of the small quantities, and our cost of labor and engineering were proportionally high because of the difficulties of learning a new technology and the poor efficiency of manufacturing in the crowded old plant.

Just about the time that I joined P.T.C., the decision was made to expand into the small distribution transformers, the ones that are mounted on the top of poles. Lee Butter understood that because it would be difficult to break into this market, it was necessary to have some gimmick to gain attention. The tanks in which these transformers are mounted are normally made of sheet steel, painted dark gray. Recent studies had indicated that in the southern states with bright sunshine most of the time, the transformers ran cooler if they were painted a light color. Lee had a couple of transformer tanks built of anodized aluminum, which had the additional benefit that they were lighter in weight and never needed painting. This idea did gain some attention for Precision at trade shows and, as a result, some specifying engineers added P.T.C. to the list of acceptable suppliers and some orders for distribution transformers were obtained. However, nobody was willing to pay extra to cover the intrinsically higher cost of the aluminum tanks, and no more were ever built.

Additional engineering staff was hired to cope with the added business, and that summer the sales department moved to separate offices in an ancient building a few blocks away. These offices were no less crowded and there was no air conditioning. All summer long the windows were open. All papers had to be weighted down to prevent them from blowing off the desks, and everything became covered in a film of dust. But we were happy to be away from the factory. The five of us, Lee, John and Jim (when they were in the office taking care of their paperwork), me and our secretary Sue Andersen, worked hard but also had time for some carefree chats and jokes. Jim Bonner had an inexhaustible supply of jokes. I don't know where he got them all; I never heard him tell the same one twice! We also had a continual string of temps helping out with the typing. We endured the primitive conditions throughout the autumn and the next winter, because we knew that construction of the new Precision Transformer factory in the industrial park of Elk Grove Village was already under way.

In the early spring of 1960 we moved into the brand new plant on Greenleaf Avenue. At last we had a clean factory we could be proud of with an efficiently arranged production facility and neat offices. At last we could bring consultants and architects to the factory to inspect the facilities without cringing and having to make excuses. At the same time Mel Adler succeeded in luring away from General Electric a foreman of the large transformer plant in Rome, Georgia, to whom he gave the position of production manager. Al Charbonneau brought with him a wealth of experience in the manufacture of large oil-cooled transformers, gained during many years with G.E. Through Al the engineering supervisor of large dry-type transformers in Rome, Jerry Simmons, was recruited. Jerry, in turn, recruited another engineer and a couple of draftsmen with experience in large oil-filled transformers.

Precision was now in a much better position to become a serious contender in the effort to become a supplier of transformers to the greatest market segment of all, the publicly-owned electric utility companies. In any case, our sales were expanding and we were gaining more recognition at larger industrial companies and with a wider circle of consulting engineers. I believe that if this course had been continued and we had steadily increased production in the already established product range, P.T.C. would gradually have expanded, gaining continually improved recognition.

I worked hard to do my part in developing new customers and markets for the products of P.T.C. One of my early tasks was preparing a catalog. This took many hours of intensive work, but I was pleased with the end result and so was Lee Butter. The front cover had a montage of photographs of well known sites at which Precision transformers had been installed such as the Old Orchard Shopping Center and the new Chicago O'Hare Airport and prominently listed the names of the contractors and architects.

Hopefully, this would get across to new clients that Precision transformers could be trusted if they were used at such prominent installations and approved by such renowned architects and engineers. Inside, each page described one product line in detail and provided sample paragraphs to be used in specifications. Outline drawings with dimensions were also included to simplify the work of project engineers who always needed to know how much room to allow for equipment. I had the most difficulty with these drawings, to get our own engineers to provide the needed information, since many of the sizes listed in the catalog had never been built. In most cases I just copied dimensions out of Westinghouse and General Electric literature and hoped that when we got orders engineering would be able to match the published dimensions. These catalogs were completed in time for the first mailing as we moved into our new plant.

The part of my job that I enjoyed most was traveling to places that I had never visited before for discussions with our representatives and with customers. Most of my travel was in the Midwest, but I did get as far west as Phoenix and Los Angeles, south to New Orleans and Baton Rouge and various places in Florida. Some of the trips were less pleasant because they were to deal with customer complaints and transformer problems. Considering the lack of experience of most of our people and the poor manufacturing facilities in the old Lake Street plant, it is a wonder that we had as few problems as we did. Regardless, any problem was an embarrassment.

The most interesting of my trouble calls was to the Kitt's Peak Observatory near Tucson. In this case the transformer had suffered a direct lightning hit, and we were not required to make good under the warranty. The main purpose of the visit was to determine the extent of the damage and whether it would be possible to make repairs on site. It was an interesting drive through the desert, then climbing a rough, steep road to the summit 4,000 feet higher up. The view was fantastic. At the same time I got to visit the observatory and look at the sun through their special telescope.

Several times P.T.C. participated in trade shows, particularly in the Midwest. For me the most enjoyable one was in Miami Beach at the Fontainebleau Hotel in February because I managed to get some free time to go swimming in the warm ocean or lie by the pool. Nevertheless, these shows were hard work, set up the booth during the two days before the show, then manning the booth duty during exhibition hours, normally from 10 a.m. to 6 p.m. and after that, entertaining thirsty customers in the hospitality suite until 11 p.m. The shows in which P.T.C. participated were oriented towards the contractor market and electrical contractors all appeared to be big boozers. Some of them got pretty rambunctious towards the evening's end. Hookers loved these shows and because the contractors expected entertainment, they were tolerated by the staffs.

I remember one show in Chicago at the Conrad Hilton Hotel. We had a large hospitality suite and three pretty, well dressed young women were in constant attendance each evening and were very popular with our guests. I suspect that they had been encouraged by Mel to enliven the activities. Periodically, each of them would leave with one of the guests and return alone half-an-hour later. At the last evening of the show, things started getting rowdy. John Hogan had to forcibly eject one loud-mouthed drunkard from the room. Even before the usual time of 11 p.m., we started nudging our guests towards the door and closed up shop. We ordered up coffee and sandwiches, took off our ties and coats and shoes and prepared to relax.

Suddenly, we heard a loud commotion outside in the corridor and then screams and finally, a banging at the door. We opened it and in tumbled the three girls in disarray. After leaving the suite, they had been accosted by some drunks and, unable to get away from them, had fled back to the safety of our suite. After repairing the damage to their dresses and hairdos, they sat down with us and shared our sandwiches and coffee until it had quieted down and they felt safe to go back to their rooms. We learned that they were from Detroit, two were office workers, the third, a married housewife. They told us that from time to time they went to some city where a show or convention was being held, far enough away from home to minimize the risk of being recognized. After paying their air tickets and hotel rooms, they cleared enough to keep them in "pin money" for awhile. The housewife was saving up for a down payment on a home.

The last show I participated in was when P.T.C. was already in financial difficulties. It was a small show during an REA convention in Washington. This time there was no fun, only three days of hard work. I was by myself with only part-time assistance from the local Washington area representative (who, of course, had to spend time also with his other principals). After spending the entire day at the booth without any relief, I was in no mood to entertain in the hospitality suite. Although I sat there for an hour or so, I had few visitors. Farm country electricians were not on the prowl looking for free drinks. So I closed down quickly, had dinner and went to bed early.

Although Precision was the only manufacturer in the Chicago area of oil-filled transformers of the type used by the electric power utilities, Lee had been quite unsuccessful in getting Commonwealth Edison to even test one of our transformers, let alone buy one. I had met the engineer who was responsible for purchasing at one of the many meetings of AIEE that I had attended, in fact, at the one at which I had presented a paper on the use of aluminum in transformer design. I took advantage of this to get an appointment to see him in his office. I tried hard to get him to agree to at least test a transformer, which we would supply at no charge to Commonwealth. I pointed out that many bulk users of electric power were connected to the Commonwealth network by means of a Precision transformer, and that they worked successfully. He was adamant that it was Commonwealth's policy to purchase only from a limited number of suppliers who were capable of providing extensive technical support.

"What advantage can you offer to justify purchasing from you?" he demanded.

"First of all, lower prices, at least 5% below the price of equivalent G.E. or Westinghouse transformers," I replied. "Secondly, we are a local manufacturer and can provide instant service, whenever needed."

"You have no research, nor technical development," he responded, "The major manufacturers all spend at least 5% of their gross income on developments in the electrical field which, over the years, have been of great value to the power utilities. It behooves us to support these efforts; therefore the 5% price reduction is not important to us. We also expect them to maintain a local stock of standard transformers, available for immediate delivery in the event of some emergency or disaster." With this comment, he dismissed me.

At this time the three major manufacturers provided the basic pricing structure for the whole industry. Anti-trust laws had been set up at the beginning of the twentieth century to prevent collusion between manufacturers to fix prices, either to gouge the customers with high prices or to force smaller competitors out of business by dropping prices too low. Nevertheless, any time G.E. or Westinghouse changed a price for one of the standard products, the rest of the industry followed suit. These were the so-called list prices, which were published and widely known. That is how companies such as Precision Transformers were able to print price lists even for products that we had not manufactured or designed and consequently had no idea of their costs. We just copied the published G.E. price sheets. Hopefully, the large manufacturers knew their costs well and were making a good profit on the published prices. Therefore, we believed that whenever we got an order, engineering would be able to come up with a good enough design that we would, with luck, make some profit for the company.

In actual fact, no one bought equipment at the list prices, an extensive range of discounts was available to different classes of buyers such as distributors, contractors, power utilities, and the U.S. Government. There were also quantity discounts available to qualified buyers. Frequently, we quoted prices over the phone in a shorthand fashion, if the ratings were standard ones (that is, power size and voltages in accordance with national standards). For example the standard contractor discount for small dry-type transformers was at that time 37% off list, with another 5% for a quantity in excess of 10 of the same size.

A contractor called us to request prices for some construction job. He listed the quantities and sizes that he needed, and then asked, "What is your best price?"

"37% and 10% across the board for the total lot," I answered.

"That's no good. I've already been offered 37 and 12," he responded.

"We'll do some calculating and let you know."

"You'd better sharpen your pencils and give me an answer by Friday." The contractor hung up.

I called our local sales representative to sniff around, to find out, if he could, who had quoted the lower price, if any, or whether the contractor was just pulling our leg, to get a lower price from us and increase his own profit.

This was a well-structured system which allowed an orderly business atmosphere. It also allowed many small regional manufacturers to become established and prosper serving limited markets. There were at least a dozen companies across the United States manufacturing oil-filled transformers of one kind or another, a couple of dozen more smaller companies manufactured only the smaller dry-type transformers. Some of these small companies were exceptionally successful and had grown significantly during and after the war to become a major factor in the industry, although smaller than the big three. Obviously, Precision Transformer was aspiring to grow along these lines.

In the cases where the transformers (or other electrical equipment) were purchased directly by some government authority, the prices had to be quoted in writing in sealed bids. If the quantities were modest, small manufacturers with low overheads, such as Precision, could bid a lower price than the big three, and if they were the lowest bidder and the engineers did not reject them on some technical basis, they could get the order. If the quantities were large, at least one of the major manufacturers would drop the price far below the normal level and obtain the contract. In that case the small manufacturers were not in a position to match these low bids. However, the important point is that the existing system made it possible for small companies to enter the market and challenge the big guys and get enough business on small quantity jobs to grow and thrive.

Then the bottom fell out. A congressional committee or some publicity hungry government attorney (I don't remember the details) started an investigation into why each of the major companies was getting a share of all large public contracts roughly proportionate to their size. Suddenly, the Big Three and several of the second tier companies such as Federal Pacific and Pennsylvania Transformer were indicted for alleged conspiracy to fix prices in violation of the anti-trust laws. In the media it was called the "Phases of the moon conspiracy." According to the newspaper stories, some executives of the indicted companies had met at a resort and agreed on a formula by which each, in turn, would put in a low bid on public tenders, while the others quoted standard prices. Which company put in the lower bid was supposedly determined by the phase of the moon at the time of the bid opening. Anyway, the case never came to trial. The companies involved plea bargained to avoid court proceedings which would have gone on for years and cost each of them (and the taxpayer) millions of dollars. Several vice-presidents went to jail for short terms. The end result of this case was that all the pricing rules went right out the window. The Big Three and the other three or four started a bidding war for _all_ large and medium sized projects. This drove all the small manufacturers such as Precision, Uptegraff, Central Transformer, (to name a few) out of business. They did not have the resources to last out a long war with prices at, or below, their costs. Ostensibly the anti-trust laws had been set up to prevent this kind of thing from happening. However rigorous enforcement of the statutes ruined the very companies that they were supposed to protect. Ironically even some of the defendants in the government prosecution, such as Allis-Chalmers, Pennsylvania Transformer, and Federal Pacific Electric, no longer exist today, they all went under, unable to survive the price wars that were unleashed by this case. Consequently the number of suppliers of electric power equipment has been sharply reduced and eventually the cost to the consumer increased.

Theoretically, the general public is served best when free enterprise is allowed full rein; government intervention, for whatever reason, only hurts. At least that is what the Republican conservatives preach. Nonetheless, history shows that some incentives are needed to assist small enterprises and also to provide some protection against crooks who would use their muscle to take over the markets. And once some regulations are introduced to protect or assist any group, whatever it might be, minorities, small business or small farmers, there will always be some politician or lawyer who will take advantage of the system to bolster his own personal ambition or fortune regardless of the consequences.

Ironically, the same purchasing engineer at Commonwealth Edison called me and asked me to come to talk to him. This time he sang a different tune. He claimed to be shocked by the revelations of the scandal. Now he was interested in buying transformers from Precision Transformer. However, the conditions he proposed were stiff. First we had to supply free units for evaluation by their laboratories. If approved, we would negotiate an annual supply agreement for some small range of transformer sizes and would have to agree to build and maintain a stock of transformers ready for immediate delivery of value equal to the value of the contract. But we would not get paid until units were actually requisitioned by the operating division. I passed this proposal on to Lee. By this time Precision was already in financial difficulties and was unable to make such a large investment in inventory.

Unfortunately, a decision had been made just before these events occurred, which led to financial disaster and the collapse of the company. Mel and his financial backers were unhappy with the low profit margins of the products that we were selling and kept complaining about the low prices at which we were getting contracts. The price levels were set by the market. The only way to increase profitability was to reduce costs. This meant we had to strive for larger production runs of essentially similar products which, in turn, would give greater purchasing leverage in buying all the materials and components that we bought from others, and lower unit labor costs with higher efficiency. We were saddled now with higher overhead rates to pay for the new factory building and all the new machinery and the larger engineering staff. This made it even more essential to concentrate on increasing the volume of existing product types.

However, someone convinced Mel that we should expand production into the medium power range, that is in the size range 1,000 - 5,000 kVA and with input voltages up to 115,000 volts. The argument was that in this size range the number of competitors was small and the potential profit margins much larger. Unfortunately, this also meant that even larger and riskier expenditures had to be made for new designs, which became ever more complex. It required substantial additional capital expenditures for larger machines for winding the coils, larger tanks for vacuum impregnation of the units and expensive new testing equipment. Furthermore, the market expansion necessitated a concentrated effort on the part of the sales staff to gain access to this restricted market. This took away from the efforts needed to expand markets for existing products.

If there were any problems, which have to be expected any time a major expansion of design capabilities is made, the costs of repair would be very large. Installation and transportation costs of such large units ran into thousands of dollars. The company, which was already overextended financially with the recent expansion, was unable to sustain this new venture.

Finally, with a very low bid we obtained a contract to supply three large transformers for the Bonneville Power Administration. As might be expected, we did have problems with the units. As a result not only did P.T.C. sustain heavy repair expenditures, but a substantial part of the contract price was not paid but put in escrow as a reserve for any future problems during the warranty period. This additional burden finally lead to bankruptcy, initially reorganization under Chapter 11; finally, in 1963 to total shutdown.

LADY LUCK DESERTS ME

In every commercial building there is a requirement for small transformers in the power range of 1/4 KVA to about 15 KVA. These small transformers are typically totally enclosed and are designed for mounting on vertical surfaces such as walls and partitions. Precision Transformer did not build these units but purchased them from an outside supplier. We made very little profit on them, but they were essential as no contractor wanted to go to another source for a small part of the transformers used on a single contract. If we didn't supply the small units, we could easily lose the whole contract. We purchased them from a small manufacturer in Chicago called Captran. In 1961 they started having financial troubles and deliveries became erratic. To obtain the best possible prices, we bought them in quantity and carried in stock. As our stock ran low a new order was placed on Captran, but delivery was never made on time. This caused us a lot of trouble with our customers.

In November 1961 the Captran salesman informed Lee Butter that the owners needed additional cash to continue operations or they would sell outright. At this time Precision Transformer was already pretty shaky itself and was in no position to do anything. Lee had the idea to make an investment in the company himself. He got all the financial records, customer lists and gave them to me to study. Captran was one of hundreds of small manufacturers of miniature transformers made mostly for the electronics industries — controls, television, hi-fi and commercial sound systems. There were at least two dozen such companies in Chicago alone. But only a handful besides G.E., Westinghouse and Hevi-Duty Electric made anything bigger than about 100 watts. At that time consumer electronics was still big business in the United States. None of us understood that the Japanese planned to destroy this business within the next few years. At that time Japanese cheap radios were being sold by drug stores and Woolworths but had not made much of an impact in the market place because of their poor quality. The transistor was a wonderful new invention, but most radios, TV's and sound systems still used tubes which required transformers. Most of Captran's business was in this field, but the company also possessed the capability to make larger units, for which we knew that there was a growing industrial market.

Analyzing the figures, it became clear that one of the problems was that Captran had a large salaried overhead which was draining cash. They had many good customers but also some, particularly in New York, that were not paying their bills. They had virtually no sales to the industrial market, Precision Transformer was their only significant industrial customer. We knew that we had lost a lot of business in the smaller sizes recently because Captran refused to quote prices on any new designs and was always late in making deliveries. Therefore, I judged that, if the expensive overhead were eliminated and the bad accounts were cut off, it would be possible to build up the industrial side of the business utilizing the contacts of Lee and the Precision sales representatives and turn the business around.

Then Lee asked me whether I would be interested in running the business. I was already concerned that before long I would not have a job, the way things were going at Precision Transformer. But, on the other hand I was scared of getting into an undercapitalized business because I knew that was the certain road to disaster. He asked me how much capital the business needed. I spent several days at the Captran plant checking records, machinery and inventory. Then I prepared a detailed financial plan. I concluded that the maximum that should be paid for the goodwill, designs and equipment was about $20,000, considerably less than what was being asked. I also listed the equipment required for building the products sellable in the industrial market and stated that a minimum investment of $100,000 was required. I estimated that under those conditions a break-even point could be reached in one year by concentrating on the industrial markets, while maintaining present production for the credit worthy consumer electronics customers.

In January 1962 Lee got several people interested in investing in this business and hoped to get the entire $100,000 together shortly. After discussing the matter with Lili, I agreed to run the business, under condition that the stipulated capital was available. I promised to invest $5,000 myself. At the end of the month the owners of Captran announced that they were closing the doors of the plant and ceasing operations. Lee felt that it was essential to keep the company going, that it would be difficult to start up again and regain the customers once operations ceased. He was also afraid that the equipment and designs might get sold off to competitors. Although only half of the required capital was committed, he assured me that he would obtain the balance within two to three months. Captran agreed to sell all the assets and the goodwill for $25,000.

I had considerable misgivings, but after a long discussion with Lili, who was interested in the possibilities of making a lot of money if everything went well, I agreed to go ahead. We had a couple of meetings with Lee's lawyer, Theodore Stone, in downtown Chicago. The Acts of Incorporation were issued and signed by all the initial investors, which included a couple of Precision salesmen. On February 5 the assets of Captran Corporation were acquired by the new company, Preferred Transformer Corporation. The following day I started work as president of the new company.

Lee did not want me to keep on Captran's previous sales manager. But I needed him for his contacts with the electronics industry customers in order to maintain the volume of orders essential for the business plan that I had prepared. I did however reduce his salary substantially, giving him instead a commission on business that he brought in personally. At the same time I put him on a tight rein regarding expense accounts and personally reviewed the credit history of each customer. All the plant workers, mostly women doing coil winding and assemble work, were kept on, as well as the plant foreman.

I found that the majority of the employees were first rate, were all experienced in their work, and because I made a point of getting to know each of them and discussing the details of the jobs we were doing, they became very loyal to me. In any case, they were all interested in helping me keep the company and their jobs going. It was a union shop, and to my dismay, I found that I was obliged to continue with the existing contract. Ironically, if we had delayed with the purchase and allowed Captran to go out of business and then after an interval of a few weeks had started business again, we would no longer have been obligated to maintain the contract. In actual fact, it had little effect. When the union organizer tried to force me to negotiate a new contract with higher wages and benefits, virtually all the workers sided with me and agreed to continue working for the same wages with only a small cost of living adjustment. However, under the contract I was saddled with granting paid vacations to all the employees based on their length of service in the previous company. The number of employees was about 20 at the time, of which all but three were covered by the union contract.

The first few weeks went well. I was learning new skills; I had no previous experience in the production of small electronic transformers nor in designing them. Running a plant was a new experience for me too. It didn't matter how much one read from books, or had learnt from management courses at G.E., the reality continually introduced new problems for which I had to find a solution. I worked hard to regain the confidence of our suppliers. At first I had to pay cash for all supplies which quickly ate away at the meager cash reserves, but gradually I got the most important suppliers to give me a credit line. To protect our credit, I had to make sure the bills were paid on time but not too quickly, because we didn't have the cash. Gradually my credit limits were extended and it became easier.

The second problem was collecting from our customers. Irving was no help here. He was a typical salesman, get an order at any cost, but don't annoy the customer by demanding payment! I started holding up shipments until invoices were paid; some orders were canceled as there was always some other supplier willing to provide the goods on credit, and Irving would get mad.

"That's how Captran went down the drain and their predecessor too!" I cried out in exasperation. "Our suppliers won't give us the material unless we pay. The same rule has to apply to our customers. How else can we keep going?"

My days were the longest I had ever worked in my life. Normally, I arrived at the plant, on the fourth floor of a large loft building at 1910 North Elston Ave, no later than 7:30, before any of the employees. I started by checking the daily work assignments, normally the job of the foreman, but I did not trust her. I was always looking for ways to improve efficiency. Then I'd check the materials needed for the jobs, what inventory was running low and what needed to be ordered to make sure production would not be held up in the next few days. I negotiated with suppliers and looked for new sources. I dealt with the accounts. Ginny, the secretary and bookkeeper, was very conscientious, but nevertheless had to be checked and coached all the time. She had no previous bookkeeping experience but learned from our accountant. Checks had to be signed and mailed, or put in the wait basket if they could be delayed a few days. I made sure invoices were mailed out promptly and that no mistakes had been made. I reviewed requests for quotation, made cost calculations and provided pricing. The latter was basically the job of Irving, but I had already discovered he had little understanding of costing and was only interested in quoting a low price to ensure getting the job and his commission.

When the plant closed at 4:30 and everyone went home, I put on my other hat and started preparing new designs. I had to learn how to design the small electronic transformers, so that I could find ways to improve them to reduce costs, if at all possible. I had the greatest problem with so-called audio output transformers, the ones that were used in audio amplifiers for commercial and hi-fi sound systems. They constituted a sizable part of the production of Captran. The old engineer, who had done all Captran's design work on a contract basis, told me how to design them, but he could not explain the methodology. I studied books on the subject to get a better understanding of what made a superior audio output transformer. Only if I could understand that would I be able to come up with a better or a cheaper product that would increase our business without bankrupting us. I designed a series of small industrial transformers and made samples, tested them and developed cost sheets, then designed a catalog sheet. I also reviewed all the designs of the commercial lighting transformers that Captran built for Precision. I made a number of design improvements to reduce costs and improve performance.

Some nights I did not get home until 9 or 10 o'clock. Often I was so exhausted that I would leave the car parked in the street and take the train to Highland Park from the Chicago & North-Western station close by on Elston Avenue. Lili picked me up, but then would have to take me back to the station to catch the 7:05 train the next morning.

The only help I got from any friends or family came from my kids. Mark, Peter and Annette all came in one weekend to help make a complete inventory. This meant ticketing each item, recording it in a book, then counting or weighing each item, the time consuming part. It was dirty work and took all Saturday and part of Sunday. Annette was only nine years old but gave moral support and was very helpful counting small items.

Ginny was an interesting woman. Black and considerably overweight, she always complained about climbing the four flights of stairs and whenever she could, she rode up in the freight elevator. Always cheerful and friendly with the other women in the work force, she served as a useful conduit for information about attitudes on the floor. She had learned the intricacies of bookkeeping very quickly and required less and less supervision. She kept me informed who were the hard workers, who were the lazy ones.

She lived on the south side. She had two children and, although she was not Catholic, she paid to send her children to parochial schools, because, as she told me, she wanted to give them a chance in life, and the conditions in the public schools on the south side with the high crime and generally bad attitudes were harmful. She worked hard and tried her best to help out as much as she could. She stayed until a couple of weeks before the end when she received an offer of another job, and I had to advise her to grab the opportunity. Sometime during the winter her father died. I went to the funeral in a Baptist Church, which was different from any funeral service I had ever been to. It was not so somber; the singing and hand clapping made it seem almost a festive occasion. I was the only white face in the whole congregation. Everyone looked at me, wondering, "What is he doing here?". I understood then how it felt to be "different."

A CPA recommended by Lee came in for a couple of hours each week to help set up the books and teach Ginny how to make all the necessary entries, a job that had been done at Captran by a permanent employee. He also came at the end of the month to balance the books and prepare financial statements. In January 1963 he quit. I wasn't upset because I didn't need his help any more and certainly was happy to reduce expenses still further. Anyway, he wasn't a very good accountant, although he had been very helpful teaching us the mechanics. In the fall I had a problem with the I.R.S. which disallowed the tax loss that I had taken for the home on Fort Wayne. I asked him for advice and he said that, in his opinion. the I.R.S. was right!

I had no desire to pay the back taxes plus penalty and interest amounting to over $2,000. I made two trips to the tax office in Waukegan. They refused to discuss the matter. I owed the money, that's it, "Don't waste our time." Finally I succeeded in getting a delay and a transfer of the case to Chicago. I talked to our neighbor Sandberg about my problem and he sent me to a friend, a tax lawyer in an office across the street from the Federal Building. The lawyer had me send him the files, then talked to me on the telephone. He told me to come in to his office fifteen minutes before the hearing was scheduled.

"Don't we need to discuss the matter?" I asked.

"Don't worry, Mr. Biega," he replied. "There's no problem; trust me."

We walked into the tax inspector's office. The inspector seemed surprised, he obviously knew the lawyer well. The lawyer said right away, "Joe, you know you don't have a case against my client. Let's not waste my valuable time, settle this right now."

He told me to sit on a chair in the corner, while he sat at the inspector's desk. They spent about five minutes going over the paperwork. Then he said to me, "Mr. Biega, I suggest that you agree to write a check for $37.22. I hope you have your check book with you."

I started to ask a question. He frowned, shook his head. I understood that there was no point in asking questions. I wrote out the check, handed it to the inspector, who took it and gave me a receipt.

When we walked out of the office, the lawyer explained that to save face the inspector made an issue of the amount of depreciation that I had originally calculated. He claimed that my calculation was in error. The amount was too small to waste time arguing about it. To my surprise, the lawyer billed me only $35. The moral of the story is that tax people are more interested in proving how good they are than they are in helping the average citizen who pays their salaries. A poor slob who doesn't have a good tax lawyer never has a chance.

During the first two months things were going well and I felt optimistic. New orders were coming from the old customers. In a few instances I was able to negotiate a small price increase. Suppliers were, on the whole, cooperative. But requests for quotations from industrial customers were slow in coming; this was the area on which my hopes for increased, more profitable business were based.

As the end of the first quarter approached, there was still no sign of the remaining half of the capital that was essential to our continued existence. We were still far from the estimated $300,000 annual sales level needed to break even and start making a profit. I needed money to develop some new products for which I had ideas and to prepare proper catalogs and promotional literature. Preparation and printing of proper new catalogs required an expenditure of a couple of thousand dollars, which I was loathe to do until the promised extra cash became available. In the meantime, I was still using up supplies of Captran catalogs with the name Preferred Transformer over-stamped on them. The data sheets for the lighting transformers and industrial control transformers that I had designed were duplicated typewritten sheets and their crude appearance was not very confidence inspiring. I had procured a couple of laminating machines and some sorely needed test equipment at an auction sale of a transformer manufacturer in McHenry that had bitten the dust. Most of our customers were paying reasonably promptly, but the money rarely came in less than 40 days from date of invoice. At the same time I was paying for supplies within a few days of delivery to us. I was running out of cash.

According to Lee most of the remainder of the promised $50,000 was to come from our lawyer. But, for two months he had been ill and the money was not forthcoming. Suddenly he died. I was in a panic. I tried to get a credit line from our bank, the Harris Trust, where our accounts had been set up by our lawyer. To no avail — this big bank had no interest in small accounts. I moved to a local bank, Manufacturers National Bank, on the corner of Milwaukee Avenue and Ashland, which was easier for me to get to, to make daily deposits, but as far as credit lines were concerned, Preferred Transformer was an unknown and doubtful quantity in their equations.

I tried to get a small business loan guarantee through the Small Business Administration, which had been set up to help small start up corporations like ours to get on their feet. But this required a great deal of paper work. I spent many hours preparing all the necessary statements and forecasts for one year, two years and five years, hours taken away from managing the company and designing transformers. Then many weeks elapsed waiting for a response. I was now desperate. I got my own bank in Deerfield to give me a personal loan to tide us over. Finally, the SBA turned us down; I don't recall what reasons they gave, if any. I have often wondered whether the fact that all Lee's shares were registered in my name had any effect on the difficulties in obtaining bank credit or an SBA loan. Lee had done this because his contract with Precision Transformer did not allow him to have any outside interest in another transformer company. But during background credit investigations it must have raised questions whether the claimed $50,000 initial investment, over half of which was in my name, had ever existed, or if it did, where it had come from. Any checks into my own credit background would have revealed that there was no way I could have come up with this money myself in any legitimate way.

There was no other way to continue except by borrowing against invoices, otherwise known as factoring. Precision Transformer, which was now in bankruptcy under Chapter 11, was getting its daily operating funds by these means from National Acceptance Corporation, one of the largest factors in America. Lee arranged for me to get a loan from the same organization. A couple of auditors appeared at the plant and went over the books with a fine tooth comb. A complete inventory was made of the factory stock and work in process under their supervision. Then they took all the outstanding invoices that were less than 15 days old and made a loan of 85% of the total value of these invoices. This suddenly gave me an infusion of about $5,000 cash. The catch was that the percentage paid was fairly high, about two to three percentage points higher than the 5% that banks were charging at the time. As more goods were shipped, each week I sent over the invoices and got additional advances. National Acceptance collected from our customers and credited our account with the proceeds less the interest. I was not obligated to send all invoices. For example, one of our customers was the Hotpoint Division of General Electric which always paid within ten days. I held on to these invoices.

During the summer volume gradually improved, Irving was bringing in new business, not all of it very profitable, but I was desperate to increase volume to make the business more attractive to potential investors. Lee and the Precision representatives provided some industrial business. I hired a Polish woman, Alina, as an engineer to help me with the increased design load. She had some experience with electronic transformers and generally was quite helpful, but most important was that she was willing to work for the minimum wages that I could afford to pay.

I had been forced to fire the forewoman after discovering that she was completing work for customers that had been discontinued, using my labor and material and pocketing whatever these customers paid her. I was lucky to find a new foreman, Joe Pizza, who was very energetic and gave me a great boost. He did not have much transformer shop experience but seemed to be able to deal with all the problems and find solutions. He came from a family with local political connections and could easily have gotten a political job paying much more than the meager salary he received from us. He told me many amusing stories about these types of work, such as being a bridge tender on one of the bridges that had to open only a few times a year or counting cars going down a street. He said that his family couldn't understand his desire to do an honest day's work!

We started experimenting with epoxy moldings to give us an entry into the more profitable military electronics market. I did a little dabbling in electronic circuits. I had some ideas for new products such as marine battery chargers using the solid state SCR's (silicon controlled rectifiers — or thyristors), which had recently appeared on the market. Another idea I had, which I spent a lot of time on, was an inverter which would run off a car battery and provide enough power to run refrigerators and freezers or in winter time the furnace. My idea was that this product would be useful to people in isolated rural communities which were frequently subject to short power outages during summer thunderstorms, tornadoes and winter blizzards. I drew up the basic design which would work in reverse as a charger to recharge the car's battery when power returned. Unfortunately, all the daily problems of business survival never allowed me to complete the project, or even to build a working sample[*].

The increased volume and the fact that I got paid fast for 85% of the value of each shipment had stabilized our cash position, and I was able to hold my own, although I was unable to do many things I wanted to do because I had to be extremely careful about making any expenditure other than for material and wages, and, of course, rent and utilities. Incoming orders in August and September were running close to my projected break-even point. I breathed a sigh of relief. I felt much more confident. Even the employees realized that things were looking up and their mood was buoyant.

Suddenly, in October, National Acceptance Corporation announced that they were canceling our account, would stop loaning against invoices immediately and that the loan balance was payable in full in 30 days, which meant that we would have to buy back any invoices not collected by that time. They gave no explanation for this step. Perhaps they had advance knowledge of the coming changes in the consumer electronics market, which is where most of our business still lay. Anyway, it was a catastrophe.

About this same time Lee had come up with a potential investor who spent some time going over the business with me. Finally, he made a proposal which in principal involved giving him a controlling interest in the company. Lee refused in spite of my pleas. I no longer cared about control of the company. I just wanted to have a chance to salvage it and our own investment. Without more capital, I warned Lee, it was impossible to do what was necessary to try to break out of the consumer electronics transformer business, and under existing

---

[*] A few years later a similar product appeared on the market and has been very popular with owners of boats and campers.

conditions I was unable to keep the company going much longer. Lee made some kind of counter proposal, but the prospective investor lost interest.

I was almost out of cash to buy materials, pay wages and bills. I was no longer able to take advantage of prompt payment discounts and, in fact, delayed paying any but the most vital accounts. I dismissed Irving. I was unable to pay his salary, but kept him on as a commission salesman, paying commission only when the clients paid for the shipments. Anyway, I didn't trust him, but I had no one else to get me business from the consumer electronics customers. I certainly didn't have the time to go out myself (as Lee suggested) to visit customers. I stopped paying myself my own salary, much to Lili's distress. I only paid an advance — just enough to take care of groceries, mortgage and most pressing bills.

Finally, I came up with a new source of immediate cash —ABCO Finance Company. Their conditions were much worse than those of National Acceptance Corporation. I only received an advance of 75% of invoice value. The interest rate was 10% and they insisted that all invoices be deposited with them, so I had no leeway. On top of that, they took out a mortgage on the equipment and inventory as security for the loan with three year interest of 12% per year paid up front. Further, I had to personally guarantee the account. Under these conditions there was no way Preferred Transformer Corporation could survive for long unless there was a miraculous increase in business. Even then, the added burden was intolerable for a business in which the profit margins were slim in any case.

However, Lee still hoped to come up with the needed capital. On my side I started vigorously searching for a buyer, just to be able to rescue at least part of our investment. At the same time I worked day and night trying to improve operations, cutting costs wherever possible, trying to get price increases from our customers. Unfortunately, the tight cash situation meant that we had to buy in smaller quantities so that we paid even higher prices for our materials.

As winter started the overall business situation weakened. Our existing customers started cutting back on orders and taking longer to pay their invoices. Instead of price increases I was being faced with demands for price concessions. I went to Hotpoint just before

Christmas to negotiate a new annual contract for the small pilot light transformers (used in ranges and washing machines) that we were supplying in large quantities. However, the price for the initial contract that we had taken over from Captran was such that we really made no profit, but it did cover some of our overhead and payment was always prompt. Instead of the price increase of 10 cents per unit that I proposed, the buyer told me that he had been given a lower quotation by another supplier. However, he said that we could renew the contract at the same price because we were a reliable supplier. But, he hinted, he was hoping to get a color television for Christmas! I agreed to maintain the same price but did not send him a television set. In January we were told to string out delivery of the balance of the existing contract over the next three months, in effect cutting monthly quantities in half. I assumed that Hotpoint was starting to phase in a new supplier, possibly someone who had given the buyer the requested television set.

February and March of 1963 were very difficult for me. To reduce cash payments, I was making local deliveries in my station wagon rather than pay for a delivery service. I was scouring surplus material markets for materials at low prices. I was no longer able to pay myself even an advance against salary. I had to let Alina go to save her salary; the work force had been cut back to about half.

But suddenly, near the end of March we received a series of orders from new industrial customers to whom I had been making proposals during the previous months. Things were looking up again. Once more I had a prospective investor looking at the business. Hope sprang up again that perhaps the sacrifices of the previous months would pay off, that we could still survive. Nevertheless, I was in a desperate cash-poor situation. Because of slow payment, ABCO returned some invoices to me and deducted their value from cash advances against new invoices. I was unable to make payment of tax withholdings to I.R.S. on March 31. I had to buy the materials needed to build the new orders we had just received and our suppliers would only deliver to us C.O.D. Our shipments in the first weeks of April were back up to decent levels, and once more I was feeling hopeful.

On Monday, April 22, I arrived at the plant at 7 o'clock to find a big padlock on the door and a printed notice announcing that ABCO had foreclosed on its loans and shut the plant down! Worse was to come; when the workers arrived some of them told me that their previous week's paychecks had bounced. On Friday morning I had deposited a large check from ABCO for the invoices for goods shipped that week. When I went to the bank to complain, I was told that payment of the check had been stopped. I rushed to ABCO's offices.

The son of the owner, who had been very cooperative with me, was apologetic, but he had been overruled by his father and uncle who felt that our company was going nowhere and they had to protect their investment. I pleaded with the old man, but he was adamant. Finally, with the help of the son, I got them to agree to let us finish off the work that was already in process for which the bulk of the material had already been paid. Several hundred dollars worth of material and expended labor were worthless unless the work was finished and shipped. They advanced sufficient cash for me to pay the workers on a daily basis. Every day at lunch time I had to go to their office on Lake Street with a list of employees working that day and wait for the cash. At the plant at the end of the day, I paid each of the girls as they walked out of the door.

On the night of May 1, about three o'clock in the morning, the telephone by my bed started ringing and woke me up. An unknown voice gave me the message that fire had broken out at the plant. By the time I got there the fire was out, leaving the smell of smoke and pools of water on the floor and on all the work benches. Apparently it had started in a trash barrel near the varnish tanks. Fortunately, someone in one of the other factories that occupied the building had noticed the smoke or heard the fire alarm. Very little damage had been done except by water and smoke in the area closest to the varnish tank. We still managed to salvage and finish off some transformers that were already in the final stages. But most of the remaining stocks of coils, insulation materials, and copper wire were too badly damaged by smoke or water to be used safely. This essentially was the end of Preferred Transformer.

A few of the customers, particularly in New York, took advantage of the situation and did not pay their outstanding invoices. Fortunately, those that did pay, together with the proceeds of the auction of the equipment, furniture and the insurance payment, completely covered the outstanding balance with ABCO, and some money was left over to repay the workers' paychecks that had bounced, pay Blue Cross premiums for them and to make a partial payment to I.R.S.. In adversity one always finds some people who will go out of their way to help. Several of the older women workers liked me and understood that I was doing the best I could to save their jobs, and when the going really got tough, pitched in and worked hard, not only at their own particular job, but to help with any other tasks to keep things going. Joe Heller, president of H&H Coil, another small transformer manufacturer and competitor located a couple of blocks away, one day had a problem and had called on me to ask for assistance. I had willingly given it to him.

In turn he became a good Samaritan in my final days. When I needed small quantities of some material to finish a job, I called him and he brought it to me personally. After the fire we had a number of transformers that needed varnish treatment and our facility was no longer usable. He came over with his truck, picked up all the material, took it to his plant, carried out the treatment and brought it back to us. He only asked for payment of the wages of his workers for the time they spent on our products. I took all the designs and customer files from our plant over to him for safe keeping. He completed a couple of our outstanding orders and he managed to get additional orders from some of my customers for our designs. He split his profit with me 50-50. This money enabled me to pay off some of the obligations of Preferred for which I was personally responsible as president of the company.

Fifteen months later, on September 25, 1964, I finally closed out the Preferred Transformer bank account because the income from these various sources had finally dwindled to almost nothing. My problems with paying off the obligations to I.R.S. dragged on for another couple of years.

Even the lawyer, whom I had taken on for Preferred Transformer after the death of Theodore Stone, turned out to be a friend in need. I used him very little, I couldn't afford his fees. He had a big office in Wacker Drive. But in the final weeks I had so many problems, I had to go to him for advice several times. He gave freely of his time, gave me good advice, wrote a number of letters to people trying to sue me or the company, but he never sent me a bill for his services during these last several weeks. The last time I saw him, I mentioned this.

He said, "Fortunately, I have clients who can afford to pay me well. You can't; I know that and I believe in you. I hope that before long you will be out of your troubles, and perhaps then you will become another rich client."

These sixteen months were the most difficult period for me in my whole life. In terms of mental stress, more difficult even than the war years or the two months of the Warsaw Uprising. During those terrible times I was in constant physical danger, and so were those that I loved. But mentally, I did not have to make any great decisions. I had little responsibility for others, there were not many alternatives to consider. My only consolation was that the practical education I received from this experience was better than any I could have obtained at the most prestigious graduate business school. This difficult educational course was immeasurably helpful in my later career. Nevertheless, it is not a course I would ever want to take again.

16

BACK TO ENGINEERING

After the collapse of Preferred Transformer Corporation, I was in a desperate situation. During the last few weeks I didn't pay myself a penny. Lili cut expenses to the bone and we lived off savings. Now there wasn't much left in the savings account, and I had no job. I wrote letters and telephoned everyone I could think of that I had ever met professionally, looking for some job opportunity. The only people I did not call were those associated with General Electric; pride did not allow me to do that.

Among others, I called Joe Sola, the inventor of the ferroresonant transformer. I had some contact with him during litigation over patents between General Electric and Sola Electric. He probably didn't remember me at all, but he did pass me on to someone else in the organization, and in a few days I was asked to come in for an interview at the Sola plant in Elk Grove Village, just down the street from the Precision Transformer building, now standing empty. I talked for a short while with the engineering manager, who then passed me on to Harry Gerdes, who was section engineer in charge of transformer design. The conversation was pleasant, but obviously I was over qualified for the job opening that Harry had and had virtually no specific experience in ferroresonant circuit design.

Another of my contacts was Jerry Frank. I had met him and had discussions with him on a couple of occasions at AIEE meetings. Now he was vice president of marketing for Hevi-Duty Electric, a manufacturer of transformers based in Milwaukee. Once more *thirteen* proved to be a lucky number for me. On May 13 he telephoned and asked me to come to an interview at the new plant in Lake Geneva, Wisconsin. I talked with Jerry and then had a brief interview with Harry Eikenberry, the recently hired new president of the company. A few days later they asked me to come back to Lake Geneva for further talks which resulted in a job offer — to be manager for a newly acquired product line of laboratory equipment.

I was deliriously happy; this was much better than I had ever expected. A great weight had left my shoulders. I felt young again, the sun was shining, my Guardian Angel was smiling at me. I returned home and broke the news to Lili; she cried with relief. The children perked up to see us both in a happy mood once more after months of gloom.

I had been so desperate I would have accepted any reasonable job to tide me over, but this looked like a really good opportunity. I would be on the ground floor starting a new marketing endeavor. My assignment was to put together a national sales organization and a major sales campaign including the preparation of literature, establishing pricing policies, advertising, the works. I was very excited. After months of bad dreams, now I couldn't sleep making plans and thinking of all the things I would do in the next few weeks. My life was starting on a fresh new course. Even the salary that I was offered was much better than I had hoped for, about $16,000 a year with promises of bonuses if everything went well.

On a sunny May day I drove to Milwaukee's west side, where the Hevi-Duty Electric sales department under Jerry Frank was located next to grain silos of the parent company. I quickly learned my way around the company. Hevi-Duty Electric was originally part of Hevi-Duty Furnace Company, a well-established old time Milwaukee industry. It and Sola Electric Company of Chicago were the first companies acquired by Froedert Malt Company, the supplier of this crucial ingredient to most of the breweries in the Midwest. This cash-rich company had realized that markets were changing and had decided to diversify into other types of manufacturing. The new holding company was called Basic Products Company. One result of the infusion of new cash was the building of new factories, for Hevi-Duty, in Watertown, Wisconsin; for Sola Electric, in the Chicago suburb of Elk Grove Village.

Most recently the rapid growth of Hevi-Duty Electric had created the need for another new factory in the resort of Lake Geneva, Wisconsin, to which the administrative staff had also moved. Hevi-Duty was not very efficiently organized: sales offices in Milwaukee, engineering and production for general purpose transformers and some other products, 40 miles west in Watertown and engineering and production for control and lighting transformers, as well as administration, in Lake Geneva, 40 miles from Milwaukee and 50 miles from Watertown. Jerry Frank took advantage of my previous experience to tap my brains in several long discussions. He complained about the problems the sales department had in getting realistic delivery information from the factory and the lack of responsiveness from the engineering staff.

Basic Product's latest acquisition was a small company on the north side of Chicago which built specialized instruments, mostly custom built. It had been attached to Hevi-Duty Electric and Jerry hoped to use it to diversify into instrumentation and other electronic products. I spent several days at the company; it was small and had only half a dozen employees. The founder, Dave Davenport, had left another instrument company, Associated Research, to start up on his own, but quickly found that he needed much larger resources than he possessed. He was much more fortunate than I had been at Preferred because he quickly found a buyer. I quickly learned that most of his products were copies of Associated Research designs with which we would be competing. I also discovered that he was not a very trustworthy individual. He was a great talker; he was always telling long involved stories about how wonderful this or that was, how much better than anything any competitor built, but it was very difficult to pin him down to specifics.

Anyway, with the help of his engineers, I got a basic understanding of the product line and the costs, assuming that the numbers I was given were accurate. (It turned out later that their methods of cost calculation were crude and full of omissions.) We designed a series of product pamphlets and got them printed. Then I started traveling around the country to put together a new network of sales representatives. Like most smaller manufacturers Hevi-Duty sold its products nationwide through a network of independent entrepreneurs called sales representatives. The existing Hevi-Duty reps were not suitable for the new product line because they handled general industrial products such as wire and cable, heavy switchgear as well as transformers. Therefore, in general, they did not call on the possible buyers of the new instrument line. My job was to set up a new network of reps who specialized in compatible products.

On Friday before the Labor Day weekend, I completed a two-week long trip which took me through the Southwest, up the West coast and finished in Florida. On Tuesday I arrived at my office a few minutes after 9 a.m. To my surprise, someone was sitting in my chair with his feet on my desk. For a moment I didn't realize who it was. I had not seen Harry Eikenberry since my job interview in May. He was a rather heavy set man, with a round face, full lips, heavy eyebrows which made him look as if he was scowling, although in actual fact he was quite jovial. He never liked to beat about the bush and came straight to the point.

"Biega, do you always come to work so late?" he asked.

"No, I am usually here early, but after a two-week long trip, I forgot that it takes over an hour to drive here from home," I answered, sitting down in the visitor's chair.

"Well don't make a habit of it. How do you like your work?"

"Fine, I'm really getting into it and I think I am making good progress."

Then I proceeded with an account of what I had accomplished during the past several weeks.

Then he dropped the bombshell.

"I don't think that this product line will fit in well with our program," he said calmly. "We are talking about it with Sola Electric. It might fit with them better."

"But don't worry," he continued. "I've got another job for you. How would you like to be manager of engineering?"

I was flabbergasted. I didn't know whether I was hearing this correctly. It didn't make sense to spend so much money and time preparing the new product line for nationwide marketing, and then just throw it overboard. After a moment's pause, I replied, "I don't think I would like that at all. I really enjoy marketing and sales, much more than engineering. That's why I left G.E."

"This isn't just engineering we're talking about. It's management. A chance to show what you can do to straighten out a department that's got a lot of good people but doesn't have any direction. Jerry Frank says he has told you about all his complaints."

"What about ___ (the present engineering manager)?" I asked.

"I am getting rid of him," said Harry very casually.

I started probing what kind of salary he had in mind for this job. He mentioned a figure. Although it was more than I was being paid now, I wasn't very excited. The engineering department was in Watertown. It would no longer be possible for me to commute daily. I would have to rent a room and live there during the week. Eventually, we would have to sell our house in Deerfield and move to Watertown. I didn't think that Lili would like living in a small provincial Wisconsin town; neither would I, for that matter. He said that we would like Oconomowoc located on a lake of the same name, halfway between Watertown and Milwaukee. Many people working in Milwaukee lived there; he and his wife did too. I suggested an addition to my pay to cover extra living expenses while I maintained a double residency. He said that something could be worked out. I don't think he mentioned at all that the new position would be a staff position and subject to management bonus.

Finally he said, "There's no point in you staying here, go home and discuss this with your wife. I'll meet you for breakfast tomorrow morning at 8:30 at the Red Carpet Inn on the Milwaukee Bypass. I'll expect your decision then."

I drove back to Deerfield, thinking all the time about this conversation. As I explained to Lili when I got home, this was a definite career advancement, a significant promotion. Nevertheless, the prospect of uprooting again, leaving the Chicago area where we now had so many friends, living in the "wilds" of Wisconsin, wasn't very appealing. How would the children respond to this; what are Wisconsin schools like? Certainly unlikely that they would be on the same level as the North Shore schools. The more I thought about the conversation with Harry, the more convinced I became that if turned the offer down, I would be without a job again. It occurred to me that perhaps I had been hired by Eikenberry with this idea in mind, that the Sales Manager position had been created just to try me out.

Conversations with Harry several months later proved this theory to have been correct. So by the end of the day we came to the conclusion that I didn't have much choice but to accept, considering our strained financial situation.

The next morning I made sure to leave home early enough to get to the Red Carpet Inn before the appointed time. Even so, as I drove up, so did Harry. After sitting down at the table, I pressed the issue of compensation for the extra costs of maintaining two households and got agreement to pay for the cost of a room until I was able to move. Then I said, "OK, Harry, I accept your offer!"

We shook hands, and then he said: "Finish your breakfast, Bill. We'll go straight away to Watertown and I'll introduce you to everyone at the plant."

"What about ___?" I asked.

"Oh, I fired him yesterday. He cleaned out his desk and left immediately," Harry said nonchalantly. Obviously, Harry had no doubts what my decision would be.

When we reached the Hevi-Duty Electric plant in Watertown, he had the entire engineering staff assembled; then he explained his dissatisfaction with the performance of the engineering department, that their previous manager had been warned several times, but had not responded. Then he introduced me, said a little about my background, and expressed his confidence that I would lead the engineering department to develop new designs and methods which would make it possible for Hevi-Duty Electric to achieve the goals set by the parent corporation.

In turn, I said a few words to the effect that I was honored to be given such confidence and that with the help of all the staff, I hoped to be able to achieve Harry's goals. Then I was introduced to each of them in turn.

Afterwards, Harry introduced me to the heads of all the other departments. To my surprise, the production manager turned out to be Al Charbonneau. After the demise of Precision Transformer he had been offered the job at Hevi-Duty Electric. Like me he was rooming in Watertown and returning to his home in Illinois during weekends.

After lunch we drove to the plant in Lake Geneva where the whole procedure was repeated. There was a small engineering staff also at this plant under Hans Kort, a German engineer, responsible for the products produced in this facility. By now it was late afternoon, so I returned home along US Highway 12, which would become very familiar to me during the next two years.

The next morning I drove to Milwaukee to take my personal effects from my office there. Jerry Frank had already been briefed by Harry. He congratulated me and assured me that everyone in the sales department was confident that I would make engineering more responsive to the needs of the market place. I spent only a few minutes with him and chatting to some of the others in the office before continuing on to Watertown to get acquainted with my new staff and responsibilities. Needless to say, the engineers were all disconcerted with the sudden change and were apprehensive about their future under this unknown new boss. Fortunately for me, the previous manager had been aloof and had no great friends, so it did not take me more than a few weeks to gain the confidence of my staff. From the beginning I made it known that I would expect complete cooperation and that I expected to make many changes in procedures, but that I did not expect to make any shakeups of people as long as everyone did his best.

I spent the next three nights in a motel in town, using the evenings looking for a room. I found one in the home of an elderly couple on the north side of the small town. It was nicely furnished and had its own separate bathroom. I also had the use of the kitchen facilities, which I used for breakfast and an occasional evening snack. During the next year and a half, I ate most of my evening meals in restaurants. I got to know every eatery within a 15 mile radius of Watertown and along the road to Lake Geneva. Those that weren't good saw me only once; about eight of them ended on my list of preferred places. In those days it was possible to eat a reasonably good dinner for about $5 in the small towns of Wisconsin, so I spent about $20 a week on evening meals. The plant cafeteria served a good lunch for about $1.50.

Engineering design was very haphazard. Just like Meeker in the old days at G.E., the engineers would start each design from scratch with little regard to what other similar designs already existed. Consequently, the paperwork involved in each new design was tremendous. What was worse, there was little standardization of parts; therefore, production runs were short and required continual setups. Likewise, purchasing could not be performed until designs were complete, which resulted in long production cycles, many delays and missed deliveries. This was the cause of the dissatisfaction of the sales department. My major task was to change the entire engineering philosophy and start a crash program aiming towards standardization with ultimately lower costs and shorter manufacturing cycles. The situation in Lake Geneva was easier. Here all the small transformers, specifically a wide range of control transformers supplied to the major industrial control companies in the United States (Square D, Cutler Hammer, Allen Bradley) were designed and manufactured. These industries required a high degree of standardization. In any case, the production runs of these units ran in the high hundreds and even thousands. Incidentally, this was the kind of market I had intended to break into at Preferred Transformer.

I settled into a routine. Leave Deerfield either Sunday evening, or if we had some social activity on Sunday, at 6 a.m. Monday morning, for the 2 1/2 hour drive to Watertown. I drove up US 41, which had little traffic at that time, to the Wisconsin state line, where it became Interstate 90. I took the by-pass around Milwaukee, which was then only a two lane road. Finally I took State 16 through Oconomowoc to Watertown. During the week I made at least one trip to the sales office in Milwaukee. Whenever possible, I arranged this visit for Monday morning and went there on my way from home.

At least once a week I drove to the Lake Geneva plant, another 50 mile drive. Harry Eikenberry, cognizant of the fact that both I and Charbonneau had to go home to Illinois for the weekend, generally held the weekly staff meeting in the conference room at Lake Geneva on Friday afternoons. From there it was a fairly easy 1 1/2 hour drive through Fox Lake to Wauconda and then across to Deerfield. I always stopped at a German store near Fox Lake to pick up good rye bread and homemade sausages.

Watertown was rather a sleepy little burg. The downtown consisted of half a dozen blocks with one small department store and a theater. Before the completion of the Interstate highway the traffic through town was heavy. The road crossed the Rock River at a point where there was a park. Signs warned traffic to beware of "Ducks crossing." The Hevi-Duty plant was the main source of income and activity in the town. There were actually two divisions, Hevi-Duty Electric and the original Hevi-Duty Furnace company, which manufactured a wide range of electric industrial furnaces and had been established many years before in Milwaukee.

I did not establish any social relationships with my engineers but did get to know a couple of people from the furnace manufacturing plant. I started playing bridge at the contract bridge club in Oconomowoc at least once a month. My partner was the wife of one of the furnace division engineers. They lived on a farm south of Watertown and often invited me to dinner. Almost every week I had dinner with Al Charbonneau and we reminisced about old times. More importantly we discussed how to best change engineering documentation to improve production efficiency. Somehow I became acquainted with a worker in the local telephone company office, Anne. She loved to dance and it became a Wednesday evening routine to go to one of the bars in the area that had a dance floor and music, generally jukeboxes. She was a divorcee with a 14 year old daughter and a boyfriend who lived in Milwaukee whom she saw every weekend and finally married.

Gradually, I got things whipped into shape the way I wanted. Efficiency improved, design time cycles improved and business was getting better. Hevi-Duty Electric was one of the few independent transformer manufacturers that was growing. The main reason for its success was that the company was heavily involved in the industrial market and had well established business relationships with several large Milwaukee-based companies such as Allen-Bradley, Allis Chalmers, Square D, Cutler Hammer and Harnishveger. Special transformers for the electric furnaces manufactured by the sister company also provided a substantial contribution to the overall balance sheet.

In addition, Hevi-Duty had a couple of special product lines for which there was little competition. One of these was a group of very special transformer systems used for providing the runway and taxiway lighting at all major airports. General Electric was the only major competitor, but Hevi-Duty had developed some features that were very advantageous and consequently provided us with a competitive edge. We had established a good relationship with Westinghouse which competed with G.E. on all the lighting systems but did not have their own control transformers. Gary Doehler was the product engineer for this highly successful product line. A retired engineer, Al Hauck, still worked as a consultant and had started developing a line of automatic voltage regulators (or voltage stabilizers as I preferred to call them in accordance with international usage), which extended the Sola Electric product line called *Solatron* into the high power sizes. I personally was interested in developing this product and worked closely with Al on putting the product line together. I was co-inventor with him on the patent application that we filed, which was subsequently granted.

We had put the Deerfield house on the market, but this happened to be a time of a housing market slump. The Fort Wayne situation was repeating itself. We only had one offer at a price which was quite unacceptable. So the situation continued into the winter with me coming home only for the weekends. Several times that winter I took the train rather than fighting the snow and ice. The Milwaukee Road train "Hiawatha Limited" from Minneapolis to Chicago passed through Watertown about 4 p.m. It stopped only in Milwaukee and then in Glenview, where Lili could pick me up. In the reverse direction I boarded the night mail train to Minneapolis at about 7 p.m. on Sunday and arrived in Watertown about 10 o'clock.

I got caught on Interstate 94 in a late blizzard in March, 1964. I had been invited to dinner in Milwaukee by the salesman for one of the suppliers of magnetic steel and laminations, whom I had known since G.E. days. It was snowing very lightly, a typical springtime flurry, or so I thought! During dinner I looked out of the window and it was snowing harder, the snow was sticking to the pavement. I told my host that I had better finish my dessert and quickly get back to Watertown. He offered to put me up for the night, but I declined; it still didn't look that bad. As I headed out of Milwaukee towards Waukesha, the snow was starting to drift and the going was getting tougher. I decided to leave the Interstate at the Waukesha exit and stop at a motel for the night. This turned out to be impossible; a tractor-trailer was stuck sideways across the exit. I tried to get off on the entrance ramp, but a drift had already piled up across it. So I continued on doggedly. I knew that there was a motel right by the expressway close to Oconomowoc, and I hoped to be able to reach it. By now it was snowing so hard that I could barely see. Fortunately, there was no other traffic on the road. I just followed the "cats-eyes" glowing in my headlights. The driving was not too bad because the wind was blowing the snow off the center of the road, but I did have to keep swerving to avoid drifts building up along the side. Suddenly I plowed in to a drift that was at least three feet high; I didn't see it in time. Ironically, the left lane was almost clear. I tried every trick I knew of but couldn't back out of it. Just two weeks before I had removed the snow shovel and bag of sand that I had carried in the trunk all winter long. I wasn't dressed for winter either. I had a full tank of gas, so I ran the engine to keep the inside warm and kept the blinkers flashing, hoping that no one would plow into me from behind. I kept the window open just slightly and periodically got out and pulled the snow away from around the exhaust pipe with my bare hands.

I must have dozed off. When I awoke the snow had let up enough that I could see lights a couple of hundred yards ahead! I sloshed and slithered through the snow to the motel, climbed over the fence and banged on the door. Someone opened the door and gave me a shovel. I returned to the car and started digging a path out of the drift to the open part of the road. I had just about finished when a snow-plow came along and piled snow up in front of me again! I cursed and swore and went back to digging. The eastern sky was just starting to lighten when I got my car out onto the cleared pavement. By now it had stopped snowing and I had no trouble after that in getting home for a hot shower and a big breakfast!

That summer changes occurred in the company. The directors hired Frank Roby as the new president of Basic Products Corporation. Frank had been vice-president of a medium sized conglomerate, Federal Pacific Electric. Apparently he promised the directors that he would speed up the diversification program and improve the profitability of the corporation. One of the first things he did was spin off the parent division, Froedert Malt, and used the cash generated by this to acquire other electric and high tech companies. Having gotten rid of the only non-electric division, he decided Basic Products Corporation was no longer an appropriate name. He chose to capitalize on the well known name of Sola, which for years had been a leader in the field of voltage stabilization. The new name he selected was Sola Basic Industries. Now all the literature, stationery and nameplates of the various divisions had to be changed because Frank insisted that all divisional logos be changed to one he had designed to create a uniformity of appearance throughout the corporation.

The first acquisition followed a few weeks later — Lindberg, a manufacturer of large industrial furnaces both gas and electric, located in old buildings adjacent to the Western Avenue station of the Milwaukee Road in Chicago. Hevi-Duty Furnace was then combined with Lindberg under a single management and name. Both manufacturing facilities were to be maintained, but many operations were to be transferred to Watertown because there was no room for expansion at the Chicago plant.

Frank Roby hired a consulting company which specialized in finding new locations for industries, particularly in the south. We received several proposals which were distributed to the staff for comments. One of the proposed locations was Goldsboro, North Carolina. We all discarded this location. It was a small town with no other industry in the middle of a rural tobacco growing area. The closest educational center and airport is Raleigh, distant some 50 miles. Harry was equally opposed to this location. However, Frank took him along on a trip to look at each of the proposed places. Frank chose Goldsboro, basically because he expected to be able to get low labor costs, and particularly because the town was so anxious to attract a major industry that they gave the land free of charge and would exempt the company from local taxes for a number of years. I don't how Frank twisted Harry's arm, but after his trip, Harry suddenly became a Goldsboro enthusiast.

Now, in turn, he started twisting the arms of staff members to make them agree to move when the plant moved. Of course, this event was still a year away. First, the plant had to be designed and built. I was quite uninterested in this move and told Harry so. However, the matter of decision was still not pressing.

Just before Christmas, one Monday morning (it would be nice if the date were the 13th, but it wasn't; it was the 14th) I came to my office after the long drive from Deerfield a few minutes after eight o'clock. This was really *déja-vu* — Harry Eikenberry was sitting in my chair behind my desk.

"Good morning, Biega. Do you always come in late on Monday mornings?"

This time I didn't try to make any excuses, just sat down in the visitor's chair and waited to hear what Harry had on his mind.

"How do you rate your engineering department?" he asked.

"In general I am satisfied; things are going pretty well now, I think. Of course, there are still things I would like to improve," and I continued to discuss various details that I thought still needed improving.

"I've already told you that I am very happy with the progress that has been made, and your last raise is proof that I'm pleased," he said.

"But," he continued, "there is another division of Sola Basic that has serious problems with its engineering department, a similar situation to that we had here at Hevi-Duty. I would hate to lose you, with the move coming up, but I have been asked whether I could let you go to do another engineering department reorganization. In principle I have agreed, but, of course, the decision is up to you. How would you like to take over Sola Electric engineering?"

I was stunned. This was the ideal solution for me, I thought quickly. I would not have to sell our house; I would not have to agonize over whether to move to Goldsboro; this would be great. After a pause I responded, "Harry, I have been very happy working for you and I would hate to leave you and all the great people at Hevi-Duty. But Sola Electric is close to my home and it would solve my personal problems, so I have to say that I am interested in this proposal."

"Whom would you suggest to take over your job?" Harry asked.

A discussion followed about the people that worked for me. I said that although I still had reservations, Roy Bancroft, the engineering supervisor, had learned a lot and had become much firmer and more decisive, and I thought should be given the chance to prove himself. Harry was always a man to make quick decisions. He halted the discussion and said, "Let's tell Glenn Konker that you are interested."

Quickly he dialed the president of Sola Electric.

"Hi Glenn," he said. "You remember our discussion at the staff meeting last week. I've just talked to Biega and he is interested in coming with you. When do you want him to start?"

There was a long silence at this end of the wire. I couldn't hear what Glenn was saying, but I imagine he was protesting that he had only raised a hypothetical question, that he hadn't yet decided on a course of action, etc.,etc., (a typical Glenn Konker reaction as I later discovered). Harry fidgeted; finally he exploded.

"Cut the crap, Glenn. Make up your mind. If you don't want Biega, say so now. That'll make me real happy. But I won't discuss it again."

More silence at this end. Finally, "O.K. Glenn, Biega will see you in your office at 10 o'clock Wednesday morning. If you two agree, then let's make it snappy and get it over with."

Harry hung up and turned to me. "Glenn wants to talk to you first, but in principle he wants to go ahead. I suggest that we make the move right after the New Year. And remember, Bill," now he got on a personal note as one friend to another, "Sola is a bigger company than Hevi-Duty in overall business. I think their engineering department is about 60 people (Hevi-Duty at that time had a total of about 35 or 40), so you should demand more money. And not a word to anyone until we are ready to make the announcement. Go home tomorrow and tell Lili, she should be happy."

I had the meeting with Glenn Konker. It went well; I got another salary increase and the starting date was set for the first Monday in January. I went back to Watertown with a briefcase full of literature covering Sola products, a listing of all personnel and other information that would be useful for me to study before starting.

The announcements were made simultaneously at Sola Electric and Hevi-Duty on New Year's Eve. Roy Bancroft was surprised at his promotion. That afternoon we had an early staff meeting in the conference room at Lake Geneva, then the staff retired to a local bar, where everyone wished me good luck. The end of this chapter in my career was a happy one for me and for Lili.

17

THE SIXTIES

The Sixties were a bad decade. The Cold War intensified with both the United States and the Soviet Union adding to their nuclear arsenals aimed at each other. Cuba under Castro became more rigidly communist and started exporting its type of revolution to other countries in Central and South America. The denunciation of Stalin by Kruschev and his visit to the U.S. in 1959 raised hopes of some relaxation. This did occur in the Soviet Union itself, but there was no sign of this in external affairs. In September 1962 it was learned that nuclear armed missiles were being installed in Cuba; after a tense confrontation, the Soviets backed down and removed the missiles. President John Kennedy stepped up assistance to South Vietnam in its opposition to infiltration by communist guerrillas from North Vietnam. After the assassination of John Kennedy on November 22, 1963, President Johnson escalated the deployment of U.S. Forces to Vietnam until they reached a peak of 543,000 at the end of his last term. Nixon became president in January 1969 and started gradual withdrawals of American troops while attempting to push through an agreement with North Vietnam to end the war. I have never understood why American liberals and the media have always called this war "Nixon's war." The involvement was started by Kennedy and escalated by Johnson. It was Nixon that finally brought it to an end.

It was a decade of continual unrest in the country — race riots and demonstrations, anti-war demonstrations, particularly on the college campuses, culminating in burning of flags and draft cards and anti-

nuclear demonstrations obstructing not only the building and shipment of missiles but also construction of electric power plants.
Massive rioting in Los Angeles (Watts) in 1965, and in Newark and
Detroit in 1967, caused extensive damage and many deaths. The
assassinations of Robert Kennedy and Martin Luther King resulted in
more outbreaks of violence. The only positive happenings in the
1960's were successes in the space program culminating in the first
landing on the moon July 20, 1969, and the continuing overall
economic prosperity.

These same problems were reflected in life at home and in
Deerfield generally. At Deerfield High School discipline was very good
at first. The students in general were neatly dressed because of the
strict dress code. One day Peter was sent home because he had gone
to school without a belt in his pants. You might say that this was
excessive, but Lili and I agreed with the policy as such. This was 1964;
the kids were beginning to run around in torn bluejeans and dirty tee
shirts. It seemed the more holes and frayed edges, the better. Fine, we
said, for playing in the park but not at the dinner table, certainly not
in school. So no big deal, Peter put on his belt and went back to school.

A few weeks later the son of a wealthy lawyer got sent home
for an infraction of the dress code. The father sued Deerfield High
School for denying his child his constitutional right to express his
individuality by dressing like a vagabond! After some agonizing
meetings the school board decided they didn't have the money to fight
a clever lawyer. They backed down and the dress code went out the
window. Some of the students went out of their way to flaunt their
new "freedom" and to annoy the teachers. Consequently, discipline
went to hell also. The new "in" thing became smoking marijuana,
particularly since this was an illegal substance. It became normal
in the evenings and at weekends to see groups of teen-agers lounging
all over downtown Deerfield in all kinds of ragged garments, most
smoking cigarettes, many of which were of the forbidden kind,
judging by the cloying aroma.

Another aspect of this new flaunting of disrespect for authority
and for all the "square" grownups was a growth in vandalism.
Antennas were torn off cars, streetlights and signs broken or defaced.
Fortunately, spray painting didn't get started in the big cities until a

few years later. One of the most spectacular acts of vandalism in Deerfield was the cutting down of the towers of the local radio station. The studios of this particular station were in Highland Park and mainly broadcast soft music. This irked the kids because its signal tended to drown out the reception of their "music" from a favorite rock station that was very close in transmission frequency. So one night a group of junior highschool students took wire cutters and severed the cables holding up the two towers. Fortunately, no one got hurt. Some of them got caught because they were so busy admiring their achievement that they didn't notice the squad car driving up. Much to the embarrassment of the police, two of the boys were sons of their own colleagues.

At home we fought this horrible trend. Nobody was allowed to sit down at the table unless reasonably dressed and clean. But it was hard, too many parents gave in. It was especially hard on Lili because for three years I was home very little, first fighting my own battle to save Preferred Transformer, then working at Hevi-Duty, coming home only for weekends. However, at the beginning it wasn't so bad at our home. Peter always tended to be neat and rather conservative, Mark was used to the routine of getting dressed up for Sunday dinners and all festive occasions and didn't resist. The problem really didn't get out of hand until Annette and Philip were going to junior high and later high school.

Peter had made fantastic progress with his asthma since coming to Deerfield. In Fort Wayne Lili took him regularly to an allergist who had given Peter a series of shots but with no obvious improvement. He was on a continual diet. Because of his particular allergy to fish, we never ate it at home. After coming to Deerfield, he joined the local scouts. One Friday he went with the troop to a camp; fortunately, not too far distant. About 10 that evening the scoutmaster brought him home violently ill. In those days Catholics still religiously ate fish on Friday nights and because so many of the boys were Catholic they had fried fish on the campfire. Just the odor was enough to bring on an attack.

Lili found an allergist, Dr. Rappaport, in the Ravinia section of Highland Park. When Lili told him about the treatment that Peter had received in Fort Wayne, he didn't believe her until he obtained the files. He was astounded that someone claiming to be an allergist could have handled this severe case so badly. Peter was given a series of tests and then started on a rigorous treatment schedule: first, a series of shots three times a week, then twice a week , then weekly. After about a year they were cut back to every other week, finally monthly. Each series consisted of a number of injections of carefully controlled amounts of antibodies to the various things Peter was allergic to. After four years Dr. Rappaport pronounced Peter essentially cured. He was very proud of his success in this difficult case. Peter, who had been thin and underdeveloped, at age 15 started growing rapidly not only in height but in breadth too. Now he could eat almost everything, although he always remained sensitive to certain kinds of fish and to cats and dogs.

Mark managed to get through high school but with rather poor grades. He had problems with doing homework, and most of the time I was not home to help him. He was too involved with more interesting activities. He played football and was on the school basketball team. He also played in the school golf team. He had caddied at the Fort Wayne Country Club and learned to play with the other caddies; this was the sport that he seemed most interested in. Like all Illinois high school students he took driver's education classes and just after his 16th birthday he got his first driver's license.

Only a few months later he had a horrifying experience. It so happened that Baba and Bill Murray-Lawes were visiting us in October. During the weekend I had let Mark take the car, the Dodge, to go somewhere or other. We were sitting having a drink when the phone rang; it was the State Police. Mark had had an accident. I rushed to get him. He was shaken up and in shock. It was a miracle that neither he, nor his friend, had suffered any injuries because the car was a total wreck. He had been driving south on US 12 near Lake Zurich and had just started up from a traffic light when he was hit hard from behind by a speeding, drunken driver. The impact from the rear was so powerful that the front seat collapsed; the bolts holding it pulled right out of the rusty floor, so that they both fell backwards. The car was then catapulted into a tree at the side of the road. But for the collapse of the front seat they probably would both have been badly injured from the subsequent impact. There were no seat belts in those days.

After this traumatic experience, Mark bought a second hand motorcycle, in spite of our protests. But he needed transportation, and we now only had one car and momentarily were unable to buy another one. I was up to my neck in financial problems at Preferred Transformer and I used the station wagon every day to go to work. Once more Providence was watching over Mark; he had two more narrow escapes. After the second one, in which a car made a left hand turn right in front of him, Mark lost his enthusiasm for riding motorcycles. Lili sold it for him and got almost as much for it as he had originally paid. He used the money to buy an ancient Buick which served him for quite a long time.

With Peter we had no problems. He had a very friendly disposition and everybody liked him. He was a natural salesman and he never had any trouble earning pocket money. He got odd jobs, even did some babysitting. For a while he had a newspaper route in the neighborhood which required him to collect payment weekly from his customers, who tipped him liberally. Like Mark, Peter started caddying as soon as his health had improved. At the Jewish Country Club in Deerfield, he became the favorite caddy for a number of the matrons who gave him big tips. He always knew how to charm the ladies with compliments on their game. At school he was unable to participate physically in the sporting activities, but he attended all events and was chosen as manager of the high school basketball team. He was more selective than Mark in hise choice of friends and thus kept out of trouble most of the time.

His best friend was Jim Goulka, who was in the same class. We liked Jim too; he often came over to our house and wanted to learn some Polish words. His mother was of Polish origin from a large Milwaukee family. We became good friends of Sylvia and Jim Senior and partied together several times a year. Jim was the owner of a small company which made plastic extrusions for the automobile and electronics industries. Sylvia worked with him in the company, which fortunately was doing very well. Their daughter Joanna also came over frequently to learn Polish phrases from Lili.

In his junior year Peter and a friend decided to go to Florida during the spring break to join the thousands of young people from eastern colleges that swarm like lemmings down to the beaches of Fort

Lauderdale every year at that time. They suspected that they would not get permission for such an escapade, so they decided to take off without telling anyone. Peter didn't come home from school at the usual time that Friday and Lili was already worrying when the phone rang. It was Peter calling collect from Hammond, Indiana. Lili was very angry, but at this point there wasn't much we could do about it except exact a promise to call every day to tell us where he was. That same night they got a ride as far as some small town in southern Indiana where they decided to stop for the night. It was cold and they had no money for a motel, but they had a bright idea. They went to the police station and good salesman Peter talked the local police into letting them sleep in an unused cell in the jail! They were fortunate and got rides all the way down to Fort Lauderdale, arriving Saturday evening. After spending two days on the beaches, they found some students heading back to a Wisconsin university who gave them a ride all the way back to Deerfield. They were let off on the toll road close to our house, climbed over the fence and were welcomed back home by parents relieved that this adventure had come off without any trouble.

Unfortunately, Peter had problems with school subjects. It was probably a side effect of his long time disability with asthma and allergies that he had a reading difficulty. He took some special courses which didn't help much. As a consequence, he had problems keeping up with his studies, reading assignments and homework. He probably got better grades than most other students would have done, under the same conditions, particularly from female teachers, because of his charming personality.

The Sixties didn't spare Lili and me although we tried to hide the strained relationships from the children. I was under severe mental stress during the Preferred Transformer period. Lili, of course, was also very worried and during 1963 had to keep the home going with very little money available. Tempers got short; Lili seemed to blame me for all the problems, even though, as I reminded her, she had taken part in the decision to get involved in this unfortunate venture. She kept putting pressure on me to throw in the towel, to just walk away from the problems and find another job. She couldn't, or wouldn't, understand that I was tied in knots. I felt an obligation to Lee and the others who had put money in the venture to do my utmost to find a solution which would allow at least part of their investment to be recouped. I couldn't just ditch my responsibility to them because the going was tough. After Lee refused the offer from a potential investor because it would have meant losing control, I was sorely tempted to give up. I could justify in my own mind doing that because I had made it clear at the beginning the minimum amount of investment needed, which Lee had promised would be available. The plight we were in was largely a direct result of the failure to get that capital. But I also knew that nobody else would see it that way; they would just blame me and say "Biega wasn't able to handle a tough job. He's a quitter". My pride wouldn't let me do that. I kept on fighting a losing battle, grasping at straws to keep my head above water

I desperately needed some loving words of support and reassurance, but I did not get them. Likewise, I got no support from Lee and John, who had their own serious personal problems now that Precision Transformer was on its last legs, sinking fast and taking their jobs and expectations with it. I was fighting the battle of Preferred Transformer very much alone, worn out mentally and physically with fourteen hour days, six days a week. When I came home I was faced with new problems and complaints; Mark and Peter both needed help with their school work. They were having a difficult time in high school. Lili blamed me for not giving them the time and help they needed. They say that the age of 40 is a stressful time for most men; for me it was a disaster.

At the few parties that we did go to during the weekends I needed relaxation, to take my mind off my problems. Lili liked to spend the time gossiping with other women. I found solace with those women who preferred to dance, be merry and flirt too. Irka, who was a great dancer, and Diana, a flirtatatious cuddly, blonde, provided consolation and distraction from my problems, even if it was only for an evening. After each party there were more quarrels.

Finally, the nightmare ended; matters were taken out of my hands by events over which I had no control. Soon I had a new satisfying job and the money started coming in again, although it took many months to clean up all the obligations I had been saddled with. Lili was relieved that I had a job and was happy that pay checks were coming in again but continued to be dissatisfied because I was away from home so much. This theme would continue for the next 30 years.

In May 1964 Mark graduated, the first of many high school graduations. It took place in the school gymnasium. The ceremony was impressive and Mark was very happy, as were we. Unfortunately, the overall atmosphere at school had caused Mark to apply himself less than needed during the crucial final two years. The poor grade averages that resulted reduced the range of colleges he could get into. I had registered to vote in Wisconsin and had a Wisconsin driving license, so he qualified for in-state tuition fees at any Wisconsin college. I tried at the University of Wisconsin in Madison without success. It was recommended that he enroll in one of the State colleges, then if he did well, he could transfer. So in September 1964 Mark enrolled in the state college in Whitewater. This was convenient, being about half way between Watertown and Lake Geneva, so I could visit him regularly. He did reasonably well so that a year later he was able to transfer to Southern Illinois University in Carbondale. During the summers he worked as a delivery man for Sun Valley Dairy in Highland Park. This was a good job, even though he had to start work at 5:30 in the morning. It provided him the satisfaction of earning good money while driving around in the open air and he got home early in the afternoon and had all evening to play around with his Deerfield friends.

The threat that hung over him was Vietnam, but as long as he stayed in college with passing grades, he had a deferment. Then he was required to register for the draft. To our relief he drew a number that was so high that he was virtually assured that he would never be called up. The disadvantage was that this removed any incentive for him to continue his studies. Although he continued to be enrolled in the university, he failed in a couple of subjects. I drove down to Carbondale to plead with him to continue his studies, to retake the failed courses, not to be discouraged. Finally, I got angry and told Mark that if he dropped out I would no longer provide any financial support. These pleas were unsuccessful. He quit college.

During the next few years, Mark drifted and traveled around. But wherever he was, whatever he was doing, Mark always turned up at home for Christmas. We were very happy that he did, regardless of our feelings about his lack of interest in pursuing what we thought of as a meaningful direction. These annual visits were our only contact with him for a couple of years, although we did occasionally receive postcards from strange places.

After Mark's graduation, our finances had improved sufficiently that we could plan an extended vacation. We decided to go for a trip out to California. Peter and Mark both had summer jobs and were not interested in traveling with their parents and young siblings. While they stayed home, the remaining five of us took off early one morning in June. The steel-gray Chevrolet station wagon, which I had bought at a used car lot when I got the job at Hevi-Duty, had no air conditioning. The weather was hot all through the Midwest and we drove with the windows open. Philip soon got into a fight with Annette and throughout the remainder of our trip, he rode by himself in the rear-facing back seat. Interstate 80 had already been completed almost all the way to Denver, so we were able to cover 700 miles the first day arriving, very tired and hot in North Platte, Nebraska. Lili was exhausted and went to bed immediately, but the kids and I had a swim in the pool to freshen up and enjoyed hamburgers before turning in.

Our next stop was in Boulder, Colorado, at the house of friends from prisoner-of-war camp. They took us on an excursion into the mountains to collect mushrooms. We had never seen such big ones and in such quantities in our life. Americans never picked them, only the Rosinski's and a Czech professor. Their neighbors looked askance at them every time they came home with baskets full and expected them to all drop dead from food poisoning. These were the best quality boletus, called *porcini* in Italy. We came home with two big buckets full to the brim and enjoyed a delicious dinner.

From then on we drove through beautiful country, the Rockies, to the ancient cliff dwellings at Mesa Verde. Then we took photographs standing together at the corner of Arizona, New Mexico, Colorado and Utah, each of us in a different state, before proceeding to fascinating Monument Valley. A Navajo on horseback allowed us to take his picture, for a fee, against the backdrop of the towering buttes. Nothing we had seen so far on this trip prepared us for our first view of the Grand Canyon. We all stood on the edge, looking down, awestruck. None of us spoke for a long while. Lili and I had, of course, seen many photographs and movies of the great chasm. None of them give more than an inkling of the sheer majesty of the view, and all the shades of color — reds, vermilions, purples, browns, russets, greens, ochers, ... I have never, in all my travels, seen any sight that can compare in grandeur. Of course, we took more photographs, all of which were disappointing when we looked at them. Even a superb artist like Ansel Adams cannot do full justice to the Grand Canyon.

Our next scenic wonder was Yosemite, where we spent the night and watched the spectacle of the waterfall of fire[*], in which a gigantic bonfire was set ablaze at the top of one of the cliffs, various Indian ceremonies were performed, then finally the glowing embers of the fire were pushed over the cliff. Nothing can match the majesty of Grand Canyon, but Yosemite is certainly a close second. The 2,400 foot series of waterfalls was still full of water. We then visited the giant sequoia trees in the Tolumne Grove and drove through the tunnel cut through the trunk of the Dead Giant. From there we climbed to the high meadows. Philip and I braved the icy waters for a very brief swim. We crossed the pass and descended the eastern slope of the Sierra Nevada and continued northward.

Then we recrossed the mountains to visit our friends the Thomases, who had moved from Detroit several years earlier. Janek had built their home in the foothills of the Sierras in the bush on a mountain slope. Wild life was abundant; Janek told us about the puma that often lay on their porch sunning itself on cool winter mornings. On another occasion he had caught a big snake. Not being sure whether it was a harmful or a beneficial one, he coaxed it into a sack. Then he drove all the way to Sacramento to get an identification. It turned out that it was indeed a good snake which helped keep various rodents under control. He took it back to his property and let it out into the woods.

Here we left the children in the care of Anielka and the company of her children while Lili and I drove to San Francisco where I had to attend an IEEE[**] conference. Here, too, we met old friends, Nina and Alex Lempicki. Alex , my friend since high school and now a well known physicist, had come from New York to deliver a lecture.

---

[*] This ceremony is no longer performed for environmental reasons.

[**] IEEE — Institute of Electrical and Electronic Engineers — resulted from a merger of AIEE with the Radio Engineers.

Together we talked up a storm in the evenings while visiting San Francisco's then famous topless nightclubs. After all the beautiful places that we had visited, the drive home through Reno, Salt Lake City and Cheyenne was an anticlimax. This was the most ambitious excursion that we ever made with our children, full of exciting experiences and pleasant meetings with old friends. Unfortunately, Eileen was too young to appreciate most of them, but I think both Annette and Philip learned a lot from this journey through America. Two years later we had another trip to Florida and enjoyed the beaches and visiting various interesting and scenic places, but it was not as exciting.

Another result of improved financial circumstances was that we could now afford to go skiing. eter and I were the first to get skis and boots, which were still fairly simple and not as exorbitantly expensive as they are today. There were several places not too far away with ski hills. The best were Wilmot, on the border of Wisconsin close to Fox Lake, and Alpine Valley, another half an hour further north in Wisconsin. They both had a number of tows and at least one chair lift with runs ranging from beginners to intermediate. Of course, none of them were very long or difficult, but they were well groomed and provided good fun and exercise. Soon the remaining three got their skis and we went together at least once each weekend during the season as long as the weather was nice. Lili never went with us, not even to watch. Both Philip and Eileen became quite proficient and later joined the Snow-flakes club, which provided bus service and ski trips for children up through high school.

Our last skiing trip together was in February 1971, Annette and Philip were both in high school, Eileen in 6th grade. I had promised to take them on a long weekend to Northern Michigan where the slopes were more challenging. Unfortunately, the weather turned bitterly cold. At night the temperature dropped to 30 below zero and even at noon it was not possible to make more than a couple of runs without going into the lodge to warm up. The first night the car froze up and we weren't able to start it in the morning until a tow truck arrived to take it to a garage to thaw it out. The remaining two nights each of us got up in turn every hour to start the engine and run it for a few minutes. The snow was deep and soft, conditions that we were not used to. Eileen got into trouble trying to make a turn and fell, breaking her leg. Fortunately, it was a clean break with no complications, but it put an end to skiing for Eileen for that season. This was when I started wondering whether skiing was worth the misery of being cold most of the time!

Peter graduated from high school the next summer in 1965, but his grades were sufficiently poor that it was a problem finding a college that would accept him. Once more Wisconsin State Colleges came to the rescue. In September 1965 I drove with Peter to Duluth on Lake Superior to enroll him in this northern school. He enjoyed school but, unfortunately, the same problems held him back. At the end of the first year he had failed in at least one subject and he decided to take a rest and look for a job. In the fall of 1966 he started working for NorthWest Airlines at O'Hare airport. He continued in this job for the next three years, most of the time working as a passenger agent, where his personality made him very popular, both with his supervisors and fellow employees, as well as with the customers. At first he lived at home. But as soon as he had settled down in his job he moved out and shared an apartment with some fellow airline employees in Melrose Park, not far from the airport.

It was now 1967. Only three children were left at home. Annette was in high school, doing well in her studies, Philip was in junior high, which was still located in the old building at Wilmot Road and Eileen was at grade school in Woodland Park. Then Philip, in turn, went to high school and Eileen to junior high in the new building on Castlewood. This building was controversial; it was built without any windows and designed for year round air conditioning. I never found out what the architect's reasoning was for this aberration. However, funds ran out and the air conditioning did not get installed in the first year. Needless to say, when the first hot weather came the classrooms were unbearably hot. The kids had to be let out of school early every warm day.

Although both Philip and Annette were doing well scholastically in high school, the pressures of the times adversely influenced their behavior. All the unrest in the collleges and inner cities influenced the attitudes and conduct of high school students. The disappearance of discipline in the schools and lack of respect for any authority influenced their behavior and caused continual problems at home. Lili became increasingly exasperated, which caused angry exchanges with Annette and Philip, but also caused friction between us. Lili continually blamed me for being too lenient. I tried to be tough and insist on proper manners and respect but also felt that it was necessary to bend a little with the changes. I felt that I would lose control completely by being a martinet continually laying down the law. I sought to be reasonable and to talk things over whenever problems arose, hoping to create an atmosphere of mutual trust, although I still insisted on respect for the basic tenets of social behavior.

Both Lili and I got angry if any of the kids didn't come home when they had promised but for different reasons. Lili worried. I objected to the lack of respect for us, the lack of understanding of our feelings. I also got angry if any of them did not fulfill obligations, for example not going to a job on time or staying away from it without giving notice. The message eventually got through, all of them started calling regularly if they were going to be late. Annette decided that she wanted to go to California to stay with one of her school friends whose parents had moved to the San Francisco Bay area. She wanted to drive out with some boy. Lili was very angry but Annette was adamant; she wanted to leave home. I talked to her and when I got her promise that she would find a college to go to in California, I took Annette with her two bags to the place in the western suburbs where she was going to meet the boy. Annette lived up to her promise and enrolled in the Foothills College, south of San Francisco. After three years, she returned to Illinois to Lake County Junior College, then after several tries was accepted to the Chicago Medical School from which she graduated.

I had many arguments regarding Vietnam, not only with the children, who were all, except Peter, more or less influenced by the radicals in the anti-war movement, but even with some of our neighbors. On one hand I was violently anti-communist and supported a tough stance against Soviet and Chinese aggression and their exploitation of every element of unrest anywhere in the world to further their expansion. I was convinced that the anti-war and "Ban the Bomb" movements were being fostered and financed by communist agents. On the other hand, I agreed with Eisenhower that Vietnam was the wrong place to get involved in a land war. The French disaster at Dien Bien Phu was best proof. The British had been able to defeat communist aggression in Malaysia because of the narrow peninsula separating it from the rest of the Asian continent and their ability to cut off supplies to the guerrillas. For a similar reason, in Korea America and her allies were able to contain the communists along the mountainous neck of land separating north and south.

In Vietnam there were no natural borders and the dense jungle favored the guerrillas. I felt we should support the anti-communist people of South Vietnam with material, training, air support to destroy the invading forces and their infrastructure, but no more. However, I was absolutely opposed to the demonstrations, flag and draft-card burning and every other kind of behavior which encouraged the communists in their belief that the United States would back down. This was particularly true once peace discussions began. One can only negotiate from a position of strength. Unfortunately, the growing anti-war movement encouraged the North Vietnamese not to concede anything, just to drag out the discussions in Paris forever, if necessary, because events convinced them that eventually America would give up.

Of course, I was very concerned about Mark being sent to Vietnam and both of us were relieved when he drew a high number. Peter was, of course, in no danger of being drafted because of his asthma. Regarding Philip we just hoped that the whole unfortunate war would be over, one way or another, before his turn came up. Indeed on January 27, 1973, the Vietnam Peace agreements were finally signed in Paris, and the same day the end of the military draft was announced by President Nixon. The last U.S. ground forces were removed from Vietnam on March 29, although fighting in the region continued for another two years until April 1975 when Saigon was overrun by the North Vietnamese, who had never adhered to the Paris agreements they had signed. So the danger was over when he did graduate from high school in 1974.

During the sixties my father continued with his work in the Assembly of Captive European Nations (ACEN) in New York and in the Polish Council of Unity. He made several trips to Europe to visit various Polish organizations in London and Paris and for brief holidays.

In 1965 I was present with him when he gave a short speech while presenting Carol Rozmarek, president of the Polish National Union, with a medal on behalf of ACEN. This took place in Chicago during the annual commemoration of the Polish Constitution of the Third of May*. The principal speaker at the ceremony in Humboldt Park was Vice-President Hubert Humphrey. I and Dad sat on the main platform with the Humphreys and all the local political notables, such as Mayor Dailey. My father's political activities came to an abrupt end when he slipped on a patch of ice in January 1971. He suffered multiple fractures of his leg and spent several months in hospital. Subsequently, he lived for several months with us in Deerfield while he was recuperating. After his recovery he moved from New York to a residential hotel on Chicago's north side.

The decade ended with one very cheerful event — Peter's wedding. He followed in his father's footsteps, getting married at 22! The bride was Jeanette, a United Airlines stewardess (as they were still called in those days) who lived in the same apartment complex in Melrose Park. She was one of four daughters of the Gilberts who lived in Marin County, north of San Francisco. We all went out west for the ceremony, flying on cheap tickets provided by the young couple's respective employers. We all stayed in a motel close to the Gilbert's large home. Babette and Wesley were extremely hospitable. Wesley enjoyed cooking and we ate several excellent meals, before and after the wedding, in their comfortable home.

At the reception in a country club on top of a hill with a wonderful view, there seemed to be a limitless supply of champagne. I think that this is where Eileen acquired her love of this bubbly drink. It was a great party, we all had fun dancing. All members of both families attended, except Mark who was traveling somewhere in the Caribbean at the time. The Gilberts originally had lived in Connecticut. Then they had moved west to California and he had started his present company, a package delivery business. Earlier that summer they had both stopped in Deerfield to get acquainted with us, and, I suppose,

---

* This happened in 1791, two years after the adoption of the American Constitution.

to check out whom their daughter was marrying. It seems they were pleased with what they found. He offered his new son-in-law a job in the company, starting from the bottom. Thus, Peter started his new career in the transportation and courier business.

A new Polish immigration to America started in the late sixties. Since the end of the Stalinist period in 1956, the new head of the Polish communist party, Gomoulka, had started a slow relaxation of the rules that virtually prohibited travel out of Poland. At first, a number of the Jewish population that had survived the war were allowed to emigrate, ostensibly to Israel. Then many professionals were allowed to take jobs in "friendly" socialist countries such as Libya, Algeria and Syria. Subsequently, others managed to obtain passports for "visits" to friends and relatives in the West, mainly England and America, from which many of them never returned. Some of them worked for several months at whatever menial jobs they could obtain, principally repairing houses, or as servants. Even the low paying illegal jobs they obtained sufficed to make them wealthy when they returned home, given that the dollar had become the only currency for which one could obtain many scarce goods in Poland such as appliances, cars and building materials. Under these circumstances the black market exchange rate was about 100 times the official rate. To assist in the rebuilding of the ruined infrastructure, the Polish government desperately needed hard currency and Poland became the only country in the communist block in which the possession of hard currency was not a crime. On the contrary, people were encouraged to set up hard currency bank accounts, so called *Konto A*.

However, a large number of the professionals, once they were safely abroad, immediately requested political asylum. In the U.S. and Canada these requests were generally granted. Doctors were welcome in the big city hospitals. They needed many years of work as interns, for which they were paid minimal salaries, in order to be able to sit for State Board accreditation examinations. Engineers and architects were in a better position. Many of the large consulting and contracting companies were receiving lucrative construction contracts in the oil rich middle eastern countries. Consequently, they desperately needed extra personnel, particularly those familiar with European standards, to cope with the increased workloads.

Our circ̲ [...] ̲siderably. Several of them, for example the [...] were architects, did very well in a short peri [...] buy nice homes on the North Shore.

The Kryn̲s̲ [...] ̲hey were both doctors who had come with [...] ̲. In spite of several years of grueling interns [...] ̲ing the State examinations, for some reaso̲ı̲ [...] ̲aining residence permits. Consequently, tl [...] l became very successful there. However, [...] ̲ed for service in the U.S. Army and receiv̲e̲ [...] ̲nd ultimately became a citizen.

Most of the ne̲ [...] ̲ smoothly into society; nevertheless there were some who [...] less grateful for the chance for a new rich life. Typical of this cate̲g̲ory was one architect with whom I nearly had a fight at a party. After a few drinks this ingrate started telling everybody how terrible it was in this country.

"There is no culture, no theater, no music," he grumbled. "I have to work long hours and then the government steals my hard earned money. More than a third of my salary is taken from me for taxes and stuff. This is terrible! I don't know why you all put up with it."

I couldn't stand it any longer. I burst out, "*Do cholery jasnej* (God damn it), if it's so bad in this country why don't you just pack up and go back where you came from?"

He rushed over and tried to hit me. Others held him back and tried to quiet him down. I just walked out of the room.

There were only a few like that. Most of the new arrivals worked hard, did very well, and appreciated the opportunities given them by their new home. A typical example was our friends Bogdan and Lila Grzybowski. They had endured great hardships in Warsaw because of their resistance to political demands made by their supervisors. Finally, after years of waiting, sponsored by relatives, they arrived in Chicago in the early sixties, together with their two small boys. Bogdan immediately went to work in a small tool and die shop. Being very clever in mechanical things, he quickly made enough money to enable him to set up his own shop in a small building next to the North Western railway tracks that run between Highland Park and

Deerfield. They also bought a small house close by. Because of his adroit ideas he quickly developed a clientele among the pharmaceutical companies in the northern Illinois area, such as Abbott Laboratories. He developed and produced many smart semi-automatic production tools and machines. The business grew so rapidly that in ten years he bought a much larger building in Northbrook. The two sons, George and Andrew, inherited their father's mechanical abilities and, after graduating from university, took over the operation of the growing business. Another Polish immigrant success story like ours, I could list many others.

During this period many official visitors also came from Poland. They generally had a very difficult time because they were only allowed to take five dollars with them. Most such visitors tried to sell things like amber bracelets and necklaces to get extra cash. For example in 1962 the Polish National Athletic team visited Chicago for a competition with an American team. The match took place in the stadium of University of Chicago. All the Chicago Polonia* welcomed the athletes with open arms and helped them as much as they could. I brought three women home for dinner one evening. Two were shot-putters, the other a javelin thrower, all hefty girls with tremendous appetites. Before departing home they wanted to do some shopping. I picked them up at their dormitory at Chicago University and took them shopping in State Street. Of course, I knew they had very little money, so, obviously, I took them to cheaper stores such as Wieboldt's and then only to the bargain basement. These three girls mostly wanted to buy underwear. I was their interpreter. It was not easy to find underwear to fit them in the price range they could afford.

The dance and choral groups "*Mazowsze*" and "*Slask*" also came to Chicago several times and encountered the same warm welcome. Although the Polish government was charging theatrical agencies the same fees that any other professional groups of similar stature did, the performers were housed in cheap, sleazy hotels and fed in greasy spoon cafeterias. They were given only a few dollars spending money. Once more Polish organizations and families came to the aid of the girls and boys in these troupes with invitations to private homes and with gifts of various kinds.

---

* People of Polish descent.

All these visitors were watched carefully. In most cases they had families at home who were, in fact, hostages for their safe return. Even so, over the years, a number of performers managed to seek asylum. I ran into another example of visitors being accompanied by watchful companions. One evening in the Polish Club, I noticed a man sitting at the bar who looked familiar to me. He also looked at me. After a while someone who had been talking to him came over and asked me, "Is your name Biega?"

The man at the bar was a friend of mine from high school in Rydzyna. He came over to talk to us and told us that he had come with a trade mission to sell Polish machine tools. Naturally, we invited him to dinner. The following evening I went to his hotel to pick him up and another man got into the car with him, came to our home, ate dinner and hardly said ten words all evening long. I immediately understood the situation, the stranger was a member of the political police. Therefore the conversation with my friend was very stilted. There were many things we would like to have talked about, but, of course, couldn't. This situation was typical during those years of all relationships with visitors from communist countries.

Ever since I had sailed in a dinghy at the age of twelve on the south coast of England, I had dreamed about boating, specifically sailing. Thirty years had passed by and I had never had the opportunity to realize these dreams. As soon as I was safely settled down in my job at Sola Electric, this dream became more tangible. That summer, almost every weekend we drove down to the harbors along Chicago's lake front, and I enviously watched people on their boats, sailing, working, or just relaxing with friends on deck. I didn't just dream; in the summer of 1967 I enrolled in a sailing class. I participated in the classes every Saturday morning for ten weeks and very quickly got the knack of keeping the sails properly filled, of coming about, picking up moorings and coming alongside a dock. Then I started looking at boats, used ones, of course.

A number of times Lili went with me to look at the boats; I thought she was interested and I was pleased. Finally, I found a Gladiator 24 which I liked and which was affordable. It was about a year old and had only been used as a demonstrator and, most important of all, the dealer was anxious to get rid of it and was willing to sell for a small down payment and the balance of his payments to the bank, $5,000 over three years. In addition, he had a mooring in the principal yacht harbor of Chicago, which he was willing to give up. This was a great plus because there was a waiting list of several years for moorings in the Monroe Street Harbor. Lili raised objections, but I was so excited that she couldn't stop me.

The next question to be resolved was a name. I suggested various names to Lili, her response was, "Choose any name you want, I don't care."

None of the names, that I came up with, seemed to have the right pizzazz. They sounded just like so many other boat names. One day I was having a drink after work with a friend and I was bubbling over with excitement telling her about my new boat. Marilyn listened patiently, smiling as I rattled along about the beauty of its lines, how wonderful it would be to be sailing again.

She interrupted me, "You talk about your boat as if she were your lover! No wonder your wife is jealous!"

That gave me an inspiration, a lover or mistress is *Kochanka* in Polish. So that is how my boat got christened.

That spring, almost every fine weekend, I was at the boat-yard doing work on *Kochanka*. Unfortunately, the yard in Blue Island was over 60 miles from Deerfield and required a lengthy drive clear across Chicago, roughly 1 hours each way. The boat was essentially new, but there were numerous small things that had to be done, including installation of lifelines and installation of a holding tank to meet the new anti-pollution regulations. At that time most of the towns were still draining raw sewage into the lake, not speaking of all the industries, steel mills, etc., that were doing the same. It seemed grossly unfair to put such a burden on the owners of small boats, particularly since the large ships that entered the Great Lakes all dumped their sewage and ballasts directly into the water. In addition, pump-out stations were almost non existent. I remember one day waiting for hours in the line to the only pump-out facility then existing in Chicago. I walked over to the pumps and followed the hose line. The sewage being pumped out of our tanks was draining right back into the lake! *Kochanka*, like most boats her size, did not have an engine. To provide the necessary power for moving down river, getting to moorings in the harbor, or to proceed when there was no wind, I bought an outboard engine from the same dealer, a used British 5 HP Seagull, designed specifically for sailboat use.

Finally, everything was ready for the first voyage from Blue Island to the Monroe Street yacht harbor on a fine day in the second half of May. My crew consisted of Annette, Philip and an older Polish friend who also owned a small sailboat. Lili drove us down to Blue Island with sandwiches and thermos bottles with soup. At first we had to traverse the canal, passing through one big lock, past the large commercial port of Chicago and many steel mills, a distance of 12 miles, which took about 2 hours. There were several bridges too low even for my small 30 foot mast. We had to traverse this part with the mast lying down on the deck secured on top of cushions. Just before entering Lake Michigan, we pulled up to a dock and raised the mast. In a small boat this was still possible for the four of us. A bigger boat would have needed the services of a crane.

Then we raised sail for the first time and proceeded out into the open lake. Lake Michigan is like the open sea, extending 400 miles from north to south and more than 80 miles wide. It can be very rough at times but on this day the weather was perfect. Nevertheless, once we got out into the open water, there was a light chop. It wasn't long before both the kids were seasick. To make matters worse, they insisted on lying down in the V-berth of the forward cabin where the motion is always worst. Fortunately, this part of the trip took only a little more than two hours as we had a good wind. I was in heaven at the helm of my own yacht flying across the small waves, the white sails full and fluttering in the ideal breeze. We soon found our mooring which was at the south end of the big harbor, close to the Aquarium. As soon as we had made everything ship shape, we boarded the harbor tender* which took us to the Columbia Yacht Club, which I had already joined. Once on firm ground (actually the yacht club was on an old ship that was permanently moored) with a Coca Cola in front of them, the children quickly recovered.

---

* A motor boat that ferries people out to their yachts attached to moorings in the harbor.

Before the first summer was over I became proficient and was able to come up to mooring under sail, even single handed. I went sailing virtually every weekend and occasionally midweek evenings accompanied by any friends who wanted to share my pleasure. In nice weather it was not difficult to find crew among my various Polish friends. Frequently, a couple of engineers and their families joined me. I also participated in some of the club races particularly on Wednesday evenings. We never won a race, but we always had plenty of fun. Eileen was the only family member who loved it and was a frequent companion. She joined the junior sailors program at the club and took part in dinghy racing. Lili and the other children only came when accompanied by their own friends. I also made several longer voyages across the lake to harbors along the Michigan shore as well as northwards to Waukegan and other harbors to the north. One of these cruises to the beautiful area in Door County, Wisconsin, was two weeks long. *Kochanka* gave me a great deal of pleasure every summer for seven years.

18

REWARDING YEARS

The day after New Year 1965 I drove up to the Sola Electric plant on Busse Road in Elk Grove Village. Glenn Konker introduced me to the staff. He and the vice presidents of production and marketing had taken over only about a year earlier. All three had previously worked for a management consulting company in Cleveland and had been hired by Basic Products Corporation to make a study of operations at Sola Electric. They had issued a report with many recommendations, apparently suggesting that they should be hired to run the division!

The engineering department at Sola Electric was much larger than that of Hevi-Duty Electric. It was divided into three design groups, each responsible for a different range of products and each with its own test laboratories. The supervisor of one of these groups, Harry Gerdes, was very disturbed to discover that his new boss was the job applicant that he had rejected two years earlier! My first problem was getting sufficiently acquainted with the design methods for the various products so that I could better assess the problems involved and why top management, particularly marketing, was so disturbed about engineering performance.

Joseph Sola, an immigrant from Argentina, had developed the ferroresonant transformer as a means of providing a stable voltage source some twenty five years earlier and owned the basic patents in the U.S. and the principal industrial countries. The basic patents had long expired but many additional patents for various improvements of the original idea were still in effect but nearing the end of their lives. This long hegemony in the field had lead to an arrogant approach to the customers and to a lazy engineering staff slow to make changes and improvements. During the previous five years the company had, as a result, lost a considerable share of the market for voltage stabilizers which were so necessary in the growing electronic and computer industries. One of the major customers that had left Sola was I.B.M. With the expiration of the basic patents, several competitors had come into the market with substantial design improvements and lower prices. My job was to try to turn this trend around.

I soon discovered that part of the problem was the same engineering syndrome that had existed at Hevi-Duty Electric. It took a while to convince the older engineers that the measures that I proposed should be adopted in order to provide better service to the customers. A certain amount of arm twisting and subtle threats were needed before all of them got on my bandwagon. There was a very specific difference between Hevi-Duty and Sola. The principles of transformer design are well established, and except for radical new innovations there is no great need for building and testing prototypes or models. At Sola we were dealing with non-linear magnetics and special electronics, in which the design principles are less clearly defined.

Therefore the building and testing of prototypes is essential before releasing a design for quantity production. Frequently, prototypes had also to be supplied for customer approval. A model shop, which was under the control of production, built these models and they were considered a nuisance. Consequently, engineering schedules were at the mercy of disinterested people in the production department. I was able to convince Glenn Konker that in order to get engineering schedules under control it was essential to put the model shop under my authority. Soon I had another section working for me, the Engineering Model Shop with several clever and resourceful technicians under the leadership of Bob Czarnecki. This shop became so efficient that I had to resist pressures from the sales department to produce small quantity production runs.

Before the year was out, Engineering was running fairly smoothly. We were maintaining promised schedules for special custom designs and getting prototype samples for customer approval out on time. New product development was proceeding and I had introduced a reporting system to keep other departments, particularly marketing, aware of what we were doing. I tried to have good honest relationships with the people that worked for me, particularly those with whom I had the greatest contact, the supervisors of the various sections. I made it clear that any of them should feel free to discuss any problems or complaints with me at any time. It was company policy that, at least once a year, each supervisor was required to make an evaluation of each direct subordinate which was discussed with the individual before being turned in to the personnel department. These evaluations were generally tied in with salary increases, or lack of them.

I also kept an eye out for openings elsewhere to reward the best performers. I won the appointment of Harry Gerdes to general manager of a new plant that Sola Electric built in Alabama. I learned that Rux Tucker, a talented, ambitious , young electronics engineer who had obtained an MBA degree at Chicago University by studying nights, had marketing ambitions; I got him transferred into the position of products manager. I obtained promotions to other operations of the corporation for several other members of my staff during my six years at Sola Electric.

Joe Sola was no longer active in the operation of the company. He was basically retired but had an office at the north end of the second floor with his own personal secretary, Alice Marshalek, who looked after his investments and personal correspondence. He did act as a consultant for research and new product development. This work was carried out by a separate Sola Basic Research department with laboratories on the upper floor. It had been set up two years earlier to provide new product development for the entire corporation and was operated under the direction of Dave Davenport and included some of the engineers who had worked for his small company, which had been closed down after I had become chief engineer at Hevi-Duty Electric. Carl Peterson, who had been Joe Sola's chief engineer was in charge of Magnetic Research.

In actual fact, no research in the true sense of the word, was carried out, but some development work on possible new products was being done. However, none of the other divisions of the corporation indicated much interest. A certain amount of friction developed between my engineering staff and the people "upstairs." Several new product ideas were sent down to us for implementation, unfortunately, all of them needed redesign to make them suitable for production. The new president of Sola Basic Industries, Frank Roby, soon decided that the corporation did not need a separate research department and that each product division should be responsible for its own new product development. I fully agreed with that conclusion. Dave Davenport and most of his people were let go. Carl Peterson and a couple of engineers who were working on projects of potential interest to us stayed on, but under my overall supervision. Carl Peterson wasn't very happy with this and a few months later he left to establish a new company to manufacture small transformers, particularly constant voltage transformers to the old Sola patents which had now expired.

I believed that the days of the ferroresonant constant voltage transformer were limited, that advances in electronics would make them obsolete. Events have proven me correct, although still today, 25 years later, Sola Electric continues to enjoy a small market in them. Consequently, I wanted to build up the capability of Sola in the field of electronics, power supplies and other devices such as uninterruptible power supplies to provide instantaneous power for computers and other sensitive equipment in the event of a failure of normal mains power. I started a search for experienced engineering talent in this field. Today UPS have become a billion dollar market, and Sola Electric has a share of that market.

Also, I believed that computers would play an increasing role in engineering design, replacing, to a large extent, the trial and error methods of engineers armed with slide rules and calculators making laborious calculations on paper. I got one of the engineers to learn engineering programming and to start working on methods to design transformers and non-linear circuits. In those days personal computers were unknown. Only large main-frame computers existed that cost hundreds of thousands of dollars. Sola Electric had one, of course, but it was used entirely for inventory control and financial matters. All input was by means of punched cards; there were no terminals to give interactive access to the machine.

It was not suitable for the type of work that we wanted to do and I convinced Glenn Konker to provide funding so that we could access a large scientific computer, somewhere in Chicago, on a time share basis. A teletype machine in the engineering library was the only means of access to this remote computer. Hank Borkovitz wrote out his program statements using pencil and paper in Fortran, which was the most popular computer language for engineering and scientific work in those days. It consisted of English-like words and phrases strung together with mathematical and similar symbols. However, the syntax rules were very specific. The slightest error, even adding an additional space, would result in the computer refusing to work or spitting out a lot of gibberish. The only way for Hank to test his work was to type in his statements on the teletype machine and wait. If he was lucky, after several minutes had elapsed, the teletype would start chattering and a result would be printed out. More often than not, an error message would come back or a lot of rubbish. Hank persevered and after many months he started getting good results.

Once my engineering department was operating smoothly, I was able to spend more time on other activities, particularly the IEEE. In June 1965 I participated in the organizational meeting of the Chicago Chapter of the Industry and General Applications Group. Groups provided the structure for IEEE members to meet others of similar professional interests and to have meetings at which speakers presented papers on subjects of particular interest to them. So there were many such groups under the overall umbrella of this enormous organization. In large metropolitan areas such as Chicago the various groups organized chapters for their local meetings. I was elected vice-chairman of this new chapter and became very involved in its early period, arranging meetings with programs of interest to its membership.

Shortly afterwards, John Ferguson, a manager at S&C, a large manufacturer of electrical switchgear on the north side of Chicago, got in touch with me. He had been selected by the national committee of the Industry and General Applications Group to be the chairman and organizer of its first annual meeting to be held in Chicago the following year. He asked me to serve on his committee. For such an undertaking I had to obtain the approval of my boss, Glenn Konker, as it would involve a lot of work and would require company support. Glenn was reluctant but finally agreed. I served as secretary-treasurer and with the help of many other volunteers, arranged a very successful meeting. It took place in the Conrad Hilton Hotel in October 1966, lasted four days, and was attended by close to 1,000 from all over the United States and Canada. A few months later I was asked by the national headquarters to be the organizer and chairman of the 1968 Annual Meeting. This time Glenn Konker agreed without hesitation. I was able to put together a very good group of volunteers and in October 1968 we had another successful conference, this time in the La Salle Hotel with attence by over 1,100. Lili was chairwoman of the committee which arranged entertainment for the wives of the delegates.

Organizing an endeavor of this kind is a time consuming but also a very satisfying job. There is no payment, the only reward is the satisfaction obtained from the recognition of one's peers for a successfully completed task, and from working with a diverse group of people each of whom performs an assigned portion of the overall effort. Needless to say, not all the co-workers are equally well motivated nor talented and a considerable amount of follow up, cajoling, prodding is necessary. The very first task that must be performed, at least a year in advance of the event, is the selection of committee members; each of whom is responsible for a specific function. These functions include program, dinners and luncheons, publicity, finance, registration, entertainment. The chairman's staff also includes a secretary-treasurer and a vice-chairman, who assists and would take over in the event of the chairman's disability.

The best candidates for these positions are the engineers who had worked on the previous annual meeting. Since I had been secretary-treasurer, I knew who had been the most enthusiastic and efficient workers, these were the ones whom I invited in the first place. For various reasons, personal or work-related, some declined and new volunteers had to be found. Each of the sub-committee chairmen, in turn, recruited their own co-workers to help with various details. Many of these were co-opted at a later date. By the conference time about 50 individuals were actively involved. In our case the responsibility for the technical program, that is, the papers that were presented, lay with the national committee of the organization. However, we were responsible for getting advance publicity, registrations, printing of programs, reservations for hotel space, all of which were dependent upon the program. So we had to continually follow up to get the necessary information on time. This required some frenzied activity and numerous long distance phone calls, in the weeks preceding various deadlines.

For example, the advance programs had to be printed in time for a general mailing to the entire national membership 10-12 weeks before the date of the Conference. As the date of the Conference approached the activity of all sub-committees increased. So did the pressures from the hotel management for guarantees for the number of guest rooms, conference rooms, meeting rooms, attendances at luncheons and banquets. Engineers are typically tardy in making advance hotel registrations (in part because generally they have to get company approvals for time off and travel expense), so about four weeks before the conference date the hotel management started pressuring me to reduce the number of rooms set aside. I would counter with statistics from other engineering conferences to prove that the bulk of reservations did not usually come in more than one week before the deadline. In Chicago there was always a shortage of hotel rooms so I had to fight hard to hang on to the room assignments to the last possible moment. Financially the conference was self-supporting, so that registration fees, prices of tickets for luncheons, dinners and other events such as tours, had to be set high enough to ensure that all costs would be covered with an allowance for no-shows and unexpected items. Since all the workers were volunteers and speakers were free (except perhaps the principal dinner speaker), we were able to hold the registration fees relatively low.

Companies generally paid the costs of their employees attending such conferences; therefore, it was very important to keep them as low as possible, otherwise the attendance numbers would drop, particularly in any bad economic times. The employers of our volunteer workers had to allow them countless hours away from their normal duties. They probably did not realize how much additional, non scheduled, secretarial help they also were providing! The only benefit for the companies concerned was that they were all named in the published programs. Fortunately, our planning was right on target, everything went off well, there were no major snafus, and we were able to deliver several hundred dollars surplus to the treasury of the IEEE.

As a result of this accomplishment, I was asked to become National Meetings Chairman. I served in this capacity until my resignation in 1972 when I started extensive international travel. I was responsible for the selection of locations and chairmen for all subsequent annual meetings and also for providing the necessary guidance, overseeing finances and publicity for the numerous smaller meetings organized by various Technical Sections of the Group*. My very first activity was selecting the hotel for the 1970 Annual Meeting which was to be in Chicago once more. It was already rather late and I was unable to get sufficiently large space allocation in any of the downtown hotels. The new Regency O'Hare hotel was just under construction and due to be completed in the spring of 1970. It was the first of the new style hotels with soaring atriums around central banks of exposed elevators. I had several meetings with the newly appointed hotel manager at the job site, wearing hard hats. I was impressed by the architectural drawings and, working from blueprints, blocked out the space we needed for our various meetings and reserved a block of 700 guest rooms, becoming the first major convention to book space in this first large hotel in the rapidly growing O'Hare area. Having learned from this experience, I went ahead and booked space for the following two years in Los Angeles and Toronto. From then on, hotel arrangements were made five years, rather than two years in advance.

Another project I got involved with was more business oriented. Sola Electric and most other divisions of Sola Basic Industries belonged to a trade organization called National Electrical Manufacturers' Association (NEMA). Its principal activities were setting standards for products and collecting and disseminating statistical data.

---

* The Group was renamed Industrial Applications Society in 1970.

I represented Sola Electric at several meetings of NEMA, in particular at meetings of a group which was writing standards for electronic power supplies. In turn, this latter group represented the United States in the committee which was preparing a similar international standard. These activities were directed by the international standards body IEC (International Electrotechnical Commission with headquarters in Geneva, Switzerland). In the spring of 1968 I went to a committee meeting in Paris as a member of the U.S. Delegation. In this specific committee the most active countries were France, West Germany, Great Britain, Sweden and the U.S.A., although several other countries were members and sent delegates to the annual meetings. A Dutch engineer was chairman of this committee.

Shortly afterwards some personality conflicts arose in the NEMA committee and I was asked to take over as chairman. The purpose of the standards, that we were working on, was to unify definitions, provide uniform test methods and establish basic requirements for performance and safety tests. Representatives of several manufacturers met every couple of months at NEMA headquarters in New York. In between meetings various members worked on assigned portions, which were then discussed and approved at the meetings. It was very fortunate for future exports that both American and international standards were under study at the same time as this ensured that there would be no conflicts between the two. The work on these two standards, the American and the International, continued in parallel for four years. Documents and draft proposals for the international set were exchanged by mail through the Geneva headquarters of IEC. The international committee met for six days once a year. The successive meetings were in Zagreb, then Washington and finally Stockholm in 1971. After that, the completed Standard was circulated to all member countries for ratification. I enjoyed this work as it gave me the opportunity to meet a number of influential people in the American electronics industry as well as various other countries. It also provided the opportunity to travel to New York, where my father was living, and to other countries. Lili went with me to all the international meetings.

The procedure at these annual meetings was normally as follows. Various national committees had been assigned sections, or chapters, of the proposed standard to prepare a draft proposal.

These drafts had been circulated many weeks beforehand, and frequently written discussions or counter-proposals were then written and circulated by some national groups. At the meeting each completed section was discussed paragraph by paragraph until an overall agreement as to wording had been reached and accepted by majority vote.

There was usually a Japanese delegation which never took part in any discussion. In the 1960's they generally did not have sufficient command of English to be able to do so. At the meeting in Zagreb a humorous incident occurred. From the exchange of documents prior to the meeting, it was clear that the Japanese wished to add several sentences to the end of one of the paragraphs. At the meeting, when the discussions reached this paragraph and most of the delegates had accepted the previously prepared and circulated text the chairman paused, obviously awaiting the presentation of the Japanese proposal. A long silence, we all waited ...., then the chairman said, "As there are no objections, Paragraph *xx* is accepted. We will proceed to the next paragraph."

I raised my hand and said, "Mr. Chairman, I believe that our esteemed Japanese colleagues wished to present an addition to Paragraph *xx*."

"Thank you for drawing this to my attention, Mr. Biega. Does the Japanese delegate wish to present his proposal?"

I turned around; the three man Japanese delegation was sitting at a table directly behind the Americans. They were hurriedly searching through their papers. Obviously, they had been caught by surprise and didn't understand that it was their moment of glory.

After a long pause, the chairman asked, "Mr. Biega, would you by any chance have a copy of the Japanese proposal? If so, would you be so kind to read it to us."

"Yes, Mr. Chairman, I have the text," and I proceeded to read it.

The French delegate objected, speaking in French, "Mr. Chairman. This is not necessary. What does this proposal mean? We object to any changes. We have discussed enough."

The Chairman, who spoke fluent French as well as English, translated the Japanese proposal into French.

The German delegate in his usual diplomatic manner, suggested that although the proposed new sentences really didn't add anything to the standard, he felt that, if the Japanese really believed that their revision added to the clarity of the matter, he would propose that the additional wording be adopted.

The British said that they didn't see that it mattered one way or the other, the original wording was sufficiently clear.

I said that the American delegation saw no harm in accepting the proposed new wording.

The Chairman put the matter to vote, "Time is pressing, if there are no further discussions, we'll vote on accepting the added sentences. All in favor please raise your hand."

The motion was carried with the British abstaining, the French objecting.

I looked around, the Japanese had still not found their papers and appeared completely bewildered by the proceedings. That evening, before the banquet, the Japanese came up to me and all three bowed three times and thanked me for my assistance. So much for amicable international relationships.

Another international relationship had developed at Sola Electric. Sola Basic Industries was looking for opportunities to expand sales in Europe. An opportunity arose to purchase a majority interest in a small Spanish company located in Barcelona that manufactured ballasts for fluorescent and mercury vapor lighting. The president and principal shareholder, Senor Artigas, came to the U.S. with his wife and his English speaking sales manager. They spent two days in Elk Grove Village. We also had license agreements with a French company whose President came to Sola Electric for a couple of days when it was necessary to renegotiate the agreements. Then came a Japanese delegation from Sanken Electric with whom a joint venture was being discussed. Before that, I maintained close contact with other Sola subsidiaries in Australia, Canada, the Netherlands and in Mexico City. On the American scene, I was spending more and more time on customer negotiations with such companies as I.B.M. and Xerox, as well as with the U.S. Navy with whom we had several contracts for the supply of voltage stabilizing equipment, mainly for the electronics on aircraft carriers. In spite of the title of Director of Engineering, I was spending a great deal of time in other fields than engineering.

At the staff level there were more changes. Warren Whalley, vice president of marketing, had been appointed president of the Nelson Electric Division in Tulsa, Oklahoma, another new acquisition. Steve Speltz, who had been running the Los Angeles sales office of Sola Electric, was advanced into his position. During a downturn in business, Glenn Konker was forced to resign and was replaced with Glenn Ronk, whom Roby brought from his old company, Federal Pacific Electric. I found Glenn Ronk much easier to work with than the other Glenn. He was more direct in his discussions with people and he was more decisive in business dealings. After his arrival on the scene there, were many improvements in the daily business routines.

At least once every three months we had a general staff meeting with the president of Sola Basic Industries, Frank Roby. Frank was a small, wiry man, with a permanently dour expression on his face and was always accompanied by his treasurer Bob Meyers, who was tall, but corpulent and possessing a cheerful demeanor. They always reminded me of the characters in the silent movies, Flip and Flap. Bob was always the driver of their car. Frank was well known, not only within the corporation but throughout the electrical industry, for his penchant to indulge in long monologues. I remember at one of the NEMA conferences the president of another large company read my lapel badge and queried, "So you work for Frank Roby. Tell me, does he still talk as much and as long as he used to?"

At these staff meetings, each of us was required to make a presentation on the situation in his department. It was rare that any of us finished our presentation. Frank always interrupted with some question, listened to the answer, and then launched into a long statement of his opinion of what should be done in the department in question. Steve Speltz was a master at coming up with answers that pleased Frank. Many a time I observed how Steve would watch the expression on Frank's face, and sometimes, in mid-sentence, would change the sense of his report or the answer to a question. He was later rewarded for his positive attitude with a promotion to president of the Warren Communications Division. During the entire meeting Bob Meyers never said a word, except in direct response to a question from Frank relative to some financial performance figures. He had a tremendous memory for numbers. Sometimes it would seem that he was asleep, leaning back in his chair, eyes closed, hands folded on his prominent belly.

Suddenly Frank would ask, "Bob, what was the change in return on investment of the XYZ Division in the second quarter of last year?" Without the slightest hesitation, Bob would open his eyes, and say, "It went from 6.8 to 7.1 percent."

Frank would frown, "That's not how I remember it. Are you sure, Bob?"

Bob would open up one of his big folders lying on the table in front of him, look at a sheet, and respond, "Frank, you are quite right. It actually went from 6.81 to 7.12," close his folder and smile like the Cheshire cat in *Alice in Wonderland*.

In these staff meetings I was always too honest and outspoken, believing that it was necessary to present the facts and draw the appropriate conclusions from them to develop the best strategy for the future; as I was taught in the General Electric management school. If I felt that the numbers indicated that a certain course of action should be taken in my department or somebody else's, I would say so. I did not hesitate to take part in the discussions of other departments and make suggestions. Frequently, Frank felt otherwise and would spend half an hour explaining to everyone the proper way to proceed, generally without waiting for me to finish outlining all the available facts.

By now I was getting more and more restless in my official job. It was fortunate that I had all the outside interests to keep me busy. Once more I wanted to get back to marketing from which I had been side tracked. I was always being praised by Glenn for my work and my salary increases were satisfactory evidence of his opinion. But it became obvious that as long as Frank Roby headed Sola Basic Industries, I would not get any further promotion. I was too outspoken. My international contacts had generated a desire to get into that area of sales and when I learned in November 1970 that one of the staff at Sola Basic International in Milwaukee had left to take another job, I made some inquiries and determined that he was surely at about the same salary level as I was. Then I went to Glenn Ronk and asked for his support to obtain that position. Glenn was surprised.

"Bill, that would be a step backwards for you," he said, "Now you are head of a big department with 65 employees. You have responsibility for a budget of over a half million dollars in a product division with sales of 25 million. You are an important member of my staff. This position at International has no staff and requires a lot of travel. You will probably have to take a cut in pay, I doubt that Jim Hosler could match your present salary and bonuses."

"Glenn, I don't worry much about titles," I responded. "I have never made an issue of the fact that you made Steve Speltz a vice president, while I have always been just a director of engineering. I have always wanted to be in marketing, that's where I started at Hevi-Duty. As you know, I like travel and get on well with people, especially internationally."

Finally, I convinced Glenn that I was serious. He agreed to call Jim Hosler. As it turned out, Jim was delighted with the idea of me joining his team. He had already seen me in action during the negotiations with Artigas, the French and the Japanese. He was a mechanical engineer himself and wanted to have an electrical expert, particularly someone with such intimate knowledge of the Sola and Hevi-Duty products which constituted a major part of Sola Basic exports. In addition, he did not speak any foreign language and was keen to acquire my knowledge of French and German. He was able to match my present salary. As far as bonuses were concerned, at Sola Basic International, they were tied to success in achieving sales targets. He decided to give me responsibility for Europe, Africa and the Middle East. The only obstacle to be overcome was getting Glenn Ronk to let me go quickly.

It was agreed that I would stay at Sola until a replacement had been found. A logical replacement for me would be Hank Borkovitz, who was manager of the magnetics design section. He had done well as leader of several development projects, was heading the development of computer programs for product design. He had also obtained an MBA degree from the University of Chicago, studying evenings with company sponsorship. At the beginning of March 1971 the decision was made, Hank was given my old job.

For the second and last time I quit engineering as a career and I left Sola Electric to start my new career in international sales. It took 13 years to achieve this goal from the time that I had been turned down by General Electric International. This new career would give me great personal satisfaction and an opportunity for wonderful experiences and many new exciting adventures.

— END —

APPENDIX

NOTES ON PRONUNCIATION OF POLISH NAMES

All vowels are pronounced seperately and sound like they do in Spanish:

A is a long AA	like in "rather"
E is a short E	like in "echo"
I is a long EE	like in "see"
O is a short O	like in "pot"
U is a long OO	like in "root"
Y is a short I	like in "pit" when used as vowel in

W is pronounced	like V in "vessel"
J is pronounced	like Y in "yam",
	"Janek" is pronounced "Yanek"
L is pronounced	like L in "lip",
Ł is pronounced	like W in "wash" or "wood"
CH is pronounced	like an aspirated Scottish H
SZ is pronounced	like SH in "shell"
CZ is pronounced	like CH in "chat"
RZ is pronounced	like French J in "Jacques"
CI is pronounced	like a soft CH as in Italian "cello"
SI is pronounced	like a soft SH as in "shoe"

Polish has several additional letters, which are not printed in the text.

ą	pronounced	like ONG in "gong"
ć	pronounced	like soft CH, see CI above
ę	pronounced	like French AIN, or ENG
ł	pronounced	like W in "wood"
ó	pronounced	like OO in "wood"
ś	pronounced	like soft SH, see SI above
ż	pronounced	like hard SH.

For example:

Kraków is pronounced	"krakoof"
Lwów	"lvoov"
Pałak	"pawongk"
Jarmuż	"yarmoosh"
Oswiecim	"oshviengcheem"
Wałęsa	"vawengsa"
Łódz	"woodge" similar to "wedge"

BIBLIOGRAPHY

For anyone wishing to learn more about the history of Poland, I can recommend many books written by Norman Davies, including:
Heart of Europe - Oxford University Press, 1986 - Paperback -463pp.
God's Playground - Clarendon Press, 1981 -Oxford Un. Paperback, 1983 2 vols

Majdanek, Auschwitz, Ravensbruck, read the account of a Jewish teenage girl who survived:
Hope is the last to die - Halina Birenbaum - Twayne Publishers, Inc, N.Y. 1977

For details about the Yalta Conference and the last days of the German Reich:
The Last 100 Days - John Toland - Random House, N.Y. - 1966

For details of the Polish Underground Army and the Warsaw Uprising:
The Secret Army - T. Bor-Komorowski - MacMillan, London 1951
Warsaw Uprising - George Bruce - Rupert Hart-Davies, London 1993
For details of the civilian undergound government *Delegatura Krajowa*:
The Polish Underground State - Stefan Korbonski - Columbia University Press, NY - 1978

ABBREVIATIONS

The following is a partial list of abbreviations used in the text.

ACEN	Assembly of Captive European Nations—a political organization.
AIEE	American Institute of Electrical Engineers—a professional organization, merged with IRE to form the IEEE.
AK	Armia Krajowa—the organized Underground Army in Poland.
ATC	Air Transport Command.
DP	Displaced Person—one of the millions of Europeans displaced from their homes by war.
GG	General Gouvernement—Nazi administrative unit for occupied Poland, also used to refer to the geographical area under its administration.
IAS	Industry Applications Society—one of the many interest related groups within IEEE.
IEC	International Electrotechnical Commission—establishes Recommendatiuons for safety and testing standards.
IEE	Institution of Electrical Engineers—British professional organization.

IEEE	Institute of Electrical and Electronic Engineers—American professional organization.
IRE	Institute of Radio Engineers—merged with the AIEE to form IEEE.
NEMA	National Electrical Manufacturers Association—American industrial organization, provides statistical services and works on national standards.
POW	Prisoner of war.
SHAEF	Supreme Headquarters Allied Expeditionary Forces.
SS	Stutz Staffel—the elite Nazi organization, SS officers headed the dreaded Gestapo, the SS also provided the officers and enlisted men for elite units of the German army, the SS Divisions.
UNRRA	United Nations Relief and Rehabilitation Administration—set up close to the end of the war by the Allies to provide relief for displaced people.
UPS	Uninterruptible Power Supply—an electronic power supply which provides power from batteries in the event of a break in normal electric power supply. Used in particular for computers and emergency services.

INDEX